D0801355

UNMASKING OBAMA

The Fight to Tell the True Story of a Failed Presidency

Jack Cashill

Post Hill
PRESS

A POST HILL PRESS BOOK

ISBN: 978-1-64293-445-8
ISBN (eBook): 978-1-64293-446-5

Unmasking Obama:
The Fight to Tell the True Story of a Failed Presidency
© 2020 by Jack Cashill
All Rights Reserved

Cover design by Joel Gilbert

Post Hill Press, LLC
New York • Nashville
posthillpress.com

Published in the United States of America

Dedicated to my fellow Lilliputians

Table of Contents

Prologue:
Michael Cohen Calling

I n the spring of 2011, I received a call from a fellow named Michael Cohen. I did not recognize the name. Nor did I know how Cohen got my cell number. He explained that he was the attorney for Donald Trump—I did recognize that name—and he wanted to know what I knew about Barack Obama's origins.

I would occasionally get calls like this from people of a higher pay grade than mine. Ever since I first started questioning the authorship of Obama's 1995 memoir, *Dreams from My Father*, I had become something of a conduit between what I have come to think of as the conservative *samizdat* on the one hand and the "responsible" right on the other.

In Russian, samizdat means "self-publishing." During the Soviet era, "samizdat" referred to the clandestine copying and distribution of literature banned by the state. I use samizdat as shorthand for an alternative conservative media composed of what one Second Amendment blogger aptly called "a coalition of willing Lilliputians."[1] In truth, those in the American samizdat run few risks beyond public shaming and perhaps job loss. For American citizen journalists on the right, the gulag is not an active worry, at least not for most of us—*pace*, Jerry Corsi—at least not yet.

During the Obama years, the conservative samizdat of blogs, public forums, news aggregators, online publications, talk radio shows, and legal monitors such as Judicial Watch challenged the left—and, occasionally, the responsible right—for control of the Obama narrative. The internet gave the samizdat unprecedented reportorial power, and social media, Facebook and Twitter most prominently, gave us an ability to distribute our message in ways Soviet dissidents could only imagine.

Every Lilliputian who dug up a useful fact and shared it on Facebook enlisted in the coalition of the willing. I got to know many such people. Aiding me in my Ayers-Obama research, for instance, were a half-dozen amateur sleuths from around the world, the two most helpful being the owner of a small Nebraska construction company and the caretaker of a Colorado ski resort. Volunteers did not need a law degree or a PhD. Heck, they didn't need a GED. All they needed was common sense and a nose for the truth. In the only slightly repositioned words of Soviet dissident Vladimir Bukovsky, the struggle was "our glasnost versus their glasnost."[2]

To keep damaging revelations out of the public square, a counter-insurgency emerged on the left parallel to the samizdat. These well-funded, internet-savvy shock troops had no larger goal than to suppress the information conservatives gathered or hoped to gather. This cohort included media "watchdogs" such as Media Matters for America, "extremist" monitors, most notably the Southern Poverty Law Center, various fact-checking operations, and a wide range of left-leaning online publications, some more reckless than others.

Watching these activists go about their business, I was reminded of a scene in Ray Bradbury's 1951 dystopian sci-fi classic, *Fahrenheit 451*. In the way of background, 451 degrees Fahrenheit is the temperature at which paper burns. In the novel, the state employs "firemen" to burn paper lest the few civilians who care about books avail themselves of information the state does not want them to have. "Is it true that long ago firemen put fires out instead of going to start them?" a young woman asks her friend. The friend tells her she has been misinformed. "Strange," she answers. "I heard once that a long time ago houses used to burn by accident and they needed firemen to stop the flames."[3]

Years ago, young journalists aspired to gather information and spread it. During the Obama era, however, the firemen on the left, like those in Bradbury's novel, aspired to destroy inconvenient information before it could spread. At the risk of sounding sexist, I will use the term "firemen" both in homage to Bradbury and in recognition that men take to this dirty work with more relish than women. Every book burner I identify herein is male.

The firemen had numerous ways of protecting the Obama presidency: defaming opposition journalists, mocking their work, exposing their past sins, trivializing their information, and twisting their facts, among others. At the amateur level, firemen routinely subverted the Wikipedia pages of perceived opponents, wrote one-star book reviews of their work on Amazon, and trolled the "comment" sections of conservative journals. Former CBS journalist Sharyl Attkisson saw the mission shift up close. "After Watergate," she writes, "few would have predicted today's dynamic in which some journalists view their job not as questioning the powers that be, but undermining those who report on the powers that be."[4]

Many of the salaried firemen lived in the same world as their mainstream colleagues. They attended the same universities, hung out in the same bars, and occasionally slept in the same beds. More than a few would leave the firehouse for a desk in a major media newsroom. Among those who made this move was wunderkind Ezra Klein. As a twenty-two-year-old, Klein launched an online meeting space called "JournoList" in which bloggers on the counterinsurgent left like himself could communicate with major figures in the media.

In its first reporting on JournoList in March 2009, *Politico* described it as a site where "left-leaning bloggers, political reporters, magazine writers, policy wonks and academics" could compare notes and swap story ideas. Despite the many high-profile people who participated, *Politico* noted ingenuously, "JList itself has received almost no attention from the media."[5] This would change, but by that time, the twenty-five-year-old Klein was writing for the *Washington Post*.

The firemen took the samizdat more seriously than did many "responsible" conservative journalists. To the right's tactical disadvantage, its better-connected writers and producers at the *National Review*, *Washington Times*, *New York Post*, *Wall Street Journal*, the *Weekly Standard*, and Fox News worked to keep their distance from their irregular allies. There was no JournoList on the right, nothing like it.

Editors at the flagship publication of the responsible right, the *National Review*, have ventured warily through the media minefield since the publication's founding in 1955. This strategic caution became obvious in 1960 when *NR* condemned the less responsible John Birch Society. Rationalized an editor in an internal memo, "We can't afford to jeopardize the grudging status we've earned in the liberal community."[6] Not to deny the dazzling *National Review* founder William Buckley his due, but Buckley established a modus operandi that has endured to this day throughout the responsible right.

During the Obama years, *National Review* editor Rich Lowry never stopped worrying about the "status" the liberal community begrudged his publication. As Lowry once noted, "Mr. Buckley's first great achievement was to purge the American right of its kooks."[7]

In September 2008, when I stumbled onto the likelihood that terrorist emeritus Bill Ayers was Obama's muse, I almost wished I hadn't. I knew what I was in for. I was about to become a kook, a racist kook at that. Allow me to cite my own case here as an example of the way the media forces aligned themselves during the Obama years.

Although not inclined to say so out loud, at least a few people on the responsible right trusted my judgment. From time to time, individuals would quietly call to confirm or deny a rumor about Obama. I suspect one of them referred me to Cohen. I told Cohen I followed the birth certificate issue only from a distance. I knew no more than anyone else. I recommended instead that Trump focus on the authorship issue. Although Obama claimed to have written his acclaimed memoir by himself, he definitely had help, much of it from Bill Ayers. This I deduced from my literary forensic work in the summer and fall of 2008.

Mainstream biographer Christopher Andersen confirmed Ayers's involvement in his Obama-friendly 2009 book, *Barack and Michelle: Portrait of an American Marriage*. Andersen's sources in Obama's Hyde Park neighborhood told him that Obama found himself deeply in debt and "hopelessly blocked." At "Michelle's urging," Obama "sought advice from his friend and Hyde Park neighbor Bill Ayers." What attracted the Obamas were "Ayers's proven abilities as a writer" as evident in his 1993 book, *To Teach*.[8] Ayers himself took credit for *Dreams* on multiple occasions, usually, but not always, with a wink and a nod.

My conversation with Cohen reaffirmed that Trump was the un-Obama, a creature of his own creation: crude, bombastic, and as subtle as a truck bomb. Unlike most on the right, Trump refused to be intimidated. He was eager and ready to vet the nation's first unvetted president. On April 15, 2011, Sean Hannity of Fox News gave him the opportunity.

"I heard he had terrible marks, and he ends up in Harvard," said Trump in his inimitably artless style. "He wrote a book that was better than Ernest Hemingway, but the second book was written by an average person."

"You suspect Bill Ayers?" said Hannity.

"I said, Bill Ayers wrote the book," Trump replied.

Trump had made the claim earlier in a public forum. He doubled down on Hannity's show. For all the outrage about Trump's questioning of Obama's birth certificate, the mainstream media (MSM) were noticeably silent about Trump's much more tangible challenge to Obama's literary skills. As was their wont, the firemen noticed and filed away Trump's "astounding racist projections" for another day,[9] but at the time, there was negligible pushback to Trump's remarks about *Dreams*.

The mainstream media were equally silent about Andersen's revelations. Indeed, at least fifty publications reviewed Andersen's book, and not a one mentioned the six pages he spent on the book's most newsworthy revelation. Relentless Obama defender Chris Matthews interviewed Andersen on MSNBC's *Hardball* and did not address the authorship issue. Said Matthews at the end of the interview, "You're amazing, successful guy. You have a winning streak here."[10] If Matthews did not read the book, which is likely, someone on his staff surely must have but chose not to notice the damning Ayers revelation. The MSM have been silent on this issue not because they think Trump was wrong, but because they think he might have been right. Contrary information frightens them.

The election was still in play that September. By late in that month, I had gathered enough evidence to make a strong public case for my thesis, but I needed a lot of words to make it and ideally some high-profile space to put those words. After much back and forth, *Human Events* passed on my research. True to form, the *National Review* editors did too, as did those at the *American Spectator*. The Fox News producers showed some interest, but the suits blanched.

The managing editor of the *Weekly Standard*, who had earlier published several of my articles, sent me to the magazine's literary editor. His response nicely reflected the widespread fecklessness that allowed Obama to win the 2008 election: "An interesting piece, but I'm rather oversubscribed at the moment, the length is considerable, and cutting would not do it justice. (Also, we had a long, rather critical, piece on Obama's oeuvre not too long ago.) So permit me to decline with thanks for allowing me to take a look." The kind of editors who would use a word like "oeuvre" in the heat of an election proved themselves so responsibly disdainful of Donald Trump in 2016 that they oeuvred themselves out of business.

Through some combination of naiveté and courage, the genuinely responsible writer and attorney Andy McCarthy came to my defense in *National Review Online*. McCarthy called my analysis of Obama's *Dreams* "thorough, thoughtful and alarming—particularly his deconstruction of the text in Obama's memoir and comparison to the themes, sophistication and signature phraseology of Bill Ayers' memoir."[11]

The "liberal community" quickly pounced on McCarthy and the *National Review*. In the *Atlantic*, then fireman and now mainstream darling Ta-Nehisi Coates took the first swipe at McCarthy. He extracted one of his quotes in my defense and introduced it with the barb, "How desperate can it get? This desperate."[12] The *Atlantic* added another quick review that began thusly, "At The Corner, Andy McCarthy evaluates Cashill's argument and proves himself to be an idiot."[13]

These exchanges took place a month before the 2008 election. *New Yorker* editor and Obama biographer David Remnick later observed about my theory and McCarthy's endorsement, "if ever proved true, or *believed* to be true among enough voters, [it] could have been the end of [Obama's] candidacy."[14] Having acknowledged the samizdat as a force, Remnick attempted to negate its power through ridicule and outright contempt. Although he demeaned many of Obama's critics, he reserved what neoconservative scholar Ron Radosh called "his most extensive and nasty comments" for me.[15] In his Obama biography, *The Bridge*, Remnick introduces me as "a little-known conservative writer, magazine editor, and former talk-radio-show host."[16] The "little known" part speaks for itself. The "talk-radio-show" detail is code for "not to be taken seriously." Radosh, whom I do not know at all, introduced me a shade more accurately: "Cashill has solid bona fide academic credentials. He has a Ph.D. in American Studies from Purdue University, and [is] author of a respected book on American intellectuals, *Hoodwinked*."

Remnick then reviews my theory that Ayers played a major role in the writing of *Dreams from My Father* by cherry-picking the least significant evidence and overlooking the most compelling. My theory, he insists, would have remained "a mere twinkling in the Web's farthest lunatic orbit"[17] had not more influential conservative voices echoed it. True to form, Remnick makes no effort to find some hole in my argument. He simply attacks me personally and concludes, as Radosh noted, "by playing the race card in an absurd way." Remnick would play that card until the spots wore off, explaining for the naive that mine was a "racist insinuation," one with a "particularly ugly pedigree."

There was a price to be paid for criticizing Obama. Everyone on the responsible right understood this. I am told McCarthy caught heat internally for jeopardizing *National Review*'s "grudging status" among liberals. What I know for sure is that the link from Coates's article to McCarthy's goes nowhere. I suspect McCarthy's review was scrubbed almost immediately. I was unaware of it until I read Remnick's attack on it two years later. In the final month of the campaign, no one on the responsible right would give me change for a dollar.

What made Trump's entry into the public square so memorable in 2011 was that he showed no concern about his status with liberals or the responsible right, grudging or otherwise. He bulled right in. Race had little, if anything, to do with his appeal. Boldness had everything to do with it. Although Trump's impact on the Obama presidency was minimal in 2011, he showed what a force he could be should he ever become president. To preserve their own version of events, as shall be seen, Obama and his allies would go to unprecedented lengths.

During the Obama years, an asymmetrical war was waged for control of that critical first draft of American history. There is no fair way to record that history without first acknowledging the war. The field of battle shaped up as follows: on the right, the samizdat and the responsible right, occasionally working together, often working at odds; on the left, the mainstream media, the social media giants, Hollywood, Broadway, the federal bureaucracies, the national security apparatus, and the ubiquitous firemen, amateur and professional. Rarely at odds, these forces routinely worked together to amplify what Obama adviser Ben Rhodes called the White House's "messaging campaign."

If push came to shove, the left had the most powerful ally of all in its corner, the U.S. government, particularly Obama's Department of Justice (DOJ) and a politicized Central Intelligence Agency (CIA). At least five of the truth tellers profiled herein were arrested for their efforts. Several more were harassed or threatened or subpoenaed by the DOJ, the FBI, the IRS, the Drug Enforcement Agency (DEA), and unknown others. A few expressed reluctance in going on the record for fear of further retaliation.

Money, resources, and power overwhelmingly favored the left, but the right had the equalizer on its side—the facts. By book's end, this dichotomy will not seem simplistic. From the moment of Obama's emergence in 2004, journalists, mainstream and left, have relentlessly disgraced their profession and betrayed the American people. The histories they write will not be worth reading.

The Front Man

"We quickly settled on him," wrote John Kerry of Barack Obama. Kerry and his advisers had selected Obama to give the keynote address at the 2004 Democratic National Convention. "It was an easy decision—a clean slate, someone fresh who could articulate a new vision, someone who was unexpected."[1]

In reality, Obama's slate was anything but clean in 2004. Knowing little about the man, Kerry and other Democrats preferred to imagine Obama as pure and noble, much as they imagined themselves. In the years ahead, court historians and Obama's everyday enablers in the mainstream media refused to cloud the Democrats' imagination. They deferred instead to team Obama and allowed his handlers to fashion an image of their man that best suited their purposes. Unfortunately for history's sake, that image warred with reality, not only in regard to Obama's objectives and accomplishments, but also in regard to his style and his very soul. In hindsight, it is remarkable how enthusiastically our nation's elites—political, academic, tech, media—could conspire to twice elect a man president they understood so little.

They failed to understand the reality of the Obama presidency in part because of their failure to understand the political transformation that occurred during Obama's tenure in the White House. "Liberalism," as understood in the post-war era, died on Obama's watch. Replacing it was "progressivism." This was much more than a casual rebranding. If liberals could envision a harmonious future, benign and paternal, orderly and safe, progressives could not. "Progressive," in fact, represents the rare bit of leftist nomenclature not cushioned by euphemism. At the risk of tautology, progressives "progress." Like the sharks of our imagination,

1

they move forward or they die. If liberals are to have any relevance, they follow, however uneasily, in the shark's wake.

In its current permutation, American progressivism is fundamentally improvisational and anti-intellectual. American progressives owe less to cultural Marxists such as Antonio Gramsci, the Critical Theorists of the Frankfurt School, or even Karl Marx himself than they do to activists such as Alfred Kinsey, Gloria Steinem, and Jesse Jackson.

In the post-Soviet era, with no one hand guiding the international left, American progressives have moved forward on numerous fronts: black, brown, green, feminist, LGBT, Islamic, globalist, and socialist. Despite all the talk of external manipulation from the likes, say, of a George Soros, the evolution of these movements has been largely organic with the civil rights movement serving as paradigm. Almost always intentionally, these movements eroded the power of traditional institutions—church and family, local governments, and private businesses—and consolidated it in the federal government and judiciary.

Barack Obama led none of the left's movements, but he enabled them all. He was supremely positioned to do so. Born to an African Marxist father with Muslim roots and a progressive American mother, Obama learned from leftist mentors throughout his life and sampled a wide range of socialist causes before finding himself, like a turtle on a fence post, keynoting the 2004 Democratic National Convention. Once on stage, Obama was able to turn the nation's racial guilt against friend and foe alike, immunizing himself in the process against meaningful criticism.

Obama's bourgeois lifestyle and cool demeanor made him all the more effective as a front man for a movement that had grown increasingly strident, even punitive. He was prepared to sell what he lacked the stomach to lead. For eight years, he would serve as the nation's conscience-in-chief, assigning liberal doses of shame to those who defied America's promised transformation, and encouragement to those who promoted it.

Given his origins and his education, there was no front in the progressive march through the institutions that Barack Obama could not credibly represent. His timing was excellent. "Intersectionality" was emerging on the left as more than just a buzzword. In theory, intersectionality meant that marginalized groups shared common oppressors and thus had common political interests. Schooled in street-level Critical Theory, activists from various fronts were forging alliances with those in other fronts who also saw themselves as oppressed. These activists, whether they knew it or not, would be expected to subordinate their own interests to the larger progressive cause—seizing and sustaining national power. Obama managed this entente well. Arguably his most useful contribution to the leftist cause was to shepherd the fractious coalition partners more or less along the same path.

The emotional force that held the movement together was a shared contempt for the enemy. Movement leaders showed less interest in celebrating the many colors of their multicultural rainbow than they did in punishing those who resisted the celebration. On Obama's watch, and occasionally at his urging, progressives found common cause in imputing hatred to others—hatred of blacks, of gays, of transgenders, of immigrants, of Muslims, of women, of poor people, even, yes, of mother earth. If hate defined America's deplorables, love and justice defined the good. A calculus this delusional would ultimately prove to be unsustainable, not to mention unmarketable.

The media helped pave the high road of good intentions. By the early 1960s, the mainstream media were prepared to accommodate leftward thrusts that did not put too much pressure on the "Overton window"—the range of ideas tolerated in public discourse. By the end of that decade, in all but the largest cities, one newspaper stood unchallenged. There were but three major television news networks, all in New York and Washington, two news magazines of significance, and three newspapers with national clout. Newsrooms everywhere had begun to skew left, even their sports departments, but gently at first and not without internal opposition.

As leftists consolidated their power in universities, journalism schools included, newsrooms shifted leftwards with each new graduating class. For a variety of reasons too complex to explain in this space, the internet accelerated the shift. By 2008, conservatives had almost no voice in any newsroom of significance other than those of Fox News and the *Wall Street Journal*. Given license by the media, progressive activists felt comfortable in making claims that they knew would go unchallenged regarding all manner of presumed problems: global warming, wage gaps, hate crimes, sex crimes, AIDS, police brutality, gender differences, income distribution, homelessness, illegal immigration, and discrimination of all sorts. "Narratives" were constructed around strategic omissions and half-truths, and movements were built on narratives.

The victim in these narratives—most narratives had at least one—was inevitably some "marginalized" person or group; the culprit some privileged branch of corporate and/or conservative America. This strategy was more Sharptonian than Gramscian, more pop culture than Critical Theory. In Obama, this evolving Hydra-headed movement found the perfect front man to represent its many, often conflicting, interests. As a "clean slate," at least from the media's perspective, a multiracial, international charmer like Obama could be all things to all people.

Never has a president-elect entered the White House with higher expectations. Indeed, within weeks of his inauguration, Obama would be nominated for the Nobel Peace Prize. None of his Democratic predecessors, not FDR, not even JFK, enjoyed a major media as agreeably one-sided as he did. Throughout Obama's tenure, and with his support, leftist elites attempted to suppress criticism of the president, his policies, and progressive causes in general. As Angelo Codevilla has observed, these elites presided "over nearly all federal, and state, government bureaucracies, over the media, the educational establishment, and major corporations."[2] They did not like, nor expect, to lose. Their control of the academies, the social media giants, and the major media outlets was very nearly monolithic.

Codevilla, perhaps the shrewdest observer of the contemporary left, contends that progressives today struggle not so much "to create the promised new realities as to force people to speak and act as if these were real."[3] For all of Obama's control of the media during his tenure, the samizdat remained beyond his reach. Its irregular journalists routinely threatened to expose what Codevilla called "the *gap* between political correctness and reality." And working as many did on their own dime and on their own time, they had neither careers nor pensions to protect. There was power in that independence.

Scandal Free

// I am proud of the fact that we will—knock on wood—leave this administration without significant scandal," said Barack Obama near the end of his second and last term in office.[1] The use of the word "significant" scarcely dimmed the wattage of this boast. Obama quickly added, "In terms of just abiding by the rules and norms and keeping trust with the American people, I will put this administration against any administration in history." Two years later, Obama felt free to repeat the claim, telling a tech audience, "I didn't have scandals, which seems like it shouldn't be something you brag about."[2]

Obama was not alone in thinking his administration was uniquely unblemished. Prominent media gatekeepers had been encouraging him to think along these lines for years. In 2011, Jonathan Alter headlined a *Bloomberg* story, "The Obama Miracle, a White House Free of Scandal."[3] In 2014, *New Yorker* editor and Obama biographer David Remnick thought it a "huge" achievement that "there's been no scandal, major scandal, in this administration, which is a rare thing in an administration."[4] In 2016, *New York Times* columnist David Brooks insisted the Obama administration was not just scandal free, but "remarkably scandal-free."[5]

A CNN discussion on the eve of Donald Trump's inauguration showed how likely it was that fake news would soon become fake history. "He is almost unimpeachable," said presidential historian Douglas Brinkley. "He has governed with such honesty and integrity, and he's not only leaving with that 60 percent [approval rating] we keep talking, but a growing reputation. And the legacy of having eight scandal-free years is going to look larger and larger in history."[6]

The saying goes that a scandal is not a scandal until the *New York Times* calls it a "scandal" on the front page, and by that definition, yes, the Obama administration was scandal free. By any sane definition, however, the Obama administration was awash in scandal. Just on its own, the mischief surrounding the passage and implementation of the Affordable Care Act (ACA)—also known as "Obamacare"—puts Obama in the Harding-Grant strata of scandal-plagued presidencies. Again, the major media contributed little, if anything, to uncovering the fundamental corruption at the heart of Obamacare. As was normative during the Obama years, the conservative media did almost all the digging. Among those who deserve credit is one unsung citizen journalist, a new recruit to the ranks of the samizdat. In the age of informational overload, this fellow showed how routinely big-name journalists overlooked the information that mattered.

Before the samizdat discovered him, Rich Weinstein dwelt in the peaceful anonymity of the everyday suburbanite. An unassuming, middle-aged investment adviser from metro Philadelphia, Weinstein had no aspirations to make waves, let alone make news, at least not before he received that fateful email from his insurance company. The year was 2013, and the message was simple: his health care plan was not ACA compliant. In a June 2009 speech introducing the Affordable Care Act, Obama assured Weinstein and his fellow citizens, "If you like your doctor, you will be able to keep your doctor. Period. If you like your health care plan, you will be able to keep your health care plan. Period. No one will take it away. No matter what."[7]

Obama made this claim, or a variation of the same, no fewer than thirty times during the months that followed, and he did so every time without equivocation. The lack of qualifiers convinced Weinstein that Obama had to be telling the truth. "I believed him," said Weinstein. When Weinstein learned he could keep neither his doctor nor his health plan, and that his insurance premiums were about to double, he began his own personal probe into the mischief-makers behind Obamacare.[8]

Had he a mind to, the average fifth grader could have done what Weinstein did. There was nothing complicated about his search. He identified several of the reputed Obamacare "architects" through Google and found their video presentations on YouTube. A consultant with the Dickensian name "Jonathan Gruber" intrigued Weinstein more than the others. An MIT professor of economics, Gruber had also helped design "Romneycare," the Massachusetts health plan implemented while Mitt Romney was governor. What struck Weinstein about Gruber were his ship-sinking lips. On one occasion, for instance, Gruber publicly admitted his fear Romney could become president, a rash comment for a guy who had made his reputation on Romney's back.

Gruber, Weinstein soon came to appreciate, was much more candid than his client in the White House would have liked. In July 2014, Weinstein found a highly revealing video clip of Gruber from January 2012. Said Gruber at the time, "I think what's important to remember politically about this, is if you're a state and you don't set up an Exchange, that means your citizens don't get their tax credits."

This video was more than a little awkward for the White House. Gruber's comments echoed those of the plaintiffs in a pair of cases whose defendant in each case was Health and Human Services (HHS) Secretary Sylvia Burwell. In brief, the plaintiffs argued that citizens in states that had not set up their own exchanges were ineligible for Obamacare tax credits. The ACA language was so hastily and sloppily written, they had a good case. Gruber, an Obamacare architect, agreed with them. More awkward still, Gruber later signed on to an amicus brief that argued exactly the opposite of what he had said in the video two years prior.

Weinstein posted the video in the comments section of a relevant *Washington Post* article. Michael Cannon, health care expert at the libertarian Cato Institute, knew a bombshell when he saw one: here was an Obamacare architect making the plaintiff's case against the White House that hired him. Cannon posted the video on his *Forbes* blog, and it proved to be a sensation among those who cared. It's just that not that many people cared.[9]

Almost everyone cared about Weinstein's next find. He calls it the "stupid video." Weinstein traces the day of discovery to November 2, 2014, his wedding anniversary. The video recorded an October 2013 panel discussion at the University of Pennsylvania. Said Gruber of the Affordable Care Act, "This bill was written in a tortured way to make sure CBO [the Congressional Budget Office] did not score the mandate as taxes. If CBO scored the mandate as taxes, the bill dies." After some explanatory remarks, Gruber sawed the rest of the limb out from under himself. "Lack of transparency is a huge political advantage," he told his audience. "And basically, call it the stupidity of the American voter or whatever, but basically that was really, really critical for the thing to pass."[10]

Weinstein sent the video link to activist Phil Kerpen, who posted it on his American Commitment website on November 7. While the video slowly gained traction, Weinstein reached out on the morning of November 9 to his "first real reporter," veteran *New York Times* health correspondent Robert Pear. Weinstein was hopeful. He met Pear a few weeks earlier at a Cato Institute conference in Washington, and Pear had written about Gruber's health care exchange comments just a few days prior.

"Thought you'd be interested in this," Weinstein wrote in his email to Pear. "If this isn't a complete slap in the face of the American voter, nothing is. He calls the American voter 'stupid' and explains how lack of transparency get [*sic*] the ACA passed. This video should be seen by EVERY AMERICAN." Weinstein included a link to the video.

"Would you happen to know the time and place of the panel discussion?" Pear responded. Weinstein filled in the details, and Pear signed off with a simple, "Thank you." And that was the last he heard from Pear.[11] "Every American" may have needed to see this video, but the *Times* would not help them find it. The samizdat assumed that burden. Indeed, by November 12, "Gruber" had become a household word.

Forced to address the growing controversy, the White House gave Gruber the Bill Ayers "guy-in-the-neighborhood" brush-off. "The fact that an adviser who was never on our staff expressed an opinion that I completely disagree with in terms of the voters is not a reflection on the actual process that was run," said Obama when asked. Gruber's title was irrelevant. The Obama administration paid Gruber, the acknowledged designer of the individual mandate, nearly $400,000 for a year's work. As even the *Washington Post* acknowledged, Gruber met at least once with Obama in the Oval Office. The reason for the meeting was simple:

"His advice was important at critical moments when the bill's survival was in jeopardy."[12]

The *Times* finally weighed in on November 12. In a patronizing column on its "Upshot" site, economic correspondent Neil Irwin insisted Gruber's comments were "completely commonplace." Wrote Irwin, "Legislators frequently game policy to fit the sometimes arbitrary conventions by which the Congressional Budget Office evaluates laws and the public debates them." To put *Times* readers further at ease, Irwin assured them, "This kind of gamesmanship is very much a bipartisan affair."[13]

Working off Irwin's interpretation, the firemen at Media Matters for America helped douse the flames with an article a day later headlined, "The Fraudulent Media Campaign To Scandalize Obamacare's Passage."[14] Scandal? What scandal? The Obama administration deceived the American public at every turn to create a monstrously confusing program, rife with fraud, that did not work and whose rollout was an admitted fiasco. None of this moved the *Times* to utter the S-word.

To put Obamacare in its proper perspective, three of Obama's more prominent speechwriters—David Litt, Jon Favreau, and Jon Lovett—shared their feelings in May 2016 with the not yet disgraced Charlie Rose. Although something of a comedy writer, Lovett told Rose he was "most proud" of his more serious speeches, particularly those on health care and economics. At this point, Favreau interjected, "Lovett wrote the line about, 'If you like your insurance, you can keep it.'" Lovett shot back in faux outrage, "How dare you!" They all laughed, Rose included.[15] Lovett, by the way, was twenty-six years old when he conceived the "if you like your doctor" flimflam. In 2016, he and his pals were still young enough to see the hilarity in Politifact's 2013 "Lie of the Year." Perhaps if they had to dig into their kids' college funds to pay doubled health care premiums as Weinstein did, they might not have found Obamacare all that amusing.

Obamacare was just one non-scandal out of many during those underreported eight-plus years. To find another of similar heft, a curious party need only enter "IRS scandal" on the Wikipedia site. Thanks to the volunteer firemen who edit at Wikipedia, he or she will then be redirected to "IRS targeting controversy," one more reminder there were no "scandals" during the Obama presidency.

The samizdat first became aware of the "IRS targeting controversy" in early March 2012 when David French of the *National Review* began reporting on the work done by his colleagues at the American Center for Law and Justice (ACLJ). Although admitting their research was preliminary, French, a Harvard Law grad, had seen enough evidence to know how serious the problem might be. "The early indications," wrote French, "are the IRS is using the routine process of seeking and granting tax exemptions to undertake a sweeping, top-down review of the internal workings of the tea-party movement in the United States." French concluded, "Such a review is far beyond its mission and directly implicates the First Amendment rights of all citizens."[16]

The lawlessness, however, went deeper than French knew. The IRS was not just reviewing and monitoring the various Tea Parties. It was using its formidable power to suppress them. French was a serious writer. The ACLJ was a serious organization. The use of the IRS to discourage a highly successful grassroots political movement should have stirred the nation's journalists from their collective slumber. Predictably, it did no such thing.

As the ACLJ would come to see, the political class had sunk its roots deep into the IRS. In 2008, the IRS union, the National Treasury Employees Union (NTEU) by name, gave 96 percent of the $641,950 raised from its employees to Democratic candidates. Obama promptly repaid the favor. In December 2009, he issued Executive Order 13522, allowing employees and unions to have "pre-decisional involvement in all workplace matters." That same month, he and wife Michelle invited the NTEU president to their Christmas party at the White House.[17] These were Obama's people.

With the rank-and-file support assured, the political appointees put their game plan into action. In April 2010, according to a 2013 Inspector General (IG) report, the new IRS Acting Manager, Technical Unit, "suggested the need for a Sensitive Case Report on the Tea Party cases." In May 2010, the IRS Determinations Unit signed on, issuing a BOLO (Be On the Look Out) "for Tea Party or similar organizations." The motives of the IRS were not hard for the Inspector General to discern. Observed the IG, "Early in Calendar Year 2010, the IRS began using inappropriate criteria to identify organizations applying for tax-exempt status to review for indications of significant political campaign intervention."[18] The unmistakable goal was to discourage Tea Party activists from organizing.

If the media were looking for a victim to personify abuse by the IRS, they could have found no better candidate than Catherine Engelbrecht. The attractive, well-spoken entrepreneur represented everything gender-sensitive editors looked for in a heroine, except, of course, her Republican sympathies. The nightmare she endured is straight out of Kafka. A year after breaking the news of IRS targeting, *National Review* told Engelbrecht's much too real tale of woe. Aware of the mainstream's aversion to the S-word, *NR* editors mischievously titled the article, "True Scandal."[19]

Prior to the 2008 election, Catherine and her husband, Bryan, had been too busy running their small manufacturing plant in Rosenberg, Texas, to get political. Her experience as an election judge that year prompted her to find the time. A natural organizer, Engelbrecht launched two new organizations. The King Street Patriots, a classic Tea Party group, set about to enlighten citizens on economic freedom and constitutional government. The second, True the Vote, worked to prevent voter fraud. From the perspective of the Obama White House, it was hard to say which of these two outfits presented a greater threat. To give her organizations credibility with potential donors, Engelbrecht filed for tax-exempt status in July 2010.

In December 2010, Engelbrecht received a strange request. The FBI Domestic Terrorism Unit wanted to meet with her, ostensibly to talk about an attendee at a Tea Party event. This visit would prove to be the first of *six* by the FBI. Prior to the uneasy get-together with the FBI, no agents of the federal government had shown any interest in the Engelbrechts or their business going back twenty years. But once the Tea Parties showed their clout in the November 2010 midterms, the benign neglect era came to an abrupt end. In January 2011, the IRS descended on the Engelbrechts' shop to audit both their personal and business returns. In March 2011, the IRS began a deep probe into True the Vote. A few months later, the IRS was back asking more questions.

The *New York Times* first took notice of Engelbrecht in December 2011 when she organized a peaceful protest of an Austin event featuring Attorney General Eric Holder. Reporter Charlie Savage let Engelbrecht have her say. He noted her objection to Holder's "voter suppression" smears and listed voting irregularities she felt needed attention. Savage did add, however, that Engelbrecht had not witnessed these irregularities herself. This observation fit a pattern. Going forward, the *Times* would expect citizens to provide hard documentation of voter fraud in order to be taken seriously. Newspapers used to do that job themselves.

As an aside, Savage told his readers, "Mr. Holder has been a popular target for Republicans, most recently because of a disputed gun-trafficking investigation called Fast and Furious."[20] Nearly a year after this "controversy" flared to the surface—no scandal here—Savage still felt the need to remind his readers what "Fast and Furious" meant. He knew their limitations well.

In February 2012, the IRS put Engelbrecht and True the Vote through the ringer for a third time. Its agents demanded to see all her tweets and Facebook posts. As Engelbrecht testified before the House Oversight and Government Reform Subcommittee in February 2014, the IRS also wanted to know "the names of groups that I had spoken with, the content of what I had said and every word I intended to speak in the coming year."[21] The IRS started hounding the King Street Patriots as well.

The feds were just warming up. The Bureau of Alcohol, Tobacco, and Firearms (ATF) suddenly took an interest in the Engelbrechts under the pretext that their business had a permit to manufacture gun components. The Occupational Safety and Health Administration (OSHA) took the next swat at the Engelbrecht piñata, and the agency walked away with $17,500 in prize money disguised as fines. If the feds weren't problem enough, Texas's environmental agency came knocking based on a lead from an unnamed source.

Elected Democrats upped the pressure on Engelbrecht. In September 2012, Democratic California Senator Barbara Boxer wrote to Assistant

Attorney General Tom Perez, "As you know, an organization called 'True the Vote,' which is an offshoot of the Tea Party, is leading a voter suppression campaign in many states." Boxer added glibly, "I don't believe this is 'True the Vote.' I believe it's 'Stop the Vote.'" In October 2012, with the election looming, Democrat Representative Elijah Cummings played the race card for the *nth* time in his dubious career, questioning whether True the Vote was part of a "criminal conspiracy to deny legitimate voters their constitutional rights." Not easily intimidated, Engelbrecht filed an ethics complaint against Cummings.

In September 2012, the *Times* took renewed interest in Engelbrecht, not to report her ordeal at the hands of the government, but to ridicule her drive to "true" the vote. In a maddeningly dismissive article, Stephanie Saul's lede set the tone, "It might as well be Harry Potter's invisible Knight Bus, because no one can prove it exists." Saul was referring here to a bus alleged to be moving Democratic voters to a designated voting site. Rather than prove or disprove the bus's existence, Saul mocked Engelbrecht *a priori*, an admittedly more cost-efficient style of journalism than digging up facts. "There have been few cases of widespread fraud,"[22] she insisted. To prove cases of fraud, of course, someone has to look. The major media had not done so in a serious way since *Chicago Tribune* reporters went undercover in 1972 to shoot fishes in the hometown fraud barrel.[23]

At the outset, Engelbrecht had been told it would take four or five months for her organizations to be approved for 501(c)(3) status. Two years later, with approval still pending, two years during which she had endured twenty-three distinct audits or inquiries, Engelbrecht said, "Enough is enough. Let's take it to them." She sued the IRS. "I had no real expectation or preparation for the blood sport that American politics is," Engelbrecht would tell a congressional committee in 2014. "It's all been a through-the-looking-glass experience."[24]

Although the harassment of Engelbrecht was extreme, the targeting was not exceptional. The IRS stalled or rejected the applicants of hundreds, if not thousands, of comparable groups. In concluding her testimony, Engelbrecht asked Congress "to end this ugly chapter of political intimidation. There was a time when people of good will were encouraged to participate in the processes of government, not targeted because of it."

Finally, in June 2019, after six years of IRS stalling, U.S. District Court Judge Reggie Walton ruled emphatically in Engelbrecht's favor. "To have the court come out now and say, not only did True the Vote win, but the IRS has to pay a premium because of the way that they handled this whole process, is just incredibly vindicating," Engelbrecht told Virginia Allen of the *Daily Signal*, an online conservative publication.[25]

Engelbrecht would have been happy to tell her story to the major media if reporters had shown even a spark of interest, but they never did. Having collectively chanced upon the phrase "dog whistle," journalists found the one metaphor they needed to defame people like Engelbrecht. Indeed, she is featured prominently in *Dog Whistle Politics: How Coded Racial Appeals Have Reinvented Racism and Wrecked the Middle Class*. The author of this book-length slander, no surprise, is a distinguished Berkeley law professor and occasional *Times* contributor by the name of Ian Haney López. (No innocent at the race game, López uses the maiden name of his El Salvadoran mother as his last name.) Writes López, "Despite intensive, highly motivated efforts to find voter fraud, the data suggests that voter impersonation happens with roughly the same frequency that persons are struck and killed by lightening."[26] Having had a catbird seat on one mayoral election in my hometown of Newark, New Jersey, I can assure López his comments are dangerously naive. Forget about lightning strikes. Hurricane Sandy did not wreak as much havoc in New Jersey as has voter fraud.

Without major media support, the Republicans in Congress could get no real traction in bringing the IRS malefactors to justice.

The public face of the scandal, political appointee Lois Lerner, eventually apologized to the Tea Parties, testified before a House committee, pled the Fifth Amendment lest she incriminate herself, and was declared in contempt of Congress. When the House subpoenaed Lerner's emails, the IRS told House members the hard drive had crashed, and the emails were irretrievable. Unable to access the emails, a Department of Justice investigation came to naught. It probably would have in any case given the way Obama "wingman" Eric Holder dispensed justice. Wrote Assistant

Attorney General Peter Kadzik in summary, "Not a single IRS employee reported any allegation, concern or suspicion that the handling of tax-exempt applications—or any other IRS function—was motivated by political bias, discriminatory intent, or corruption." A credulous media took him at his word.

They shouldn't have. Kadzik first made the national news as the attorney who prodded the Clinton White House to pardon fugitive financier Marc Rich. Eighteen years later, Kadzik made the news again. This time, the Inspector General scolded him for not recusing himself in the investigation into Hillary Clinton's emails. His close ties to campaign chair John Podesta and his attempts to get a job for his son with the Hillary campaign made a joke of Kadzik's claims to objectivity.[27] In between those two sterling moments of public service, he helped cover up the IRS scandal. If there were a deep state all-star team, he'd be on it.

In retrospect, the failure of the major media to press the White House on such blatant harassment shocks even a cynic. It would have taken no great effort. All the information was within walking distance of the *Washington Post* offices and the Washington bureau of the *Times*. In May 2013, the now disgraced *Times* reporter Jonathan Weisman ("racist" tweets) wrote an article headlined, "I.R.S. Apologizes to Tea Party Groups Over Audits of Applications for Tax Exemption," but the headline promised more than the article delivered. Weisman accepted Lerner's "bureaucratic mix-up" excuse at face value.[28]

Collectively, conservative journalists, salaried or citizen, online or on air, did not have resources enough to track the IRS scandal to its source. Insulated by layers of faithful sycophants and protected by a complicit media, "no drama" Obama never needed to break a sweat. His secrets were safe. As I have learned firsthand over the years, there is almost nothing a conservative journalist can offer a witness to any deep state mischief to compensate for ruining his or her career. Whistleblowing has no currency with a Democrat in the White House. As a consequence, phone calls go unanswered, leads peter out, and miscreants walk away unscathed. If proof of the latter be needed, best estimates place Lois Lerner's federal pension at about $102,000 a year.[29]

In the case of Obamacare and the IRS Tea Party shakedown, the responsible right and the samizdat worked toward the same goal. Together, they were able to make at least half of America aware that the "scandal free" Obama mantra was less a reality than the punch line to a bad joke. Without the support of the responsible right, however, potential scandals can die aborning.

As an illustration, let me cite the work of Susan Daniels, a licensed private investigator from Ohio. Although now in her seventies, Daniels remains sufficiently lively and attractive to get hit on in airport bars. She is no one's fool and never has been. A movie could be made of her earlier life. In fact, one already has, but that's a story for another day.

In 2009, Daniels was asked to run a background check on Barack Obama. Working with her law firm clients, Daniels had run checks on thousands of individuals without anxiety or incident. This was different. In June 2009, Barack Obama had been president for six months. The House and Senate were both in Democratic hands, and the permanent bureaucracy skewed heavily left. What Daniels planned to do was perfectly legal. That said, she had a generalized fear of retaliation from somewhere within the federal government. Had Daniels been younger, had any of her seven children still depended on her, she probably would have punted. But with her sixty-seventh birthday looming, she figured, if not now, when?

Daniels had access to proprietary databases denied to ordinary citizens.[30] She entered "Barack Obama" and "Chicago" into one database without result. She tried with another and again came up empty. The third entry paid off. Up popped Obama's name, his date of birth, an address in Chicago, and his Social Security number (SSN). The SSN immediately struck her as fishy. She knew the prefix "042" had to have an East Coast provenance. Inquiring further, she traced its issuance to Connecticut somewhere in the years between 1977 and 1979. Up until June 2011, and that date has meaning, Social Security numbers were distributed geographically. In 1977, as Daniels easily discovered, "042" SSNs were assigned only to individuals who applied from the state of Connecticut.

Intrigued, she entered Obama's SSN into another database and came up with a list of his past addresses in Illinois, Massachusetts, and the District of Columbia. Daniels learned that Obama was twenty-six years old when he first used this SSN. At that time, he was living in Chicago. She found the same Connecticut-based SSN for Obama with the Massachusetts driver's license bureau in 1989 when he was at Harvard and on a 2009 tax return that a staffer carelessly posted online.

The mystery deepened with Daniels's discovery that the SSN was first assigned in March 1977 to a person born in 1890. As she knew, the Social Security Administration never reissues a used number. The fact that a number had been assigned to an eighty-seven-year-old did not strike Daniels as extraordinary. She had handled cases in which widows of that generation applied for Social Security in their own names only after their husbands had died. In March 1977, however, Obama was a fifteen-year-old living in Hawaii. Obama's half-sister, Maya Soetoro, was about that age when she received her SSN in 1985 or 1986 with a standard Hawaiian prefix of "576."

To firm up her case, Daniels traced the ten SSNs preceding Obama's and the ten following. All of them were issued in March 1977 in Connecticut. In fact, she was able to pinpoint Monday, March 28, 1977, as the day Obama's SSN was authorized. There was no getting around the obvious: President Barack Obama had been using an anomalous and possibly fraudulent SSN for more than twenty years. Daniels would have loved to get her hands on the original application for that number, but her efforts in that regard fell short. Insiders know better than to leak information damaging to a Democrat.

Alarmed by what she had found, Daniels contacted her local congressman, a Republican, since deceased, but he ignored her entreaties. She wrote to any number of other members of Congress with comparable results. She looked to see if there was a lawsuit in process challenging Obama's identity, but the lawyer to whom she volunteered her information did not strike Daniels as reliable.

"Reliable" will be a key word throughout this book. There are independent investigators who are every bit as reliable as the best professional journalists. Daniels is one of them. She has little use for reporters or producers who finesse facts to fit a narrative, even if they are political allies, *especially* if they are political allies.

At the samizdat online publication WorldNetDaily (WND), Jerry Corsi began writing about Daniels's findings. In June 2010, WND reporter Les Kinsolving managed to raise the question of Obama's SSN at a White House press briefing.[31] "Investigators Susan Daniels and John Sampson are asking why the president is using a Social Security number reserved for Connecticut applicants," Kinsolving said to then press secretary Robert Gibbs. Gibbs tried to laugh off the statement, but Kinsolving persisted, "Do you know of any record that the president ever had a mailing address in Connecticut?" Gibbs mockingly linked the question to the birth certificate issue. When Kinsolving tried to refocus the discussion on the SSN, Gibbs abruptly ended the briefing. This was as close as the story ever came to surfacing in the major media.

On the right, one less-than-reliable researcher concluded that the SSN Obama was using belonged to a French immigrant named Jean Paul Ludwig, who was born in 1890 and reportedly died in Hawaii in 1981. Daniels promptly and publicly challenged this story, but the researcher had given the firemen in the fact-checking industry the cover they needed to trash the larger story of Obama's problematic SSN.

Perhaps the best known of the fact checkers is Snopes. In Daniels's experience, and my own as well, Snopes seemed to have no greater purpose during Obama's presidency than to kill stories potentially harmful to the president. The Obama SSN story proved to be a classic Snopes bait-and-switch. Written by Snopes founder David Mikkelson and filed tellingly under the rubric "Birther," the piece baited the audience with a legitimate question, "Did Barack Obama Steal His Social Security Number?"[32] In the subhead, however, Mikkelson asked a red herring of a question and served up an appropriately misleading answer, "Barack Obama did not appropriate the Social Security number of a dead man born in 1890 and use it as his own." Mikkelson then planted a big red X symbol and the word "False" in bold underneath the headline. Readers who preferred to remain ignorant of Obama's foibles, journalists most notably, would have felt no need to go beyond the headline.

The disinformation continued. In the first sentence of the body copy, Mikkelson assured the curious that the Jean Paul Ludwig tale was "fantastical" and "easily debunked." The tale was not exactly "fantastical," but it was inaccurate. Daniels herself had debunked it. What Mikkelson could not debunk—he conceded as much—was the Connecticut source of the SSN.

In a different era, the grudging admission that follows would have sent serious reporters scurrying to their local Social Security office. Wrote Mikkelson in seeming wonder, "Why Barack Obama's Social Security card application might have included a Connecticut mailing address is something of a curiosity as he had no known connection to that state at the time."

Mikkelson posted this article on June 13, 2011. Two weeks later, the Social Security Administration (SSA) introduced a process called "randomization." This process eliminated "the geographical significance of the first three digits of the SSN."[33] The geographical indicator had been in place since 1935. Although likely a coincidence, this move by the SSA should have drawn attention to Obama's dubious SSN. It did not.

Unlike Obama's birth certificate, whose legitimacy may never be certified, Obama has inarguably been using an SSN that originated in Connecticut. This SSN is at least a "curiosity" and quite possibly a fraud. Reporters should have been all over this scandal in the making. They were not. Daniels surfaced the story in 2009 and was prominently attached to it in the alternative media, as well as at a White House press conference. Yet she never received a call from anyone beyond the samizdat.

Doing the White House's cleanup work, Mikkelson acknowledged a "discrepancy" but dismissed it as "a simple clerical or typographical error." He attributed the discrepancy to the fact that Obama's ZIP code in Hawaii was 96814 while the ZIP code for Danbury, Connecticut, was 06814."[34] He then speculated that an accidental switch in initial digits led to an errant SSN for Obama. To Mikkelson's humble credit, this was the best of the arguments circulating around the left side of the blogosphere. One popular trope, unfortunately echoed by Bill O'Reilly on Fox News, was that the young Obama enrolled in Social Security because his father "lived in Connecticut for several years."[35] In some versions, the young Obama visited his father in Connecticut. In O'Reilly's version, "Babies sometimes get numbers based on addresses provided by their parents." Either version would have gotten more traction if Obama Sr. had ever lived in Connecticut or if young Obama had visited him there, but Obama Sr. never lived in the Nutmeg State, and the young Obama never saw him in any state but Hawaii, if there.

The Obama faithful did not worry themselves with details, but Susan Daniels did. In researching the rogue ZIP code theory, she discovered that none of the three Hawaii ZIP codes in which Obama once lived had a viable counterpart in Connecticut. Two did not exist, and the third was reserved for the exclusive use of Union Carbide. No one in either the mainstream media or on the responsible right followed up on Daniels's research. Despite all the questions about Obama's origins, journalists had less than zero interest in exposing what could have been a career-killing scandal.

Ignored by the media, Daniels filed suit in Geauga County (Ohio) Common Pleas Court in July 2012. She demanded that Jon Husted, Ohio Secretary of State, remove Obama's name from the ballot until he could prove the legitimacy of his SSN. Not surprisingly, Husted blew her off. Neither Husted nor anyone from his office showed up for the September 2012 court date. Their absence did not much matter. After a cursory hearing, Republican Judge David Fuhry promptly dismissed the case. End of story.

As Daniels could see up close, Barack Obama enjoyed a near immunity from press curiosity. Equally incurious were those responsible Republicans whose fear of being thought racist kept them from challenging Obama on any issue relating to his origins or identity. They had reason to be concerned.

On the JournoList site, Spencer Ackerman of the *Washington Independent* shared a strategy for keeping Republicans quiet. Instead of defending Obama on racially sensitive issues, Ackerman urged his fellow journalists to take the offensive. He recommended they target a prominent Republican—"Fred Barnes, Karl Rove, who cares"—call him a racist, and badger him about his "deep-seated problem" with a black president. This accusation would cause the Republican to "sputter with rage, which in turn leads to overreaction and self-destruction."[36] Ackerman's colleagues did not need his sly advice. They had been branding Republicans as racists since white southerners stopped voting Democrat a half-century ago.

In the years since Daniels went public, three Pulitzer Prize winners have written Obama biographies. None of the three, all named "David"— Remnick, Maraniss, Garrow—so much as mentioned the Connecticut SSN "curiosity," not even to dismiss it. Neither did the fourth David, David Mendell, who wrote his biography before Obama became president. For all his sleight-of-hand, the fifth David, David Mikkelson, at least raised the issue.

Daniels's experience serves as something of a template. The reader does well to bear it in mind. Journalists who shied from learning the truth about Obama's Social Security number were not about to ask him where he was on the night the Benghazi consulate was attacked, what he knew about the IRS war on the Tea Party, or how he came to authorize "Fast and Furious," let alone what role he played in protecting Hillary Clinton from prosecution or in spying on Donald Trump's campaign.

Even more problematic for history's sake, journalists refused to understand Obama's role in the progressive revolution that redefined their party of choice. More than fifteen years after Obama first took center stage at the Democratic National Convention in Boston, the media know little more about Obama than they did back then. And that, we know, is just the way they prefer it.

The Home Front

O f the many fronts in the campaign for the American soul that Barack Obama championed—black, brown, green, and so on—none was as critical as what we might call the "home front." To become president, Obama had first to define his personal history and then defend it.

The defining part, Obama pulled off in spectacular fashion at the Democratic National Convention in Boston in July 2004.[1] Immediately after thanking those gathered for the opportunity to speak, Obama laid out his multicultural credentials. He introduced his father who grew up "herding goats" in Kenya. His mother he traced to Kansas as he always did, not to Seattle where she spent her formative years. His maternal grandfather enlisted the day after Pearl Harbor and "joined Patton's Army." His paternal grandfather was "a domestic servant to the British." Having no easily identified political value, his grandmothers, white and black, went unmentioned.

To this point, Obama was on reasonably safe ground. Then he began to stray. "My parents shared not only an improbable love," he insisted, "they shared an abiding faith in the possibilities of this nation." For the next twelve years and counting, Obama would recite variations on this story whenever the opportunity allowed and sometimes even when it didn't. Remnick called this pitch Obama's "signature appeal: the use of the details of his own life as a reflection of a kind of multicultural ideal."[2] This positioning strategy, although powerful, had its vulnerabilities. Samizdat journalists would exploit them. MSM journalists and their firemen allies would punish those who did.

In that same convention speech, Obama introduced the Democratic nominee, Sen. John Kerry. The first of Kerry's qualifications that Obama cited was his "heroic service" in Vietnam. To reinforce his position as war hero, Kerry boated across Boston Harbor to the Fleet Center as if he were Gen. MacArthur returning to the Philippines. Said the nominee upon mounting the arena's stage, "I'm John Kerry, and I'm reporting for duty."[3]

It is no coincidence that military men and politicians both use the word "campaign" to describe their presumed paths to victory. For all his military bluster, however, Kerry seemed to have no idea that his positioning strategy left him even more vulnerable than Obama's left Obama. During his time as a swift boat officer in Vietnam, John Kerry had managed to alienate a clear majority of his fellow officers. For several months prior to the convention, attorney and swift boat veteran John O'Neill— "the most public face of an effort by angry fellow veterans to discredit Mr. Kerry," per the *New York Times*[4]—had been gathering testimony from his fellow officers. O'Neill had also fact-checked Kerry's claimed heroics. Many of those tales of derring-do, perhaps most, did not hold up.

In late May 2004, I received a call from Jerry Corsi, who was working with O'Neill. Cleveland talk show host Paul Schiffer had recommended Corsi contact me about producing a documentary, my main line of work at the time. Corsi sent me the material O'Neill had gathered. It was devastating. I suggested that if he and O'Neill really wanted to make an impact, they should write a book and get it out before the Republican National Convention in late August. I recommended he send a proposal to my editor at Thomas Nelson, whose WND Books imprint had published my previous work. On May 27, 2004, I emailed Corsi, "The proposal seems like it should be enough. If they need more, I am attaching some proposal guidelines. Call me if you need any more information or intercession with WND." When my editor told Corsi he could not turn the book around in time for the convention, I recommended he and O'Neill try Regnery, a conservative publishing house. I suggested too that they compress the book's unwieldy proposed title into one word, "Unfit." Two months later, Regnery published *Unfit for Command*, a huge bestseller and a game changer in the 2004 election.

Sun Tzu could not have done a better job finding the weakness in Kerry's strength than O'Neill and Corsi did. Had Kerry not positioned himself as a war hero, he would not have been nearly as vulnerable.

Predictably, the MSM defended the Democratic candidate and attacked his critics. By 2004, this had become standard operating procedure in major newsrooms. Watching from afar, I was particularly amused at the charge that the authors were part of a coordinated Republican attack machine. I cite the email above to show just how unconnected Corsi and O'Neill were in late May 2004. Their operation was pure samizdat, the proof of which is that they were asking *me* for advice.

What the Swift Boat Veterans for Truth had on their side was, in fact, the truth. Kerry's supporters could not understand why he did not fight back or sue, but Kerry had his reasons. He knew he was not in Cambodia on Christmas Eve 1968 as he had claimed, and he knew Cambodia was just one fabrication out of the many that O'Neill had exposed. To fight back was to aggravate the wound.

In the years after Kerry's close election loss, the MSM chose to ignore the evidence and perpetuate the myth that Kerry had been defamed. Today, "swiftboating" has come to be defined as a "pejorative American neologism used to describe an unfair or untrue political attack."[5] The definition endures as memories fade. In an April 2019 *New Yorker* article, for instance, Masha Gessen dismissed Corsi as "a conspiracy theorist, a Swift Boater, and a birther."[6] Journalists never forgave Corsi for helping defeat Kerry and, worse, for embarrassing the media.

The 2004 campaign witnessed an even more memorable conflict between the MSM and the samizdat. That summer, the Democratic Party was running a coordinated round of attacks on George Bush called "Operation Fortunate Son." The major media lent a hand. On the last day of the Republican National Convention, CBS's Dan Rather signaled his intent with a question to First Lady Laura Bush: "Now that friends and supporters of the President have raised the issue of John Kerry's combat record in Vietnam, do you or do you not think it's fair now for the Kerry people to come back and dig anew into your husband's military service record?"[7] Later that same week, Rather proved himself one of the "Kerry people" by fronting a *60 Minutes* hit piece that accused Bush of ducking out on his National Guard service in 1972.[8]

Before the internet matured, Rather could have gotten away with the smear, but not in 2004. Collaborating through the samizdat, otherwise unconnected citizens quickly exposed the fraudulent documents at the heart of the CBS story. On the *Power Line* blog, one can still trace the story's unraveling. It began with a simple observation from a reader, "Every single one of the memos to file regarding Bush's failure to attend a physical and meet other requirements is in a proportionally spaced font, probably Palatine or Times New Roman."[9] Other readers, including Army veterans with specialized knowledge, augmented and refined the information stream. The evidence was damning. Rather had received a word-processed document dated from a time before word processing. He had been had.

CBS and its allies made numerous attempts to shore up the original story, the most noteworthy being an article in the *Times* headlined, "Memos on Bush Are Fake But Accurate, Typist Says."[10] The story was beyond shoring up. Four months after the initial airing of the Rather piece, and two months *after* the election, CBS grudgingly conceded defeat. An editor's note acknowledged the following: "A report issued by an independent panel on Jan. 10, 2005 concluded that CBS News failed to follow basic journalistic principles in the preparation and reporting of this Sept. 8, 2004 broadcast."[11]

It was "an important moment," said former CBS exec Jonathan Klein, unaware of how celebrated his comment would become. "You couldn't have a starker contrast between the multiple layers of checks and balances, and a guy sitting in his living room in his pajamas writing what he thinks."[12] Thanks to the internet and the development of the social media, guys in their pajamas would bedevil the Obama presidency and slow the advance of the sundry progressive fronts.

The home front was more fragile than Obama knew. In his 2008 acceptance speech at the Democratic National Convention, he once again plunged into the family saga. "Four years ago," he reminded his audience, "I stood before you and told you my story—of the brief union between a young man from Kenya and a young woman from Kansas who weren't well-off or well-known, but shared a belief that in America, their son could achieve whatever he put his mind to."[13]

Although admitting the union was "brief," Obama continued to reinforce the notion that his birth family was a real one, patriotic and forward-looking to boot. The MSM chose to take him at his word. This posturing by Obama was not incidental. It was as much his "signature appeal"—in Remnick's words—as was John Kerry's heroism in Vietnam.

In the summer of 2008, two journalists set out to tell the story of Obama's early years in Hawaii. One was Pulitzer Prize winner David Maraniss, whose research would culminate in a ten thousand-word article in the *Washington Post*. The other was citizen journalist Michael Patrick Leahy, currently a Breitbart contributor and publisher of *The Tennessee Star*, among other online journals. Leahy's research would culminate in an eight thousand-word chapter in his self-published book, *What Does Barack Obama Believe?*[14]

In his 1995 memoir, *Dreams from My Father*, Obama claimed his father left Hawaii in 1963, when he "was only two years old." In his 2007 biography, *Obama: From Promise to Power*, the *Chicago Tribune's* David Mendell sustained the illusion that Obama Sr. left the family for Harvard "when Obama was two years old."[15] Unchallenged by the media, Obama stuck with the story of a family that remained whole for two years.

Working with considerably fewer resources and without the backing of a celebrated newsroom, Leahy talked to many of the same people Maraniss did. Given his limitations, he did his research strictly by phone and internet. As a reporter, however, Leahy did have one major advantage. He was prepared to challenge the Obama myth and said so right up front. "While we can't fault Barack Obama for believing the fictional account his mother told him about his father's role in his early life," wrote Leahy, "we can fault him for failing to undertake even the most rudimentary investigation of the truth behind this fictional account as an adult, and subsequently perpetuating that fiction publicly for over thirteen years."[16]

Following the facts where they led him, Leahy concluded that Obama Sr. did not leave Obama's mother, Stanley Ann Dunham, in Hawaii. Rather, it was Dunham who "left Barack Obama Senior in Honolulu and moved into her own apartment in Seattle, Washington."[17] Leahy backed up his claim with school records from the University of Washington, as well as records from the apartments Dunham rented. He surmised correctly, "Stanley Ann Dunham returned to Hawaii from

Seattle, Washington some time between September, 1962 and January, 1964, only after Barack Obama Senior left Honolulu for Harvard."

"It was basic gumshoe reporting," Leahy told me. "It wasn't all that spectacular."[18] As "easy to find" as the information was for the samizdat, no one in the MSM wanted to find it. Journalists like Maraniss had a candidacy to protect. In his *Post* article, Maraniss made no mention of Seattle. He claimed that Barack Obama Sr. graduated from the University of Hawaii in June 1962, specifying that "before the month was out, [Obama. Sr.] took off, leaving behind his still-teenage wife and namesake child."[19] In June 1962, Obama was ten months old, not two as Obama claimed, but Maraniss made no point of the baby's age or the discrepancy in Obama's retelling. He also left intact the image of the young couple's "improbable love" and their "abiding faith in the possibilities of this nation."

As it happens, the one place where the tale of Ann Dunham's Seattle hegira percolated was on the "Capitol Hill Seattle Blog." Wrote "jseattle" on January 7, 2009, "There is no doubt baby Barack lived on the hill. It was a tumultuous time in his young mother's life."[20] Other locals happily chimed in with details, not realizing they were undoing the work the MSM had done to preserve the Obama mythology.

With the spring 2010 publication of *The Bridge: The Life and Rise of Barack Obama*, Remnick became the first of the MSM journalists to mention the Seattle exile. Although he wrote about Dunham's Seattle adventure casually, as if it were old news, he made a shocking botch of the sequence of events, his timeline a random assortment of conflicting dates and places. According to Remnick, when Obama Sr. headed to Harvard in June 1962, he "promised his wife that he would retrieve the family when the time was right." Remnick fully implies here that Dunham and the baby were still in Hawaii. "That fall," Remnick continues, referring to the fall of 1962, "Ann went with the baby to Cambridge briefly to visit her husband, but the trip was a failure and she returned to Hawaii."[21]

Pages later, however, the reader learns that Dunham was living in Seattle in spring 1962 and attending classes at the University of Washington.[22] Remnick adds, "After a year, she decided to return to Honolulu."[23] This timeline would put Dunham in Seattle from spring

1962 to spring 1963. I do not overstate Remnick's confusion here. It's as if there were two Ann Dunhams: the one left behind in Hawaii and the one who moved to Seattle. As the editor of the *New Yorker*, Remnick must have felt confident that no one of note would dare challenge him on his facts, garbled as they were.

One point on which Leahy and Maraniss agreed is that after Dunham's high school friends met her and the baby in August 1961, they did not see her again. Remnick offers a fully unsourced take of his own: "One thing Ann's friends noticed was that she was not at all reluctant to show off her baby. When she wasn't studying, she pushed Barack around the streets of Seattle in a stroller—a somewhat startling sight for some."[24] Who these "some" were, is a mystery to the reader.

In his 2007 biography, Mendell tells a fully fictional story of Obama Sr. moving his family "into a small one story white house" before leaving the family for Harvard. Mendell made no mention of Ann's flight to Seattle.[25] In her 2011 biography of Obama's mother, *A Singular Woman*, the *New York Times*'s Janny Scott allows that Dunham did go to Seattle but, like Remnick, she plays games with the timeline. "In the spring quarter of 1962, as Obama was embarking on his final semester in Hawaii, Ann was enrolled at the University of Washington in Seattle," writes Scott.[26] Like Remnick, Scott either ignores or conceals the larger truth that Ann had already been at the university for months. Instead, she speculates that a fight of some sort precipitated Dunham's sudden departure from Hawaii.

In 2011, there was no excuse for a *Times* reporter writing a biography of Obama's mother to know so little. As early as July 2009, WND's Corsi was reporting, "[D]ocuments establish Dunham abandoned Obama Sr. when she left to begin school at the University of Washington in Seattle for the fall term of 1961, which began in September of that year." Corsi reinforced that information with documentation of Dunham's address from 1961 in Seattle. Not surprisingly, Scott made no mention of either Corsi or Leahy. MSM journalists routinely discount information distributed through the samizdat.

In her 2011 biography, *The Other Barack: The Bold and Reckless Life of President Obama's Father*, the *Boston Globe*'s Sally Jacobs manufactured still another timeline. In Jacobs's account, Dunham flew to Seattle in late August 1961 on her way to Boston, then returned to Hawaii, where she and Obama Sr. "resumed their life as before," and finally returned to Seattle some "months" after the baby was born.[27]

In this account, Dunham went to Boston from Seattle in August 1961 because Obama Sr. "had been accepted into graduate school there and they would likely move the following year" and Dunham wanted to "look into job possibilities for herself." This scenario makes no sense. The baby was less than a month old at the time of this alleged cross-country expedition. Barack Sr. had not yet been accepted into Harvard, and even if he had, the idea that Dunham would have gone to Boston with a newborn to look at job opportunities defies logic. "Dunham would, in fact, enroll at U-Dub [the University of Washington] the following spring," writes Jacobs,[28] again ignoring the proof that she enrolled in fall 1961.

In 2012, Maraniss put some order back in the nativity story in his book, *Barack Obama: The Story.* He reports that Dunham left Hawaii for Seattle with baby in tow in late August 1961, when Obama was no more than three weeks old, and did not come back to Hawaii until after Barack Sr. had left for Harvard. Maraniss details the courses she took, the apartments she inhabited, and the babysitters she hired.[29] It took him four years to correct the record, but at least he did so.

In his heavily researched 2017 biography, *Rising Star,* civil rights historian David Garrow finally stripped Obama's "multicultural ideal" of all its romance. According to Garrow, "[T]he young couple never chose to live together at any time following the onset of Ann's pregnancy."[30] Dunham left Hawaii as soon as the baby was old enough to travel, and Obama Sr. may never have even seen the child. Garrow quotes approvingly one unnamed scholar to the effect that Obama Sr. was no more than "a sperm donor in his son's life."[31]

In sum, Obama's positioning strategy at the conventions in 2004 and 2008 was fraudulent. There was no "improbable love," no shared "faith in the possibilities of this nation," and little, if any, truth to the nativity story on which he had built his campaign. The samizdat exposed this fraud as early as 2008. The mainstream media grudgingly, if quietly, acknowledged it in 2012. This collective failure, however, did not stop journalists from routinely trashing the birth certificate investigation by Corsi and others, a subject about which they knew little and cared even less than they did about Obama's early years.

The Red Front

"Here are the facts and they are indisputable," writes historian Paul Kengor in his valuable book, *The Communist—Frank Marshall Davis: The Untold Story of Barack Obama's Mentor.* "Frank Marshall Davis was a pro-Soviet, pro-Red China, card-carrying member of Communist Party (CPUSA). His Communist Party card number was 47544."[1]

Indisputable too is that Davis helped shape the political consciousness of the young Obama during his Hawaii years. At least Obama thought so. In *Dreams,* Obama dedicates some twenty-five hundred words to his mentor, who, Kengor tells us, "surfaces repeatedly from start to finish, from Hawaii to Los Angeles to Chicago to Germany to Kenya…from the 1970s to the 1980s to the 1990s."[2] In *Dreams,* Obama refers to Davis only as "Frank." Had he his eye on the presidency while writing *Dreams,* Obama might not have mentioned Davis at all. In 1995, Obama's sights were set no higher than the Chicago City Hall, and in Chicago the Davis name still had cachet.

One man who remembered the name well was Vernon Jarrett, an influential African American columnist with a national reach then in his final year on the editorial board of the *Chicago Sun-Times.* When Jarrett died in 2004, the *Washington Post* published a long and laudatory obituary headlined, "Vernon Jarrett, 84; Journalist, Crusader."[3] True to form, the *Post* neglected to mention Jarrett's affiliation with CPUSA youth groups or his work with Davis to thwart congressional investigation into the United Packinghouse Workers of America.[4] In fact, so instinctive was the *Post's* bowdlerizing of leftist biographies that the obit makes no use of the words "left," "progressive," or even "liberal." To the *Post* editors,

Jarrett was just your everyday "crusader," a word that today, ironically, would raise more hackles in the *Post* newsroom than "communist."

In that same newsroom, David Maraniss would seem to have learned the fine art of scrubbing. In his August 2008, ten thousand-word article on Obama's Hawaii years, the only "Davis" Maraniss mentioned was Miles Davis, the jazz great who allegedly made Obama's adolescent playlist. The article is titled in part, "It Is Hawaii That Made His Rise Possible." Davis played a major role in that rise, not only in instructing Obama in the ways of blackness, but also in opening at least the left side of Chicago doors.

Jarrett had clout in Chicago. Two years before Obama arrived in 1985, his son William married the granddaughter of the prominent Chicago fellow traveler, Robert Taylor, the politico after whom Chicago named its most notorious housing project. By August 2008, Taylor's granddaughter, Valerie Jarrett, had already established herself, in the words of the *Times*, as "one of [Obama's] most longstanding and influential tutors."[5] The Davis connection to Vernon Jarrett should have mattered to Maraniss and the *Post*. Possibly, it mattered too much.

On the surface, Maraniss's omission of any reference to "Frank" makes no sense other than as a conscious strategy to protect the Obama candidacy. When asked by Accuracy in the Media (AIM) about his failure to even mention Davis, Maraniss replied, "My reporting conclusion was the role of 'Frank' had been hyped out of all proportion, both by Obama himself in his book and some others later. He did not play a role in really shaping Obama."[6] Of course, Davis played a role, a major one, and Maraniss knew it. In his 2012 Obama biography, *Barack Obama: The Story*, Maraniss acknowledges that college sophomore Obama wrote a poem about Davis titled "Pop."[7] As I had earlier reported, Obama likely wrote two poems about Davis, one while in high school, and Davis appears to have written one about Obama. If a teenage boy writes at least two poems about an older man, one can safely assume that the man played a significant role in the boy's life.[8]

Yes, Maraniss was protecting Obama, but he had a secondary reason for suppressing the truth about Davis, one sufficiently compromising that Maraniss should have passed on the "Obama in Hawaii" assignment. His father, Elliott Maraniss, and Davis had much in common, too much. Both were journalists who pledged their allegiance to the Communist Party and lied about their allegiance through much of their lives. Maraniss shared his father's history in a May 2019 *Post* article, whose lack of historical perspective helps clarify his misreporting on Davis.[9]

"My father had been, for a time, a communist," conceded Maraniss. That "time" lasted from the late 1930s until 1952, when Elliott Maraniss was targeted by the House Committee on Un-American Activities. That "time" included one horrendous episode after another in Stalin's drive to enslave Eastern Europe, terrorize America, and kill his own people. Although he may not have known about the genocidal terror famine earlier in the 1930s, the college-educated Elliott had to know about the Great Terror that was in full swing when he joined the party. This self-defeating madness would leave as many as one million people dead.

The 1939 nonaggression pact between the Soviets and Nazis soon followed. The soft-core Marxists in America noisily quit the party, but Elliott, like Davis, stayed the course. A student at the University of Michigan at the time, Elliott wrote editorials defending the pact. These editorials, even David found "indefensible." Maraniss *pere* enlisted in the U.S. Army after Pearl Harbor, but that proved nothing about his loyalty, at least not to the United States. Given the fact that Elliott, like Davis, stayed true to the Stalinist cause after the war, even while the Kremlin's Chinese proxies were slaughtering Americans in Korea, it seems unlikely he would have enlisted in the U.S. Army if Germany and the Soviet Union had remained allies.

Maraniss writes as disingenuously about his father as he did about Davis. In his Obama bio, he does finally acknowledge Davis's existence. He describes him, however, not as a "communist" but as "a black journalist, poet, civil rights activist, political leftist, jazz expert, and self-described 'confirmed nonconformist.'" Yes, the FBI had Davis "under surveillance," Maraniss notes, but he saw Davis, like his father, less as a foot soldier in an evil empire than as a victim of an overzealous FBI.[10]

Maraniss willfully blinded himself to the reality of what it meant to be a capital "C" Communist in the United States. Of all the communist wannabes, only the zealots took the step to swear allegiance to the Party.

The oath went as follows: "I pledge myself to rally the masses to defend the Soviet Union, the land of victorious socialism. I pledge myself to remain at all times a vigilant and firm defender of the Leninist line of the Party, the only line that insures the triumph of Soviet Power in the United States." Elliott Maraniss and Frank Marshall Davis were, beyond doubt, hard-core Communists.[11]

In 2008, when it mattered most, Maraniss must have had confidence that his peers in the mainstream media would sustain the conspiracy of silence on Davis. That they did, but the samizdat played by its own rules. Any number of independent journalists and scholars wrote about Davis before Maraniss chose not to. Gerald Horne, a Marxist scholar from the University of Houston, led the way. On March 28, 2007, a little more than a month after Obama announced his candidacy for president, Horne gave a speech at the opening of the Communist Party USA archives at NYU's Tamiment Library.[12]

Although enough of a realist to see that communism in America had taken an emotional blow with the fall of the Soviet Union, Horne saw a ray of hope in the future. He found that bright spot emanating from Hawaii. There, in 1953, tens of thousands of workers showed more gumption than their mainland counterparts by striking to protest the conviction of labor and Communist Party Leaders of Smith Act violations. Urging them on was "an African American poet and journalist by the name of Frank Marshall Davis." Davis, Horne acknowledged, "was certainly in the orbit of the CP—if not a member." More telling, Davis had left Chicago for Hawaii at the instigation of Communist friend Paul Robeson.

In Hawaii, according to Horne, Davis befriended a "Euro-American" family and took their mixed-race grandson, Barack Obama, under his wing. Said Horne, as though it were common knowledge in leftist circles: "In his bestselling memoir 'Dreams of my Father,'[sic] the author speaks warmly of an older black poet, he identifies simply as 'Frank' as being a decisive influence in helping him to find his present identity as an African-American." Horne implied that Obama "decamped to Chicago" as a way of "retracing the steps of Davis." He concluded his speech with a prediction that should have perked the ears of any real journalist following the Obama campaign:

> At some point in the future, a teacher will add to her syllabus Barack's memoir and instruct her students to read it alongside Frank Marshall Davis' equally affecting memoir, "Living the Blues" and when that day comes, I'm sure a future student will not only examine critically the Frankenstein monsters that US imperialism created in order to subdue Communist parties but will also be moved to come to this historic and wonderful archive in order to gain insight on what has befallen this complex and intriguing planet on which we reside.

The first citizen journalist in the samizdat to take note of Horne's speech hailed from New Zealand, of all places. Trevor Loudon, blogger extraordinaire, began tracking Communist influence in the west during the worldwide anti-nuke movement of the early 1980s. Upon interviewing a fellow who had infiltrated the New Zealand Communist Party for the nation's security services, Loudon learned that New Zealand's antinuclear movement had been planned and packaged in Moscow. The fellow knew because he was part of a New Zealand contingent trained at the Lenin Institute of Higher Learning in Moscow. For Loudon this was a major revelation, firsthand confirmation of what the media would have dismissed as red-baiting fiction. Hooked, he plowed deeper into the international Communist conspiracy. Over time, he came to focus on the United States because, as he put it, "America was the main enemy, the main target of the movement."[13]

When made aware of Horne's speech, Loudon posted on his blog a summary of Horne's comments under the fully accurate title, "Barack Obama's Marxist Mentor."[14] Wrote Loudon, "Now the Communist Party USA is claiming Barack Obama as its spiritual heir." With Loudon's help, author and investigator Cliff Kincaid did an extensive report on Davis in February 2008 titled, "Obama's Communist Mentor."[15] Then with Accuracy in Media, a classic samizdat outpost established well before the internet, Kincaid did several subsequent articles throughout 2008. Each time, he added new details about Davis's activities as a member of the CPUSA, a membership that remained active until at least 1956.

Kincaid also exposed Davis's work as a pornographer, unearthing *Sex Rebel: Black*, a slightly fictionalized memoir written under the pseudonym, Bob Greene. In his letters to artist friend Margaret Taylor-Burroughs, Davis admitted that *Sex Rebel* was almost pure autobiography. "You will find out things about me sexually that you probably never suspected— but in this period of wider acceptance of sexual attitudes I can be more frank than was possible 20 years ago."[16] In the book, Davis reveals both his bisexuality and his willingness to engage in sex with minors, two noteworthy traits given his relationship with the young Obama.

Among the very few entities in the MSM to acknowledge Davis before the 2008 election was the Associated Press.[17] In an article published several weeks before Maraniss's story, reporter Sudhin Thanawala gave Davis his due. "At key moments in his adolescence," Thanawala wrote, "Barack Obama could not turn to a father he hardly knew. Instead, he looked to a left-leaning black journalist and poet for advice on living in a world of black and white."

In his thousand-word article, Thanawala offered considerable information about Davis's background and detailed the relationship between Obama and Davis. That said, he refused to give any credence to the research Kincaid and Loudon had done on Davis's proven Communist Party history. "Left-leaning" was as far as Thanawala was willing to tilt. As Maraniss did in writing about his father, Thanawala played to his audience's firmly held belief that those keen on social justice were inevitably accused of much worse by the forces of reaction. In fact, Davis biographer John Edgar Tidwell, who knew full well Davis's history, refused to be interviewed lest he encourage what he called the "McCarthy-era strategy of smear tactics and condemnation by association."

As it happens, a footnote in Tidwell's book alerted Kincaid to the existence of a six-hundred-page FBI profile on Davis. Kincaid promptly submitted a Freedom of Information Act (FOIA) request, received the file, and made it public in August 2008, not that anyone in the MSM had an interest in reviewing it. Thanawala, for one, blinded himself to all unseemly evidence. How else could one account for a sentence as daft as this: "In spite of his writings, Davis scholars dismiss the idea that he was anti-American."

These alleged "Davis scholars" were part of the disinformation apparatus. In his Hawaii period, when the Soviet Union was busily extinguishing democracy in Eastern Europe and using its allies to do the same in Asia, Davis relentlessly and brutally attacked the United States. "For a nation that calls itself the champion of democracy," Davis wrote in his first Hawaii column, "our stupendous stupidity is equalled only by our mountainous ego." He never let up. America's plans to "re-enslave the yellow and brown and black peoples of the world" kept him perpetually agitated.[18]

Like Thanawala, presidential historian Jon Meacham, writing for the still viable *Newsweek* in late August 2008, acknowledged Davis's influence on Obama, but he too chose to portray Davis as a victim of the reactionary right. "His political activism, especially his writings on civil-rights and labor issues," wrote Meacham, "prompted a McCarthyite denunciation by the House Un-American Activities Committee."[19] Historian Paul Kengor took exception. "This statement," he writes, "was wholly inaccurate."[20] The Senate Judiciary Committee investigated Davis, not the House. The Committee called Davis "an identified member of the Communist Party," Kengor notes, because he was one. At the time, the long since censured Sen. Joe McCarthy was on his deathbed.

Obama's biographers have had no more interest in exposing Davis's background than did Maraniss or Meacham. In his 2007 biography, *Obama: From Promise to Power*, the *Chicago Tribune*'s David Mendell devoted three chapters to Obama's Hawaii years but failed to so much as even mention Davis. In his 2010 Obama bio, *The Bridge*, Remnick added enough detail to confirm the significance of the relationship, but it is what he erased from the record that caught Kengor's attention. "Remnick did not ignore Frank; he simply ignored all the negatives," writes Kengor. "His treatment is scandalous in its omissions."[21]

From Remnick's perspective, Davis was unfairly "tainted" by the House and Senate committees that investigated him. During the 2008 campaign, "the right-wing blogosphere" continued the alleged smear, accusing Davis of being "a card-carrying Communist, a pornographer, a pernicious influence."[22] That Davis was a card-carrying Communist and a pornographer is undeniable. Whether his influence was "pernicious" depends on one's perspective. Remnick believes the grandfather's introduction of young Obama to Davis was "thoughtful and consequential." Others might think that arranging playdates with a bisexual Stalinist pornographer with a taste for underage sex partners borders on child abuse.

If nothing else, Remnick helped delineate the battle lines that were being drawn across the media landscape. On the one side were respected journalists like himself with established platforms from which to tell Obama's story. On the other side were conspiracy theorists like myself adrift in "the Web's farthest lunatic orbit."[23] Remnick's condescension would have been more understandable had he been able to discern the subject of Obama's poem, "Pop." This was not hard to do, but he failed. More likely, he did not try. In *The Bridge*, he claims that the poem "clearly reflects Obama's relationship with his grandfather Stanley Dunham."[24] It clearly does not, but who in *his* orbit would dare challenge Remnick?

Remnick at least acknowledged my writing in the body of the text. Obama biographer David Garrow relegated me to the footnotes. The subject that involved me was "Pop." As Garrow notes, "Most commentators presumed that Obama had written about his grandfather, Stan Dunham, not Frank Marshall Davis." This much was true, but "hostile critics," Garrow continues, insisted the poem was about Davis. After citing one compelling example of why the hostile critics were right, Garrow concludes the discussion with Obama's forceful rejection of the Davis hypothesis. "'This is about my grandfather,'" he quotes Obama as saying.[25] To borrow Remnick's favorite adverb—he uses its twenty-two times in *The Bridge*—Obama "clearly" was lying.

The "hostile critics" Garrow cites in the footnotes are Paul Kengor and me. Instead of giving me credit for being the first to decode "Pop," Garrow writes parenthetically about me in the footnote as "someone who is cited with the greatest reluctance."[26] What I did to deserve this condescension is left unsaid, especially since Garrow knows I nailed the identity of "Pop" two years before Maraniss or anyone else in the MSM did the same.

If I speak about Davis at some length, it is not because I bear him any particular animus. To a certain degree, he was a creature of his time and place. Not to excuse his Communist sympathies or his various perversions, but as I write in my book *Deconstructing Obama*, "Growing up in small town southern Kansas in the early years of the 20th century, Davis endured more racist crap in a given day than Obama endured in his entire life." Besides, as I acknowledge, Davis was a much better writer than his protégé.

No, what makes Davis worth study at this stage is the extraordinary level of denial he provoked among the media elite. Curiously, this refusal to face reality climaxed on the pages of the *Washington Post* in 2015, at least three years after it mattered, and seven years after it mattered a great deal.

What prompted the *Post*'s interest was a comment by Rudy Giuliani on Fox News. The former New York City mayor was challenging Obama's love of country. Said Giuliani, "I'm talking about a man who grew up under the influence of Frank Marshall Davis, who was a member of the Communist Party who he refers to over and over in his book, who was a tremendous critic of the United States."[27] Reportedly, readers of the *Post* wanted this comment fact-checked. So designated fact checker Michelle Ye Hee Lee reached out to Cliff Kincaid. On February 26, 2015, Kincaid and Loudon, each well armed with documentation, met with Lee in Washington. They recorded the meeting on video.

As Kincaid tells the story, he and Loudon spoke at length with Lee. They told her that after "falling under the Davis influence," Obama associated with Marxist professors in college and attended socialist conferences. They reminded her as well of Obama's relationships with the anti-American preacher Jeremiah Wright, with communist terrorists Bill Ayers and Bernardine Dohrn, and with other socialists in Chicago. Kincaid also gave Lee a copy of Kengor's definitive book on Davis.[28]

Nearly a month after the meeting, Lee came back with her verdict: "Three Pinocchios" for Giuliani, which translates into "significant factual error and/or obvious contradictions"—in brief, "mostly false."[29] Lee's reasoning should frighten anyone who takes the *Post* seriously. "There is no evidence that Davis was a hard-core Communist who spied for Soviet leaders," wrote Lee. In fact, Davis was a propagandist and provocateur and certainly hard-core. Although Davis may have been a spy, no one on the right accused him of being one, least of all Giuliani, whose facts Lee was allegedly checking.

"[Davis] was critical of American society, but not America as a country," Lee continued as if this sentence had any real meaning. As Paul Kengor observed, "Frank Marshall Davis was very bitter toward America, period. Call it American 'society' or the 'country.' It was really both." Finally, insisted Lee, "There is no evidence Obama was 'raised' by Davis, or that Davis remained a close Communist mentor who advised him throughout his life." All that Giuliani said was that Obama "grew up under the influence" of Davis. He never used the word "raised" nor even implied that Davis advised Obama after Obama left Hawaii. Concluded Lee, "It is time to put it to rest," the "it" being the rumor that Davis was Obama's communist mentor.

This disingenuous hogwash mystified both Kengor and Kincaid. "How about this?" wrote Kengor. "If Rudy merits Three Pinocchios, then Barack Obama deserves at least 22." Kengor was referring to the twenty-two mentions of "Frank" in *Dreams* that aspiring fireman Obama expunged from the audio version in 2005, when visions of the White House first started dancing in his head. "It seems clear," Kengor continued, "that the purpose of this false finding of 'fact' by the Post was to send a message that political figures are not supposed to talk publicly about Obama's Marxist background. If you tell the truth, you can be accused of lying!"[30] The Davis suppression campaign worked splendidly. Obama's relationship to this capital "C" Communist may not have cost him a single vote that he otherwise would have gotten.

No one tracked Obama's leftward journey more thoroughly or conscientiously during the 2008 campaign than Stanley Kurtz, a Harvard PhD and a frequent contributor to *National Review*. During the campaign, Kurtz was understandably cautious in defining Obama's political identity. He writes in his 2010 book, *Radical-in-Chief,* "I put the socialism issue off as a sticky, irresolvable question of definition."[31]

To be sure, Obama flirted with Marxism during his two years at Occidental and came to New York at least amateurishly schooled in

Marxist theory. As a senior at Columbia in 1983, Obama participated actively in the same anti-nuke movement that alerted Trevor Loudon in New Zealand to the worldwide reach of the communist mission. A testament to Obama's participation was an eighteen-hundred-word article, "Breaking The War Mentality," published in Columbia's weekly news magazine, *Sundial.*

Six months after Obama was safely elected, the *New York Times* unearthed the article and reproduced it in its original format online. "Barack Obama's journalistic voice was edgy with disdain for what he called 'the relentless, often silent spread of militarism in the country' amid 'the growing threat of war,'" the *Times* insisted.[32] The *Times* did not mention that the "growing threat of war" was a KGB hobgoblin designed to scare the West out of placing Pershing Missiles in West Germany. Nor did the *Times* point out how irredeemably awkward Obama's prose style was, but there was much about Obama's New York years the *Times* chose not to know.

In late October 2007, the *Times's* Janny Scott, future biographer of Obama's mother, attempted to share with her readers an account of Obama's years in their fair city. The underdog in the race for the Democratic nomination, Obama should have welcomed the attention. He did not. As Scott reported, "He declined repeated requests to talk about his New York years, release his Columbia transcript or identify even a single fellow student, co-worker, roommate or friend from those years."[33] This refusal would have set off alarm bells in a real newsroom, but not on West 42nd Street. An unruffled Scott revealed a few minor inaccuracies in *Dreams* and called it a day.

Obama had to be relieved. Scott wrote nary a word about "the socialist conferences" at Cooper Union that, in *Dreams*, Obama admitted "sometimes" attending.[34] Although hard to believe in 2020, open affection for socialism could have dashed a Democratic candidate's dreams in 2008. The editors at the *Times* surely understood this, which helps explain their impressive lack of curiosity about Obama's New York misadventures.

Unhindered by partisan editors, Kurtz did the shoe-leather reporting that the *Times* and *Washington Post* reporters would have done if Obama were a Republican. As a result of his research, he no longer hesitated to label Obama a socialist. "I did a double-take," writes Kurtz, "when I saw those conference programs dotted with names I'd run across researching Obama's world of community organizing."[35] For those wanting an in-depth look at how these socialist boot camps influenced Obama, there is no better source than *Radical-in-Chief*. In exploring socialism's home-brewed evolution, Kurtz came to see the "community organizing" of that era as "largely a socialist enterprise—a novel adaptation of Marxist principles and practices to modern American realities."[36]

The major media did a splendid job of keeping Obama's socialist roots out of the news in the run-up to the 2008 election. Forget Davis. Forget the socialist conferences. Had they reported the endorsement of his 1996 state senate run by the Marxist, ACORN-affiliated New Party, they could have cost Obama the primary.

The media had less success suppressing Obama's then current affiliation with Bill Ayers, a self-described "revolutionary anarchocommunist, small c."[37] That relationship was a chummy one. In 2017, with Obama safely out of office, Obama biographer David Garrow addressed his subject's involvement with the radical pair, Ayers and Dohrn, in some detail. A leftist himself, Garrow describes Ayers as "a student radical" who grew up to become "well known in Chicago for the dedication to school reform."[38]

Ayers was well known for more than school reform. In 1970, his comrades in the Weather Underground, including his lover Diana Oughton, blew themselves up in Greenwich Village. Oughton and two others died. The story dominated the national news. Had these aspiring terrorists succeeded in planting the anti-personnel bomb as intended at a Fort Dix dance, Ayers would have been doing his educational reform in prison. He and Dohrn continued their bombing spree until the Weather Underground dissolved in futility several years later.

During their heyday, the two were infamous, especially Dohrn. A hottie by revolutionary standards, Dohrn made something of a splash at a 1969 Michigan "War Council" when she raised three fingers in a "fork salute" to the recently arrested Charlie Manson. "Dig It. First they killed those pigs," said Dohrn, the "pigs" being pregnant actress Sharon Tate and at least seven others, "then they ate dinner in the same room with them, they even shoved a fork into a victim's stomach! Wild!"[39] People remembered. Outside of their cloistered progressive circles, Ayers and Dohrn were still toxic forty years later.

A radical wannabe himself, Obama was unbothered. He gladly accepted an offer by Ayers and Dohrn to host a fundraiser for his state senate candidacy in 1995. This much was known in 2008, but what Garrow added in 2017 was not. He writes, "Barack and Michelle began to see a great deal more of not only Bill and Bernardine but also their three closest friends, Rashid and Mona Khalidi and Carole Travis."[40] A Palestinian native of radical bent, Rashid Khalidi will show up later in a classic tale of media suppression.

According to Garrow, Obama's relationship with his new radical friends flourished. To help promote Ayers's new book on juvenile justice, Obama organized a panel discussion. Obama served on the influential Woods Fund board with Ayers. He and Ayers teamed up on a subsequent panel discussion, "Intellectuals, Who Needs Them." Most tellingly, Barack and Michelle attended "almost nightly dinners" with Ayers, Dohrn, and the Khalidis up until the time Obama ran for the U.S. Senate.[41] A *Chicago Tribune* reporter, Mendell covered Obama up close in his 2004 run for the U.S. Senate. Yet in his 2007 Obama biography, he somehow failed to mention Ayers, Dohrn, Khalidi, the Woods Fund, the New Party, ACORN, or Frank Marshall Davis. That took forethought.

Writing for the UK *Daily Mail,* conservative Brit Peter Hitchens first breached Obama's protective media shield on the Ayers front. In a February 2008 article, Hitchens wondered out loud about whether "$200 from a certain William Ayers" might have come from the same William Ayers "who used to plant bombs in the Seventies and has said: 'I don't regret setting bombs. I feel we didn't do enough.'"

Hitchens was musing rhetorically about Ayers's donation to Obama's state senate campaign in 2001. He concluded, "Those (like me) who know the Left-wing codes notice things about Obama that suggest he is far more radical than he would like us to know."[42] Although Hitchens spent only two paragraphs on Ayers, that was enough to send the firemen at the *Washington Post* scurrying for the fire pole. Fact checker Michael

Dobbs promptly reassured *Post* readers that Hitchens overstated his case and that "the Obama-Ayers link is a tenuous one." Besides, Dobbs noted, "Whatever his past, Ayers is now a respected member of the Chicago intelligentsia."[43] And that was that.

Almost. Hillary Clinton was very much in the race for the Democratic nomination in February 2008. Her supporters in the nation's newsrooms floated the idea that although Hillary had no problem with Ayers, the Republicans surely would. "Obama's mantra, 'Yes, We Can' is inspiring and heartwarming, but in the end is an empty phrase that will founder once the Republican political attack machine spins up," wrote Larry Johnson in the *Huffington Post* two weeks after Hitchens outed Ayers. "William Ayers, in the age of terrorism, will be Barack Obama's Willie Horton."[44] The Willie Horton gambit lives on in the leftist imagination as some horrific bit of Republican mischief, much like the swiftboat gambit, but worse, given that Horton was black. It deserves a sidebar.

As a young man in Massachusetts, the real-life Willie Horton robbed a gas station, stabbed the seventeen-year-old attendant nineteen times, and left him in a trash can to bleed to death. Sentenced to life without parole, Horton got himself a weekend pass just twelve years later courtesy of an insane program favored by then Gov. Michael Dukakis. Enjoying his freedom, Horton took it upon himself to extend the weekend pass for nearly a year until Maryland authorities arrested him. Horton had knifed, blinded, and gagged one of their citizens, raped his fiancée, and stolen their car. The judge in the case, citing Dukakis's folly, refused to send Horton back to Massachusetts.[45]

Not surprisingly, the George H. W. Bush campaign featured this incident in an ad when Dukakis emerged as the Democratic presidential nominee in 1988. The ad did not show or name Horton. It simply showed prisoners, almost all of them white, passing through a revolving door while the voice-over explained the inherent madness of Dukakis's "rehabilitation" program.

Before the election, the name "Willie Horton" had little resonance inside America's newsrooms and none outside. After the election, however, the media discovered an ad featuring Horton's mug shot run in New England for two weeks by a group *not* tied to the Bush campaign.

In the years that followed, an increasingly partisan media would show the New England ad, which was racist only to the degree that it showed Horton, and attribute it to Bush.

This ahistorical madness peaked on December 3, 2018. While the body of President Bush lay in state in the Rotunda of the U.S. Capitol, the *Washington Post* published a lengthy, frenetic article titled, "How the Willie Horton ad factors into George H.W. Bush's legacy." Writer Eugene Scott admitted that an independent group created the offending ad and that the Bush campaign disowned it, but he judged the late president guilty beyond the grave for "one of the most infamous political ads in history, one that stoked racial stereotypes that continue to shape criminal justice policy years later."[46]

Not wanting to be remembered for creating Barack Obama's Willie Horton, the nation's journalists laid off of Bill Ayers, most of them anyhow. The one notable exception was George Stephanopoulos of ABC News, a one-time field marshal in Bill Clinton's "war room." While moderating a Democratic debate in 2008, Stephanopoulos asked Obama a question that any good journalist should have: "Can you explain [the Ayers] relationship for the voters and explain to Democrats why it won't be a problem?" For those in the audience who did not remember Ayers, Stephanopoulos filled in the blanks, "He was part of the Weather Underground in the 1970s. They bombed the Pentagon, the Capitol, and other buildings. He's never apologized for that."[47]

Caught off guard, Obama stuttered out an answer: "This is a guy who lives in my neighborhood, who's a professor of English in Chicago, who I know and who I have not received some official endorsement from. He's not somebody who I exchange ideas from [*sic*] on a regular basis." This was a dishonest answer, and the media should have called Obama on it. With the rare exception, they did not. They slammed Stephanopoulos instead.

The line of attack appears to have originated in one of the left's murkier firehouses, the *Democratic Underground.* A day before the debate, in order to help promote it, Stephanopoulos appeared on Sean Hannity's talk radio show. Among other possible debate questions, the conservative

Hannity had suggested one on Bill Ayers. Stephanopoulos jested, "Well, I'm taking notes now."

Immediately following the Hannity show, "Emit" posted on the *Democratic Underground* blog the highlights of the exchange and concluded, "Let's see if George takes Hannity's advice on this. More collaboration with Fox News. Hmmmm..."[48] The conservative *Daily Caller* traced the orchestration of the mugging that followed to the online meeting group, JournoList. As the *Guardian's* Michael Tomasky wrote on the site following the debate, "Listen folks—in my opinion, we all have to do what we can to kill ABC and this idiocy in whatever venues we have."[49]

The firemen at *Think Progress* found the Hannity reference, confirmed it, and ran with it, headlining their article, "AUDIO: Hannity Feeds Stephanopoulos Debate Question On Weather Underground."[50] The *Huffington Post* joined the literal "feeding" frenzy. Its article read, "Hannity Spoonfed Left-Field Debate Question To Stephanopoulos."[51] The editors at the *Los Angeles Times*, hating to see a dead horse go unbeaten, headlined its article: "Stephanopoulos denied he'd been spoon-fed the question by Fox News host Sean Hannity."[52]

For many voters, perhaps most, the Ayers question was a legitimate one, but not for the mavens of the major media, and certainly not for Obama's Praetorian Guard at the *Washington Post*. The *Post's* Tom Shales took no mercy on Stephanopoulos. According to Shales, Stephanopoulos dug through his notes looking "for something smart-alecky and slimy" and came up with "such tired tripe as a charge that Obama once associated with a nutty bomb-throwing anarchist."[53] As Garrow and Christopher Andersen later confirmed, that association was intimate. It stopped, or at least submerged, only when Obama set his sights on the presidency. Just as he edited "Frank" out of his audio, Obama edited Ayers out of his life. Once again, journalists on the left made the editing possible.

As I was writing this book, I made one final effort to reach out to Ayers. In an amiable email I wrote, "Although the authorship of 'Dreams' is peripheral to the larger story [of this book], I would really like to get your honest take on it, on or off the record." Ayers could have responded in kind and soberly refuted my thesis. He did not. He played, as he often did, the clown: "Short answer: I WROTE EVERY WORD OF

DREAMS FROM MY FATHER (including nautical references!) and IF YOU CAN HELP ME PROVE IT I'LL GIVE YOU A CHUNK (how much is enough?) OF RECOVERED ROYALTIES!"

I responded, "Say what you will, but unlike anyone from the 'mainstream' on right I did give you your due as a writer and had the good sense not to accuse you of having written 'Audacity.'"[54] I suspect Ayers will take his literary secrets to the grave.

Obama had one more red scare to deal with before the campaign was over, this one self-inflicted. At a campaign stop in a working-class Toledo neighborhood on Columbus Day, an everyday citizen named Joe Wurzelbacher asked Obama a question. Wurzelbacher wondered whether Obama's economic plan would cost his planned new plumbing business more in taxes. In an unusually candid moment, Obama's inner Marx sneaked out. "I think that when you spread the wealth around," said Obama, "it's good for everybody." This unintentionally honest remark raced through the samizdat and caught the attention of John McCain's staff. During a televised debate on October 15, McCain made "Joe the Plumber" an instant celebrity.

The media fired back. At Joe. On October 16, the *Times* struck a flurry of shockingly low blows against the defenseless Wurzelbacher. Arguing that Wurzelbacher deserved "celebrity-level scrutiny" for daring to question Obama, reporter Larry Rohter revealed that Joe did not currently have a plumbing license or belong to the plumber's union. In the lowest blow, Rohter reported that Wurzelbacher owed back taxes. He even documented the outstanding liens against him.[55] In four days, the *Times* had dug deeper into Wurzelbacher's entrepreneurial ambitions than it had into Obama's socialist ones during the past four years.

Bad journalism quickly morphed into bad history. In 2011, James Kloppenberg, the Charles Warren Professor of American History at Harvard, memorialized the major media's failings in a wish fulfillment of a book called *Reading Obama*. In its over three hundred pages, Kloppenberg makes no mention of Bill Ayers, ACORN, or the socialist conferences at Cooper Union, and fleetingly refers to Frank Marshall Davis only as "the poet whom Obama credits for helping him understand black life in white America."[56]

Kloppenberg does, however, make more than sixty references to President James Madison, Obama's presumed spiritual forebear. "Obama's approach to politics is deeply grounded in an American tradition originating in the eighteenth century, with Thomas Jefferson and James Madison," Kloppenberg insists. The imagined bond between Obama and Madison is their shared "philosophical pragmatism." In a passage that flirts with parody, Kloppenberg praises Obama for his "Christian humility, his pragmatist antifoundationalism, and his nuanced appreciation for the complexities of the American past."[57] If Obama was pragmatic, it was in his calculated embrace of Christianity. If he was humble, Kloppenberg was the first to notice. And as for antifoundationalist, Kloppenberg, I think, confuses that with "shallow."

Much of Kloppenberg's analysis derives from his reading of Obama's two books, especially the overlooked 2006 tome, *The Audacity of Hope*. In praising *Audacity* for its "provocative"[58] arguments and "penetrating analysis,"[59] Kloppenberg confirms that he ignored all information coming from the samizdat. He should never have taken *Audacity* seriously. As I had reported in 2009, two years before Kloppenberg's book was published, at least thirty-eight extended passages in *Audacity* matched passages from Obama's speeches nearly word for word.[60] These speeches were almost assuredly written by boy wonder Jon Favreau. Even Michiko Kakutani of the *Times* noticed that the prose, filled as it was with "flabby platitudes," read "like outtakes from a stump speech."[61] She was righter than she knew.

In reality, Obama had no time to write this book, but he did have a goal. If *Dreams* was written with the mayoralty of Chicago in mind, *Audacity* was designed to make Obama president. I use the passive tense here intentionally. The book was, in fact, "written." How much of it Obama wrote is anyone's guess. He had an eighteen-month window to write *Audacity* after being elected to the U.S. Senate in 2004, but as Remnick concedes, "He procrastinated for a long time." Once Obama started writing, he wrote longhand, allegedly at night after his hamster-wheel day job as a freshman senator. With a deadline fast approaching, Obama wrote, as Remnick tells us, "nearly a chapter a week."[62] The chapters average nearly fifty pages. As a writer, Remnick knows this pace is impossible, at least if we are to take Obama at his word that he "actually wrote [both books] myself."

In fact, he wrote neither book by himself. In the acknowledgment section of *Audacity*, Obama lists twenty-four people who provided "invaluable suggestions" prior to publication. Twenty-four? The book gives the impression of having been planned and written by committee, and the final product reads as such. Ignoring all contrary evidence, Kloppenberg describes *Audacity* as "a refreshingly serious and cogent account of American political and cultural history."[63] Bill Ayers called it a "political hack book."[64] Here, at least, Ayers was telling the truth.

At the end of October 2008, Obama told a Missouri crowd, "We are five days away from fundamentally transforming the United States of America."[65] In the details that followed, Obama spelled out what the transformation would look like. Smelling victory around the corner, he promised an economic empowerment of the people, "the secretary and janitor," at the expense of "Wall Street," the "factory owner," and the "CEO."

In the two years that followed, Kloppenberg watched as Obama made a good faith effort to do as promised. He spread $787 billion of other people's money around through his stimulus package. He redirected a sixth of the American economy through the Affordable Care Act. He made the federal government a major player in the auto industry. He heavily regulated Wall Street through the Dodd-Frank Act. And, as shall be seen, he took care of the special needs of every partner in the multicultural coalition.

Not everyone on the left fell in line. Among the more restive was radical black author and professor Cornel West. In 2011, West started calling out Obama publicly for his "centrist, neoliberalist policy."[66] Obama was furious. He had pushed the nation so hard leftward that in 2010, despite the full-throated backing of the media, his party lost sixty-three seats in the House and six in the Senate, the most devastating loss by a party in power in more than seventy years. In spotting West at an event in 2010, Obama reportedly came down to West's seat and hissed within earshot of others, "I'm not progressive? What kind of shit is this?"[67]

The Black Front

On November 4, 2008, I served as a poll watcher at Saint James United Methodist Church in Kansas City, the home base of Rev. Emanuel Cleaver II, my congressman. To ease any potential friction, I brought with me a huge box of donuts. And to show my good faith, I had the poll workers push the clocks back to standard time lest a would-be voter abandon the line, thinking the day through. The workers expected a lot of voters at this overwhelmingly black polling station, and they got them.

Having reconciled myself to a Barack Obama victory, I was heartened to see how thrilled people were to vote for an African American. More than a few of the older voters had never voted before and were eager to share that fact. I took their joy as a good sign. Like many of us on the right, I found some consolation in thinking an Obama presidency would ease racial tension in America. On this issue, I genuinely hoped he would succeed. He did not. In fact, Obama failed catastrophically.

As candidate and as president, Obama did nothing to discourage his allies from smearing his opponents as "racist" for opposing him, even on issues that had nothing to do with race. The itch to impute racism to political opponents swept through the Democratic faithful like head lice. Whites proved even more eager than blacks to denounce the nation's mushrooming population of bigots. The mania began as soon as Obama declared his candidacy and did not stop with the end of his presidency.

Perry Beam was one of those eager white people. In August 2013, Beam attended a rodeo at the Missouri State Fair. A self-professed liberal and nudist, Beam was horrified to see Tuffy the Rodeo Clown in an Obama mask mugging for the supportive crowd. Beam posted the video on his Facebook page. A friend reposted it on the appropriate fire-starting blogs with the comment, "I can't write anymore at how disgusting this is. All I want is some heads to roll." Roll they would. The State Fair banned rodeo clown Tuffy Gessling for life. The NAACP asked the Secret Service to investigate Tuffy for a "hate crime." And Tuffy's clown colleagues had to undergo—one can only imagine—sensitivity training. This is what racial healing looked like in the age of Obama.[1]

Two years earlier, the media tried to do to Donald Trump what they would later do to Tuffy. In all the years Trump had been a public figure, he had not faced a credible charge of racism until he questioned Obama's birth certificate in 2011. "I want him to show his birth certificate! There's something on that birth certificate that he doesn't like," said Trump in a March 2011 appearance on *The View*. Visibly angry co-host Whoopi Goldberg shot back, "That's the biggest pile of dog mess I've heard in ages. It's not 'cuz he's black is it?"[2] Actually, it was *not* because Obama was black.

Without intending to bolster the "birther" movement, the *Boston Globe*'s Sally Jacobs opened her biography of Barack Obama Sr. with the one critical fact that inspired the movement: "Every man who has served as president of the United States had parents who lived out their lives upon American soil. Barack H. Obama did not."[3] If Obama's father came from Kentucky, not Kenya, no one would have questioned his eligibility just as no one ever questioned the eligibility of homegrown African Americans such as Jesse Jackson and Al Sharpton when they ran for president.

Critics, did, however, challenge the eligibility of 2008 Republican nominee John McCain. Having been born on a naval base in the Panama Canal Zone, McCain faced lawsuits in at least three states. In May 2008, the *Washington Post* took McCain's status seriously enough to sic its "Fact Checker" on him. "The constitution is ambiguous about the precise meaning of 'natural-born citizen,'" concluded the *Post*'s Michael Dobbs. Dobbs quoted law professor Sarah Duggin to the effect that "there has never been any real resolution of this issue. Congress cannot legislatively change the meaning of the constitution." Indifferent to constitutional niceties, the U.S. Senate went ahead and declared McCain a "natural born citizen."[4] His Senate colleagues failed to do the same for Obama. Fearful of being called racist, they had to pretend there was nothing to clarify.

In the way of a spoiler alert, I have no new insights on Obama's birth certificate. What I can do, however, is illustrate the way Obama and his supporters used race to discourage all serious inquiries into Obama's background, starting with his birth. In point of fact, the original birther was Obama himself. In 1991, likely to position himself as more exotic than a garden-variety African American, Obama claimed in a promotional brochure put out by literary agency Acton & Dystel that he "was born in Kenya and raised in Indonesia and Hawaii." In May 2012, Breitbart. com surfaced the brochure. Breitbart research showed that as late as April 2007, agency promotional materials were claiming Obama was "born in Kenya to an American anthropologist and a Kenyan finance minister."

Aware of the likely blowback, Breitbart senior managers took pains to distance themselves from the birther movement. "Andrew [Breitbart] believed, as we do, that President Barack Obama was born in Honolulu, Hawaii, on August 4, 1961," they wrote. "Yet Andrew also believed that the complicit mainstream media had refused to examine President Obama's ideological past, or the carefully crafted persona he and his advisers had constructed for him."[5]

The media response to this revelation only reinforced Breitbart's charge of complicity. The *New York Times* ignored the story altogether. The *Washington Post* telegraphed its contempt in the headline, "The birthers are back! The birthers are back!"[6] After a few hapless stabs at irony, the *Post*'s Karen Tumulty embraced the explanation by Miriam Goderich, a partner at the agency in 2012 but a junior staffer in 1991, that the reference to Kenya "was nothing more than a fact checking error by me." The critical reader had to marvel at the ability of Goderich to recall a clerical error she had made twenty-one years prior.

A much more likely explanation for the Kenya reference is that Obama, like virtually all authors, provided the biographical materials himself. This would not have surprised his best friend from high school, Keith Kakugawa, or "Ray" as Obama called him in *Dreams from My Father*. No one had a better perspective on Obama's racial shape-shifting than Kakugawa. The friendship, Obama writes in *Dreams*, was "due in no small part to the fact that together we made up almost half of Punahou's black high school population."[7] Obama is famously half black. Kakugawa is one-eighth black. The pair did not exactly make prime recruiting material for the Crips' Hawaiian franchise. Says Kakugawa about Obama in his own self-published book, "He was cripplingly self-conscious about [race]."[8] At least until he ran for office in Chicago, Obama chose foreigners as his friends and presented himself to the world as something more cosmopolitan than the ordinary black guy. It would not have been out of character for the young Obama to pass himself off as foreign-born.

Tumulty flat out ignored the more obvious explanation for the "Kenya" claim and put full faith in Goderich's magic memory. Acknowledging that many on the right believed "the media failed to look into [Obama's] early life when he ran for president," she offered a series of links to *Post* articles for those wanting to know more. I confess to laughing out loud when I saw the article on the top of the list under the rubric, "His life in Hawaii." It was David Maraniss's ten-thousand-word puff piece from August 2008, the same article that failed to mention Frank Marshall Davis or Obama's sojourn in Seattle.

Trump plowed right into this controversy undaunted by the criticism that was sure to follow. It is quite likely that no one has ever been called "racist" more often or with less reason. "We have a president, and I say this without any joy in my heart, who is a racist," said two-time presidential candidate Sen. Bernie Sanders before a Harlem event in 2019. "It's hard to believe that we have a president of the United States who is, in fact, a racist."[9] When pressed as to what motivated his accusation, Sanders cited as evidence his belief that Trump "was one of the leaders of the so-called 'birther movement,' which sought to portray Barack Obama as an illegitimate president, someone not born in the United States."[10]

It was not just entertainers and politicians that made this accusation. In a *Washington Post* article rationalizing his father's Stalinism, Maraniss made a comparable claim: "Any understanding of Trump's political rise must begin with an act of blatant racism, his bogus birther claim that Barack Obama was born in Kenya and therefore un-American."[11] Of course, those who questioned McCain's birth in Panama or Sen. Ted Cruz's birth in Canada faced no accusations of racism, let alone "blatant" racism, but race was central to Obama's self-definition. He and his acolytes wielded it as both sword and shield.

Despite media assertions otherwise, Trump, like most serious people labeled "birther," never claimed Obama was born in Kenya. In September 2016, CNN ran an article headlined, "14 of Trump's most outrageous birther claims."[12] On that same September day, ABC News headlined a story, "67 Times Donald Trump Tweeted About the 'Birther' Movement."[13] Despite their best efforts, neither of these news services found a quote from Trump claiming Obama was born in Kenya. To be sure, Trump questioned the legitimacy of the birth certificate and speculated on why Obama took such pains to keep it under wraps, but he never went beyond speculation.

If Trump stumbled into the birther controversy, Dr. Terry Lakin did not. The former Army lieutenant colonel walked into it eyes wide open. In 2010, this much-honored flight surgeon questioned why he had to produce his birth certificate to be deployed overseas if the commander-in-chief sending him did not. After exhausting all military channels, Lakin took the one bold step he thought would force the president to respond. He conditioned his second deployment to Afghanistan on Obama's willingness to produce his birth certificate. For his efforts, Lakin was court-martialed, thrown out of the military, stripped of all benefits, and shipped in chains, literally, to the Army's Joint Regional Correctional Facility at Fort Leavenworth.

The media barely noticed. Those who did, such as Maureen Dowd of the *New York Times*, attributed Lakin's "craziness" to his "biases about race and religion." What else could have motivated him? Dowd concluded her mocking assessment of Lakin's gesture with "one big truth." Wrote Dowd, "President Obama doesn't have to show Terry Lakin anything. The colonel should have followed orders."[14] The media had finally found a military protestor they did not like.

I recently visited with Lakin and asked what drove him to do what he did.[15] He told me of an exchange that occurred during his intake assessment at Leavenworth. The psychologist asked him why he thought

Obama was born outside the United States. Lakin corrected the psychologist. He explained that he did not know where Obama was born or whether he was eligible to be president. The problem, he informed the psychologist, was that no one did. MSM journalists like Dowd had refused to do their job. As a result, concerned citizens like Lakin knew more about the president's background than did the naïfs in America's newsrooms.

By 2012, however, even mainstream journalists knew that Obama's mother showed up in Seattle in August 1961 with a baby in tow. Knowing this, they had to wonder how mother and baby got there and where they came from. If the baby had been born in Hawaii on August 4 of 1961, as the records suggest, he would have been no more than three weeks old when he left the island with his mother, Ann Dunham. This was possible, but improbable.

Sometime during the previous summer, Ann and her parents moved to Hawaii. In their respective biographies, the four Davids tell different stories as to why the family moved, none detailed, none particularly convincing. Readers do learn, however, that Ann was something of a wild child in her senior year and that she had a crush on the eponymous Afro-Brazilian of the movie *Black Orpheus*, a passion she would later reveal to her embarrassed son.

At the time, Hawaii was the one state in America where a biracial baby could pass almost unnoticed. At the time, too, parents routinely sent their pregnant daughters off to some distant place to conceal an inconvenient pregnancy. The fact that Ann dropped out of the University of Hawaii before her second semester, when she would have been no more than two months pregnant with the child of Obama Sr., adds weight to the speculation that she was pregnant when she arrived in Honolulu. In this scenario, the arranged marriage with an African, whether legal or not, would make sense for everyone. Obama Sr. would later tell local immigration officials his American wife was "hapa," pregnant, in the hope of extending his stay in America, and the Dunhams benefitted by having an African son-in-law. In 1961 America, oddly, Africans enjoyed a higher status than African Americans. In fact, Obama Sr. and Dunham's father became pals.

In this scenario, the Dunham family might have claimed a home birth and called it in to the authorities in August. They would have done this not to pave the boy's way to the presidency but to protect him from the shame of an out-of-wedlock birth. If, say, Obama had actually been born in February, not August, the very date would have given the Obama camp cause to resist sharing the birth certificate. It would have shattered Obama's "signature appeal: the use of the details of his own life as a reflection of a kind of multicultural ideal." Whatever the reality, the combination of moves by Obama's mother should have prompted the media to question the details surrounding Obama's birth. The media chose not to. They preferred to mock those who tried to make sense out of the available facts.

No one came in for more mockery than Donald Trump. A Trump tweet in September 2015—"Just remember, the birther movement was started by Hillary Clinton in 2008. She was all in!"—forced the media to pay some attention to the roots of the birther controversy. Concluded the Poynter Institute's PolitiFact, "It's an interesting bit of history that the birther movement appears to have begun with Democrats supporting Clinton and opposing Obama."[16] In fact, Democrat Philip Berg, a former deputy attorney general of Pennsylvania and a Hillary Clinton supporter, filed the first suit challenging Obama's eligibility. Without evidence, PolitiFact assured its readers, "There is no direct tie to Clinton or her 2008 campaign." To discover such a tie would have taken more work than the media were prepared to do.

A diligent researcher, Lt. Col. Lakin knew about the holes in Obama's birth narrative, knew about the Berg suit, and knew Obama's attorneys had invested considerable time and money fighting the plaintiffs who had sued to see his long form birth certificate. Lakin believed the oath he took as an officer in the U.S. Army to defend the Constitution mandated that he seek the truth. If Maureen Dowd knew what Lakin knew, she might not have dismissed him as crazy or denounced him for not following orders.

Lakin was down to his last two weeks in prison in April 2011 when Obama produced at least a facsimile of the long form birth certificate that Trump and others had been asking to see for several years. After considerable study, Lakin, like most who have researched the document, believes it to be a forgery. Still, Lakin wonders why the Obama White House, knowing the risk he was about to run, did not produce the document before his court-martial.

Today, Dr. Lakin specializes in occupational medicine and urgent care at a Pueblo, Colorado, clinic in which he is a partner. Soft spoken and diffident, he seems the least likely person to have taken a stand that would cost him his military career, his freedom, and several million dollars in salary and benefits. He has few regrets. He did what he felt he had to do. If he is a racist, that will come as news to his wonderfully supportive wife Pili, a native of Thailand, and their three steadfast children.

What Lakin appreciated about Trump in 2011 was his unique willingness to shrug off criticism and override the media. In this, Lakin was not alone. At the time Trump first went public with his doubts, a Tea Party leader told CNN, "The great thing about what Donald did is he said it and he did not flinch when he said it. A lot of the alleged conservative leaders have run like cockroaches when the lights are turned on from the eligibility issue."[17] To this day, the media refuse to understand that it was Trump's very real boldness that attracted heartland conservatives, not his imagined racism.

Trump critics have found it emotionally easier to accuse Trump of racism, a charge they gleefully extend to his supporters, than to accept their candidate's defeat. Actor Jeff Daniels reflected the media's moral *hauteur* in assessing the motives of a small-town crowd at a May 2019 Trump rally. "At the end of the day," said Daniels on an MSNBC panel, "it's race. It's race."[18] For the record, Montoursville, Pennsylvania, the site of the rally, is more than 99 percent white. My guess is that the residents spend very little time fretting about black people.

Progressives, by contrast, fret about race endlessly. From the moment Obama presented himself as a serious candidate for president, race dominated the conversation. The media have used it not only as a way to protect Obama from his critics but also to protect him from himself. Following a March 2007 speech in Selma, Alabama, Obama needed all the media help he could get.

Weeks after declaring his bid for president, Obama addressed the veterans of the famed Selma civil rights march of 1965. In Selma he knew that his exotic, oft told origins story would not play well. So, he adapted it. Did he ever! As Obama told the story, something happened in Selma that sent out, in the words of Bobby Kennedy, "ripples of hope" all around the world. Inspired by Selma, the Kennedys decided to do an airlift "to start bringing young Africans over to this country." Barack Obama Sr. "got one of those tickets" and met Obama's mother.

Lest I be accused of cherry-picking quotes, allow me to conclude with Obama's rhapsodic, if solipsistic, summary of his own role in African American history. Obama delivered this speech in an ersatz preacher's cadence only slightly less grating than Hillary Clinton's:

> But something stirred across the country because of what happened in Selma, Alabama, because some folks were willing to march across a bridge. And so they got together, Barack Obama Jr. was born. So don't tell me I don't have a claim on Selma, Alabama. Don't tell me I'm not coming home when I come to Selma, Alabama. I'm here because somebody marched for our freedom.[19]

Had a black Republican candidate made a claim so extravagantly false in so many obvious ways, his candidacy would not have survived the evening news. For starters, President Dwight Eisenhower launched the airlift in question, not the Kennedys. Obama Sr. arrived in 1959 when Eisenhower was president, not John Kennedy. The young African came to America through a separate program, not the airlift. These errors are forgivable. The next one is not. "Some folks" marched across a bridge in *1965*. Obama's parents "got together" and conceived the lad in 1960. Even a Common Core math teacher cannot make that equation work.

Fortunately for Obama, the *New York Times* had his back. In an article headlined, "Clinton and Obama Unite in Pleas to Blacks," the *Times* made note of his blasphemous claim only in the eighteenth paragraph and even then without a hint of outrage: "Mr. Obama relayed a story of how his Kenyan father and his Kansan mother fell in love because of the tumult of Selma, but he was born in 1961, four years before the confrontation at Selma took place. When asked later, Mr. Obama clarified himself, saying: 'I meant the whole civil rights movement.'"[20] Nothing to see here, folks, keep on moving.

Washington Post columnist Richard Cohen did not need prompting. In choosing Obama as the winner of the Selma beauty contest, Cohen declared, "It is not just that he performed better than Hillary Clinton; it's that he had something very important to say to black America."[21] Obama may have had something important to say, but he was never quite sure what it was. If Cohen refused to notice, civil rights veterans knew how desperate Obama sounded shoehorning his famed personal story into the larger civil rights narrative. Many of them supported Hillary.

Cohen missed all of this. He dedicated a column to the speech without even hinting at Obama's obviously tortured effort to fit in. "Barry [Barack] wanted desperately to belong to 'something.' He wasn't African American, at least not with the connotation that term has taken on: a meaning that includes a heritage of slavery," writes friend Keith Kakugawa, adding drily, "The only Black influence he had in his life was television."[22]

To firm up his identity as an African American, Obama allied himself with the Trinity United Church of Christ in Chicago, then pastored by the soon to be infamous Rev. Jeremiah Wright. Obama's choice of a church, like his selection of a wife, smells of calculation. Although a cosmopolitan at heart, Obama knew that his path forward politically hinged on his acceptance by a parochial black community. Having no larger political goal in his early Chicago years than the mayor's seat, Obama expected that membership in Wright's church, like his friendship with Frank Marshall Davis, would help his career. It did to a point.

Given all that is known now about Wright's racism and anti-Semitism, impressively little of that information leaked out in the first year of Obama's candidacy. In April 2007, the *Times* published a lengthy and largely positive article about Obama's relationship with Wright. "Mr. Wright has presided over his wedding ceremony, baptized his two daughters and dedicated his house, while Mr. Obama has often spoken at Trinity's panels and debates," wrote the *Times*'s Jodi Kantor. Kantor reported these milestones, one suspects, largely to confirm Obama's Christianity.[23] During that first year, Nation of Islam leader Louis Farrakhan was the guy in Obama's neighborhood causing the candidate the most problems, especially with Jewish voters. Farrakhan, however, did not baptize Obama's kids. Wright did. The media seemed unfazed.

As late as February 29, 2008, Wright was still something of an afterthought. On that day, the *Times* published an article centered on Obama's courtship of Jewish voters. Reporter Neela Banerjee mentioned Wright only in the fourteenth paragraph and then without any undue alarm. Although acknowledging that Wright had been accused of making "virulent anti-Israel remarks," Banerjee attributed that accusation to a Jewish Republican in Israel, thus negating its impact.

To counter the Republican, Banerjee cited the more authoritative Anti-Defamation League (ADL). The ADL, she assured her readers, found "no evidence of anti-Semitism on Wright's part."[24] The left-leaning ADL could not have looked very hard. In March 2018, two weeks after the ADL gave Wright its stamp of approval, ABC's *Good Morning America* aired a video clip of Wright's now notorious "chickens are coming home to roost" sermon. Preaching on the Sunday following September 11, the fiery Wright blamed America and Israel for provoking the terrorist slaughter.

Almost assuredly, ABC would not have shown the video if Obama were the nominee. At this juncture, however, Hillary Clinton was still viable as a candidate, and George Stephanopoulos had pull at the network. A month later, during ABC's controversial debate, Stephanopoulos would challenge Obama on both Ayers and Wright. Fox News also aired some of Wright's more provocative sermons, and the videos spread wildly through the samizdat. Had they surfaced before the Iowa primary in January 2008, Obama would not have won the primary or the presidency.

The *Times* may well have sat on the "chickens" video for a year. At the very least, reporter Jodi Kantor knew its content. In her April 2007 article on Wright, Kantor wrote limply, "On the Sunday after the terrorist attacks of 9/11, Mr. Wright said the attacks were a consequence of violent American policies." Kantor said no more than that. The *Times* had a president to elect.

In an opinion piece posted hours after ABC's first report aired, the *Times*'s Chris Suellentrop tried to contain the damage. He noted that the sermons were "creating a stir in blogland." In implying that "blogland" was not a land to be taken seriously, Suellentrop downplayed the story's importance, concluding with a nod to Hillary supporter and radio talk show host Taylor Marsh who argued, in Suellentrop's words, "Wright's sermons shouldn't be used against Obama."

As a reader pointed out in the comments section, however, Suellentrop fully misrepresented Marsh's sentiments. Here is what Marsh actually said: "This is a nightmare. A Democratic nightmare, especially since Obama and his campaign are intent on making divisiveness the signature remembrance of his primary campaign." Marsh added, "I've never heard any of my preachers talk about the US of KKK."[25]

In a news piece published later that same day, the *Times* tried again to douse the flames, this time comparing Wright's statements to those of Clinton supporter Geraldine Ferraro.[26] The editors had to know how specious this comparison was. Ferraro committed no greater sin than to speak honestly about Obama's meteoric ascent. "If Obama was a white man, he would not be in this position," said Ferraro. "And if he was a woman of any color, he would not be in this position. He happens to be very lucky to be who he is."[27] Unapologetic, Ferraro made another much too honest comment: "Every time that campaign is upset about something, they call it racist." That said, Ferraro bowed defiantly out of the Clinton campaign.

On March 18, 2008, just five days after Wright's wild-eyed sermons surfaced, Obama felt compelled to smother the controversy. He did so with a speech in Philadelphia that once again mined his "own story." This time he sank the shaft a little deeper, extracting relatives living and dead to fire up the campaign.[28] He spoke of Michelle and his two "precious daughters." They carried "the blood of slaves and slave owners." He spoke of the "white grandfather" who served in Patton's Army and the "white grandmother" who worked on a bomber assembly line. If that were not kin enough, Obama cited "brothers, sisters, nieces, nephews, uncles and cousins of every race and every hue."

The money line came late in the speech. Said Obama, "I can no more disown [Wright] than I can disown my white grandmother." According to Obama, his grandmother "once confessed her fear of black men who passed her by on the street." This graceless canard was manufactured for the occasion. In *Dreams from My Father*, "Toot" confesses only to being shaken by an encounter at her bus stop. "'He was very aggressive, Barry,'" she tells her grandson of the man who accosted her. "'Very aggressive. I gave him a dollar and he kept asking. If the bus hadn't come, I think he might have hit me over the head.'"[29] Hesitant to return to that bus stop alone, the "diminutive" Toot asks her deadbeat husband for a ride. It was he who allegedly tells Obama the man was black. In Obama's calculus of evil, Toot's understandable anxiety equaled Wright's twenty years of creepy anti-white, anti-Semitic, anti-American sermons.

At the time of the speech, Toot was eighty-five and ailing. This "typical white woman," as Obama described her on a radio show,[30] refused to tell reporters how she felt about the speech or about her grandson. Her opinion didn't matter. Titled "A More Perfect Union," the Philadelphia speech was a smash. Journalists competed to see who could praise the black candidate more fulsomely.

"With his brilliant speech on race relations yesterday at the National Constitution Center, Barack Obama showed why his campaign for president has the aura of a mission," gushed the editors of the *Philadelphia Inquirer*.[31] Janny Scott of the *Times* called the speech "hopeful, patriotic, quintessentially American" and commended its "frankness about race."[32] Years later, pundits were still gushing. In 2017, for instance, Roy Peter Clark of the Poynter Institute—the "world's most influential school for journalists"—praised the speech for its "power and brilliance" and shared with aspiring young journalists the reasons "why it worked."[33]

In the speech's most stirring moment, Obama promised not to disown Wright. Weeks later, Obama disowned Wright. The good pastor's claim that the U.S. government manufactured the AIDS virus to kill African Americans made him a tad too difficult to defend. Lamented the embarrassed cheerleaders at the *Times*, "Barack Obama rejected the racism and paranoia of his former pastor, the Rev. Jeremiah Wright Jr., and he made it clear that the preacher does not represent him, his politics or his campaign."[34] To be considered "brilliant" as something other than a con job, a speech should have a shelf life of at least a month. This one didn't.

On the JournoList site, Chris Hayes of the *Nation* proposed a way out of the mess. Hayes urged his colleagues, "particularly those in the ostensible mainstream media," to just move on. "If you don't think [Wright's] worthy of defense, don't defend him!" he wrote. "What I'm saying is that there is no earthly reason to use our various platforms to discuss what about Wright we find objectionable."[35] A day later, the editors at the *Times* suggested a bolder strategy, so bold, in fact, that I laugh in amazement each time I read it. Hang on—they *praised* Obama for "the most forthright repudiation of an out-of-control supporter that we can remember."

A month later, Wright provided enough "evidence of anti-Semitism" that even the ADL could not ignore it. In explaining why he had not spoken to the president, the irrepressible Wright told a reporter, "Them Jews ain't going to let him talk to me."[36] For years, Wright had been Obama's mentor. He did not take easily to the reversal in roles.

The same week that "them Jews" were keeping Wright at a safe remove, Obama made what might well have been his best speech on race. The media barely noticed. The site was the Apostolic Church of God in Chicago. The occasion was Father's Day. From the pulpit Obama spoke to the gathered voters—excuse me, congregants—with uncharacteristic audacity. He reminded his audience that too many black fathers were missing from "too many homes." He knew something of the phenomenon himself given that his father "left us when I was two years old."[37] Yes, that con again.

Putting aside for a moment his personal story, however fictitious, Obama made the traditionally conservative argument that fatherless children were five times more likely to grow up poor, nine times more likely to drop out of school, and twenty times more likely to get into serious trouble than children who grow up with both parents. Those absentee fathers, Obama scolded, "have abandoned their responsibilities, acting like boys instead of men. And the foundations of our families are weaker because of it." In that it was Obama who made this argument—not, say, Dan Quayle—the mainstream media reported the speech uncritically.

Progressives, however, were uneasy about Obama giving voice to what one wag called his "inner Cosby," and no progressive more so than Jesse Jackson. Even in a whisper, Jackson made his voice heard. For all of Obama's politically conscious life, Jackson's had been *the* face of the American civil rights movement. From the moment Jackson descended on Chicago in April 1968 wearing a shirt allegedly drenched in Martin Luther King's blood—Obama was six at the time—he showed that a movement leader with sufficient charisma and media access need not overly worry about the truth.

Jackson was not to be messed with. Three weeks after Obama's Father's Day sermon, Jackson got his message across. As reported by Jeff Zeleny of the *Times*, "He specifically took issue with how Mr. Obama had singled out black men in recent speeches for failing to uphold their responsibility as fathers."[38] In that Jackson himself had sired a love child, he took Obama's words personally. A hot mic at the Fox News studio caught Jackson whispering to another black guest, "See, Barack been, um, talking down to black people on this faith-based—I wanna cut his nuts out... Barack—he's talking down to black people—telling niggers how to behave." On saying "cut his nuts out," Jackson made a sharp slicing motion with his hands. One hopes he was speaking metaphorically, but he definitely "took issue" with Obama. There was no denying his rage.

Had any network other than Fox News recorded these remarks, they might never have surfaced, but surface they did, at least in part. Fox News edited out the "n-word" sentence. "We don't want to hurt Jesse Jackson," Bill O'Reilly told *Politico*'s Jonathan Martin. "We're not in business to do that. So we held it back. And then some weasel got the whole thing and leaked it out to the Internet, and here we are." Reporting on what O'Reilly left out, Martin began with the amusingly Orwellian lede, "It turns out Jesse Jackson whispered something even worse than his desire to cut off Barack Obama's manhood."[39] Most males, I suspect, would think the threat of castration a bit "worse" than a racial slur, but most males have not had their priorities reordered in a major newsroom.

This was a delicate moment for Obama and the MSM. To keep the heat off Obama, the *Washington Post's* Jonathan Weisman focused on the conflict between Jackson and his congressman son, Jesse Jr. As Weisman noted, however, "For Obama, still struggling to put the Rev. Jeremiah Wright's inflammatory sermons behind him, another flare-up in the African American community cannot be welcome."[40] The *Times* led with Jackson's preemptive apology for what Zeleny daintily called a "vulgar reference." That was as specific as the *Times* got. Obama promptly accepted the apology, but his spokesman promised that Obama would continue addressing the issue of fatherhood.

Canadian Suzanne Goldenberg, writing for Britain's left-leaning *Guardian,* reported boldly what the American media barely reported at all. The thrust of the headline—"'I want to cut his nuts out'—Jackson gaffe turns focus on Obama's move to the right"[41]—had to make one wonder whether his gaffe was a gaffe at all. Intentionally or not, Jackson raised the question, "What has happened to Obama since he won the Democratic nomination?" According to Goldenberg, Jackson's remarks "were mirrored on the blogosphere in an outpouring of anger against the campaign's moves to the right."

Jackson's authenticity intimidated Obama. For all his promises to address the fatherhood issue going forward, Obama never again spoke out as forcefully as he had on Father's Day in Chicago. In his faux apology, Jackson laid out the game plan going forward. Yes, it was okay to talk about personal responsibility, Jackson told the *Times,* but it was equally important "to deal with the collective moral responsibility of government and the public policy which would be a corrective action for the lack of good choices that often led to [black male] irresponsibility." Obama would honor Jackson's dictate throughout his presidency. The consequences for the black community would be downright lethal.

On that same Election Day that I handed out donuts in a Kansas City polling station, two leather-jacketed, beret-clad thugs from the New Black Panther Party handed out abuse at a polling station in Philadelphia. One of the men, Philadelphia chapter leader King Samir Shabazz, carried a billy club. When approached by civil rights attorney Bartle Bull,

Shabazz yelled at him, "Now, you will see what it means to be ruled by the black man, cracker!"[42]

Bull, a former New York State campaign manager for Robert Kennedy, had little doubt as to why the men were there. Their goal, as Bull saw it, was to protect illegally registered voters from the scrutiny of people like himself. Using his then novel cell phone camera, a citizen journalist recorded Shabazz and his colleague at work, and the video circulated widely via the samizdat.

In January 2009, with George W. Bush still in office, the Department of Justice filed a civil suit against Shabazz, two of his buddies, and the New Black Panther Party itself. One of those named was a Democratic Committee member and credentialed poll watcher. Bull submitted an affidavit in support of the suit. Career DOJ attorney J. Christian Adams called the open intimidation by the Panthers, "the simplest and most obvious violation of federal law I saw in my Justice Department career."[43] The law in question was the Voting Rights Act of 1965.

When none of the named individuals appeared in federal district court to answer the suit, it seemed certain the DOJ would prevail by default. By this time, however, Obama's people had taken over the Department. In May 2009, Adams's new bosses ordered him and his colleagues to abandon all action against the New Black Panther Party and two of the defendants. "For the first time in our lifetime the power of the administration of the United States was working against the Voting Right Act," said Bull. "They were protecting the people who were abusing the law."[44]

For the next year, the samizdat would be abuzz with the story. So too were its sometime allies on the responsible right: Fox News, the *Washington Times*, the *Wall Street Journal* opinion pages, the higher profile conservative publications. During that year, the mainstream media's most powerful voices, the *Washington Post* most notably, would remain perversely quiet.

With the MSM on the sidelines, the task of silencing Obama's critics fell to the firemen. Their best weapon was race. They used it often and effectively. When Adams quit the DOJ in disgust and went public with his charges, the firemen had their target. Among those taking a shot was one Adam Serwer. A writing fellow at the *American Prospect*—a publication whose stated mission is "liberal intelligence"—Serwer was one of the countless young J-School grads hunting DC for conservative prey.

In December 2009, Serwer condescended to write about "the infamous Black Panther case." He used the word "infamous" here with a wink, knowing his audience would catch the dig. In the article, Serwer set his sights on Adams, "a conservative partisan." As proof of Adams's partisanship, Serwer cited any number of his sins against liberal orthodoxy: filing an ethics complaint against Hillary Clinton's brother, arguing that health care reform was a threat to liberty, expressing skepticism about affirmative action, and relying on a section of the Voting Rights Act last used as part of "a massive statewide effort to disenfranchise black voters."

The defendants in the Philadelphia case, Serwer insisted, were simply "two foolish men," barely worth discussion, and the case itself "a rather perfect example of the conservative obsession with 'reverse racism' and a reminder just how corrupted the Civil Rights Division under Bush really was."[45] End of discussion.

Following Serwer's stint at the *American Prospect,* he moved on to *Mother Jones,* MSNBC, the *Washington Post, Salon,* and the *Atlantic,* where he serves as senior editor. I point out Serwer's career path only for its typicality. It was not at all unusual for young activists to make their bones in some fetid leftist tributary and flow right into the mainstream untainted. Little adjustment was needed. The *Atlantic,* for instance, would say of Adams that his "claim to fame as a federal lawyer seems to be his penchant for accusing black people of discriminating against whites."[46]

Media Matters for America (MMFA), the tax-exempt smear machine funded generously by the notorious left-wing financier George Soros, pounded Adams as well. In a brief profile, MMFA described Adams as having become "famous among conservatives for absurdly accusing the Obama-era DOJ of racism against white Americans, and more specifically for pushing a fake narrative about the department's actions against the New Black Panther Party."[47]

As the *Daily Caller*'s Matthew Boyle reported in detail in September 2012, the DOJ had been using MMFA all along to "quell news stories about scandals plaguing [Attorney General Eric] Holder and America's top law enforcement agency."[48] Through a Freedom of Information Act request, Boyle had secured hundreds of email exchanges between the DOJ Office of Public Affairs director Tracy Schmaler and MMFA staff. Many of these exchanges centered on what an MMFA staffer called "the phony New Black Panther Party scandal," and most involved attacking the reporters and whistleblowers that were trying to expose it. Reporters higher in the food chain fed off the garbage MMFA scavenged.

Incredibly, it was not until July 2010, nearly two years after the original incident, that the *Washington Post* deigned to publish an article on the case. The use of the word "right" in the headline—"2008 voter-intimidation case against New Black Panthers riles the right"[49]—told savvy readers all they needed to know. No worry, this was a partisan thing. To drive the point home, reporter Krissah Thompson used the word "conservative" eight times in the article. By contrast, the word "Obama" appeared four times, each time as an adjective, as in "Obama administration." Throughout his presidency, the media would do their best to insulate Obama from the wayward actions of his subordinates.

Three days later, the *Post's* ombudsman Andrew Alexander responded to those readers who wanted to know why the *Post* had been "virtually silent" about the case for nearly two years.[50] Although admitting the case was "significant," Alexander paraphrased the *Post's* national editor, Kevin Merida, on the reason for the *Post's* lethargic coverage: "The delay was a result of limited staffing and a heavy volume of other news on the Justice Department beat." This one sorry excuse helps explain how Obama's vice-president, Joe Biden, could launch his 2020 election campaign claiming there was "not one single whisper of scandal" during those eight long years.[51]

Once again, bad journalism quickly morphed into bad history. In his 2013 book, *The Center Holds: Obama and His Enemies,* Jonathan Alter wrote off the Panther case as a scandal only in the eyes of Fox News and the conservative media. Apparently unaware of how intimidation works, Alter insists, "Not a single actual voter there complained of intimidation."[52] That was just the point. No one dared complain, especially those too fearful to vote or to report voter fraud.

Ironically, Obama had long imagined himself a defender of voting rights. After completing Harvard Law School, he proposed to write a book on voting rights, listed voting rights as an area of expertise at his Chicago law firm, and integrated the subject into the courses he taught at the University of Chicago.[53] As a U.S. senator in 2007, Obama introduced a bill that would have increased the criminal penalty for voter intimidation, insisting,

"Both parties at different periods in our history have been guilty in different regions of preventing people from voting for a tactical advantage. We should be beyond that."[54] The *Times* used the very phrase "voter intimidation" in the headline of an article cheering Obama's initiative.[55] And yet the *Times* and its allies in the MSM could barely bring themselves to acknowledge what civil rights attorney Bartle Bull called "the most blatant form of voter intimidation I've ever seen."

The incident in question took place on the very day Obama was elected, and it set the tone for the eight years to follow. The *Times* and the *Post* chose not to notice when Eric Holder, who is black, called out Bull, who is white, for daring to compare the admittedly "inappropriate" intimidation in Philadelphia to the intimidation "endured in the South in the 60s." The comparison, said Holder, "does a great disservice to people who put their lives on the line, who risked all, for my people."[56]

In fact, Bull was one of those people who put their lives on the line. In 1966, he was serving as a civil rights lawyer in Mississippi and was arrested for his troubles. In 1966, Eric Holder was attending a prestigious high school in New York City, and Obama was building sand castles on Waikiki Beach. Holder's parents' roots were not in Mississippi. They were in Barbados. His father was an immigrant, as were his maternal grandparents.

From Holder's perspective, what made the Mississippians "my people" was their pigmentation. From a historical perspective, they were no more *his* people than they were Obama's. Neither had roots in the American slave experience. From a political perspective, however, if African Americans began to doubt whether they were the "people" of whichever Democrats were in power, the party was over. For eight long years, Obama, like Holder, would go out of his way to remind African Americans that he and they were one.

Were it not for the samizdat and whistleblowers like Adams, Obama would have walked away from the Philadelphia mess as unscathed as King Samir Shabazz. For all its independent parts, if the samizdat had a William Randolph Hearst, it was surely the late, great Andrew Breitbart. Until his unexpected death in March 2012 at the age of forty-three, Breitbart did more to undo the Democratic-media lock on the Overton window than anyone since William Buckley. A child of Hollywood and a recovering liberal, Breitbart had a preternatural grasp of the way the media worked. Crazily audacious at times, he was one of the very few high-visibility people to defend my thesis that Bill Ayers was involved in the writing of Obama's *Dreams*. For his troubles, he was slammed on air for racism, both by HBO's Bill Maher and MSNBC's Martin Bashir.[57] I had the good fortune of running into Breitbart shortly afterwards and was able to thank him for his support. He did not have long to live.

In 2009, Breitbart scored his single greatest strike against the empire through his young protégé James O'Keefe. Curiously, Obama biographer Jonathan Alter introduced O'Keefe and his "shenanigans" on the same page in his book as he dismissed the New Black Panther incident. In one of the more memorable moments of samizdat history, O'Keefe's shenanigans led quickly and directly to the complete collapse of the appallingly corrupt, five hundred thousand-member, twelve hundred-chapter Association of Community Organizations for Reform Now, better known as ACORN.

Obama had a special place in his heart for his fellow community organizers at ACORN. The relationship was special enough, in fact, that Stanley Kurtz aptly dubbed Obama "the Senator from Acorn."[58] According to Kurtz, ACORN had good reason to boost Obama's career. In 1995, while positioning himself to run for state senate, Obama represented ACORN in a lawsuit to assure Illinois enforced the federal "Motor-Voter" law. Leading up to his run for office, Obama sent a stream of money ACORN's way from the two leftist Chicago foundations on whose boards he sat. During that same time frame, he personally trained aspiring ACORN leaders. ACORN and its New Party political arm returned the favor by endorsing Obama's 1996 state senate run.[59] None of this, by the way, caught the attention of historian James Kloppenberg. It would have made his image of Obama as a Madisonian pragmatist an even harder sell.

Like Frank Marshall Davis or the Rev. Jeremiah Wright, ACORN played better on a Chicago stage than on a national one. Sensing this, Republican John McCain used Obama's affiliation with ACORN against him during the 2008 campaign, or at least he tried to. With Obama's election at stake, the media would not pursue the charges leveled by their once favorite Republican "maverick."

Late in the 2008 campaign, the *Times* helped guarantee that election by spiking a potentially damaging ACORN story. *Times* writer Stephanie Strom was about to report on the Obama camp's use of ACORN as a funding cut-out when her bosses thought better of it. Months later, the *Times* public editor Clark Hoyt owned up to the spiking, sort of. According to Hoyt, the story had not "panned out." He blamed the story's demise on Strom's failure to verify her source's evidence.

Strom's source had a different take. Earlier, she recorded Strom telling her, "I have just been asked by my bosses to stand down. They want me to hold off on coming to Washington. Sorry, I take my orders from higher up sometimes."[60] To the uninitiated, this sounds more like a "spike" than a "not panned out," but Hoyt assured the faithful that the *Times* was above that sort of thing. As proof of his sincerity, he repeated the *Times* "without fear or favor" slogan.[61] Without intending, Hoyt confirmed the old saw that the difference between *Times* readers and readers of the Soviet *Pravda* was that *Pravda* readers *knew* they were being lied to.

The slaying of the Hydra-headed ACORN beast began with a June 2009 Facebook message from an attractive twenty-year-old named Hannah Giles to then twenty-four-year-old O'Keefe. "Working on anything exciting at the moment?" asked Giles. As a postscript, Giles added, "have you ever done undercover stuff with ACORN housing???" O'Keefe had been experimenting with undercover videos since his undergraduate days at Rutgers and was looking for new targets. When he asked Giles what her plan was, she responded, "So what if two girls dressed for 'business' walk in and ask to apply for housing."[62]

Wrote O'Keefe in his memoir, *Breakthrough*, "Only a madman would have predicted that a couple of twenty-somethings working off a credit card and internship money could expose ACORN's dark heart and force it to disband." In the way of explanation, he added, "Journalism can still work when it is tried."[63]

ACORN had been allowed to metastasize for nearly forty years for one obvious reason: many journalists never bothered much with actual journalism. If the subject matter touched on race in an unhelpful way, journalists ducked and covered. With no one paying much attention, the largely minority ACORN offices had grown careless. O'Keefe and Giles quickly discovered just how careless when they visited these offices in the guise of a pimp and his prostitute.

Full of youthful moxie, the conspirators asked the friendly ACORN workers to help them arrange housing for a stable of underage sex workers the pair hoped to import illegally into the country. In every case except one, the office staff happily obliged. O'Keefe and Giles secretly recorded their interactions on hidden cameras. Despite the subject matter, the videos they produced were funny and playful, but ultimately devastating.

Knowing how the media worked, Breitbart convinced O'Keefe and Giles to release just one video at a time. "You know they are going to say it was one rogue employee," he told O'Keefe.[64] On September 10, 2009, Breitbart launched the offensive. He began by posting a video shot at ACORN's Baltimore office on his new BigGovernment.com site. As expected, the samizdat ran with this visually irresistible story, as did Fox News.

On camera, O'Keefe tells the office's tax expert, "There's going to be thirteen El Salvadoran girls coming into this house. And they're very young. And we don't want to put them on the books." The expert suggests that since the girls are underage, there would be no need to file 1099s on them. "On the other part of the return you can [list] them as a dependent," she enthuses, pleased with her own cleverness.[65]

On September 11, just as Breitbart predicted, ACORN execs dismissed the Baltimore video as a fluke. "This is not how we behave," said the ACORN execs. They claimed O'Keefe and Giles had gone to at least five other ACORN Housing offices "where they were turned away or where ACORN Housing employees responded by calling the police."[66]

Predictably, the firemen rallied to ACORN's defense. *Salon's* Joe Conason accepted ACORN's alibi without any attempt at verification. Said Conason on CNN, "It's not journalism unless [O'Keefe and Giles] report everything that happened. It's propaganda."[67] After letting the media vent for a day, Breitbart posted the video from O'Keefe and Giles's Washington, DC, sting. This video was at least as damning as Baltimore's.

The media were not ready for an operator as savvy as Breitbart or for videos as entertaining as O'Keefe's. CNN News called O'Keefe wanting an interview, but Breitbart counseled against it. CNN's goal, Breitbart explained, was not to expose ACORN but to attack O'Keefe. The media lived down to Breitbart's expectations. Four days after the Baltimore video, a fireman blogger at *Daily Kos* got personal on O'Keefe in an article unsubtly titled, "The Acorn Pimp: The bully behind the costume. (I found his blog)." He tracked down O'Keefe's online diary from his freshman year at Rutgers and detailed an incident in which O'Keefe was falsely accused of racism. "Maybe it was all a lie," the blogger admitted, but the truth no longer mattered.[68] The accusation of racism was out there, and for the left that sufficed.

Undeterred, O'Keefe and Breitbart posted one video after another, each shot in a different ACORN office—Baltimore, Washington, Brooklyn, San Bernardino, San Diego. The media's hollow words proved no match for the visual truth documented in these guerrilla videos. That did not stop the media from trying to undo the videos' effect.

The *Washington Post* weighed in with its first detailed story a week after the first video dropped and two days after the "Defund ACORN Act" was introduced in the House. Rather than explore the reasons why ACORN was about to be defunded, the *Post's* Darryl Fears attempted to divine what moved O'Keefe and Giles to skewer a cow as sacred as ACORN. He traced Giles's insensitivity to her "ultraconservative" minister of a father and allowed ACORN's chief organizer Bertha Lewis to suggest a larger motive for both O'Keefe and Giles.

By Lewis's lights, the two were part of the "relentless conservative attack" that had no greater goal than to "destroy the largest community organization of black, Latino, poor, and working-class people in the country."[69] The *Post* readers had no way of knowing that the responsible right kept O'Keefe and Giles at arm's length and would be quick to disown O'Keefe in the future for every misstep, real or imagined.

A day after the first *Post* article, Carol Leonnig joined colleague Fears to smear O'Keefe without evidence or conscience. Not until O'Keefe read the article did he learn that he and Giles had "targeted ACORN for the same reasons that the political right reportedly did," namely to subvert ACORN's "massive voter registration drives that turn out poor African Americans and Latinos against Republicans."[70] He and Giles thought they were focusing on housing issues.

Working off the *Post* article, the Associated Press edged further out on the libel limb, claiming O'Keefe "*said* he went after ACORN because it registers minorities likely to vote against Republicans" (italics added). O'Keefe never said or even implied such a thing. Throughout his career, in fact, he has advocated for no cause other than freedom of the press. He forced the *Post* to print a retraction, but who reads retractions?

Despite the media's defensive efforts, Obama was reeling. Defending this level of lawlessness was not easy, not even for him, not even if it involved his African American base. His relationship with ACORN may have been awkward in 2008, but by late 2009 it had become toxic. As a stand-alone, the video from the Baltimore ACORN office could have sunk any Republican endorsing a comparable organization. These videos were hard to explain away. While they were still being released, the Democratic-controlled House and Senate each passed the "Defund ACORN Act" with substantial majorities. Cornered, Obama signed the act into law three weeks after the Baltimore video was posted. Washington rarely moves that quickly. The samizdat had struck a nerve.

As Breitbart expected, the media used the most potent card in its deck to undermine O'Keefe. That, of course, would be the race card. In the way of example, ABC's *Good Morning America* anchor George Stephanopoulos began an interview with the overwhelmed twenty-five-year-old, thusly: "[Your critics] say you're animated by resentment over race. They point out that you've attended at least one conference where white nationalist literature and speakers were promoted. And they point to a time in college at Rutgers when you were kicked out of a dorm for using racist slurs."[71]

This interview took place in May 2010. By this time, Congress had defunded ACORN. The Census Bureau and the IRS had ended their contracts with ACORN, and in a few months, ACORN would file for Chapter 7 and cease to exist. In a just world, a TV news anchor would want to congratulate this inventive young journalist for making all of the above happen. Instead, Stephanopoulos slimed O'Keefe with a series of charges, no less deadly for being baseless.

It is not as if the media objected to undercover videos. CBS's *60 Minutes* and other news shows have used the technique for years, and no one in the major media hesitated to air the *Access Hollywood* tape that nearly sank Trump's candidacy in 2016 or the "47 percent" tape that did sink Mitt Romney's candidacy in 2012. No, what the MSM and their firemen objected to was O'Keefe's content. It had sufficient visual power to breach the cyber wall that the media had thrown up around all things Obama.

I have gotten to know the surprisingly apolitical O'Keefe through our shared interests and Irish-American, New Jersey backgrounds. A few years ago, I stopped by his studios in Westchester County, New York, and his crew recorded our conversation on the current state of journalism.[72] O'Keefe had just returned from covering the Republican National Convention in Cleveland. There he was confronted by a *Rolling Stone* reporter who did what journalists have been doing to O'Keefe since he broke the ACORN story—attacked him with charges that had long since been disproved. Together we watched the video of that encounter in wonder. "Anyone who attempts to speak truth to power in this country is systematically destroyed and maligned by the machine," O'Keefe explained to the reporter, who seemed utterly unable to comprehend that his once dissident publication had become part of that machine.

O'Keefe and I also spoke about the *Washington Post*'s reaction to the ACORN sting. It amazed him at the time that a Pulitzer Prize winner like Carol Leonnig would build an article around a complete falsehood, specifically that he "targeted ACORN" to thwart its minority voter drives. Equally amazing was that a day later, *Post* editors would toss off a one-paragraph correction as though smearing someone unjustly were no big deal.

There was an unevenness, O'Keefe mused, about how the media assigned motives. If an Islamist walked into a room yelling "Allahu Akbar" and shot everyone in sight, the media would insist the motive was "unclear." On the other hand, if he and others in the samizdat explained their motives, even on the record, journalists would routinely assign them a motive of the journalist's own choosing. In the age of Obama, the assigned motive was often, perhaps usually, race.

O'Keefe has a wall in his office dedicated to the various retractions the media have felt compelled to offer. The retractions, however, don't follow O'Keefe. The accusations do. After ten years in the trenches, O'Keefe has grown used to the abuse, but he has never learned to like it. Undaunted, he and his corps of irregulars, now thirty or so strong, happily subvert the ongoing media efforts to restrict the flow of information.

Should one of the irregulars in the samizdat make an error, especially if race is involved, no correction will appease the more respectable class of journalists, left or right. In July 2010, Andrew Breitbart made such an error. Ironically, it led to the most significant exposé of his career, one that the *New York Times* would validate after Breitbart died.

The story began with an ugly bit of Democratic agitprop. On March 20, 2010, Rep. Andre Carson and Rep. John Lewis showily walked through a crowd of Obamacare protestors from the Cannon Office Building to the Capitol. Once there, Carson told reporters that he and Lewis were "walking down the steps" of Cannon when they "heard 'n-word, n-word,' at least 15 times, hundreds of people."[73] True or not, this was exactly the story the media needed to prove the Tea Party's racism, evidence of which had eluded them to this point.

If the media chose to believe Carson, Breitbart did not buy this improbable nonsense for a second. He also understood that cell phone cameras, no longer a novelty, could confirm his suspicions. In an effective bit of gamesmanship, Breitbart offered $100,000 to anyone who could produce video showing a single person shouting a racial epithet at any member of the Congressional Black Caucus (CBC). "What [the Democrats] did not expect was that new media would successfully challenge the propaganda of the old media and the Congressmen's racial smear," wrote Breitbart.[74] He caught Carson in a spectacular lie. The CBC members were recording the event themselves, but even they could not produce any useful video. Breitbart could. He found four videos that showed the opposite of what Carson claimed and silenced the CBC, at least for a moment.

Three months later, however, the NAACP resurfaced the charges against the Tea Party as if they had never been disproved. The media predictably played along, and Breitbart fought back. To highlight the NAACP's own racism, Breitbart posted a video clip of United States Department of Agriculture (USDA) official Shirley Sherrod telling an NAACP audience, to the nodding approval of its members, how she had once consciously discriminated against a white farmer.

Knowing how the major media would pounce on any error from the samizdat, Breitbart was generally careful with his information. Not this time. He and his people made two errors. For one, they gave the impression that Sherrod worked for the federal government when she slighted the white farmer. In fact, the incident had taken place twenty-four years earlier. More consequently, they took the posted video clip out of context. Later in the same talk, Sherrod told the audience how, upon assessing her own bias, she went back and helped the farmer. In the text accompanying the video, Breitbart reported Sherrod's change of heart, but he let the video stand as an illustration of the way Obama's people instinctively filter decisions through the prism of race.[75]

As presented, the Breitbart article would have raised questions about Sherrod's judgment, but it hardly would have justified what happened next. Within hours, Agriculture Secretary Tom Vilsack, with Obama's blessing, forced Sherrod's resignation. In doing so, the White House transformed a Twitter feud into a major media fandango. Immediately, the firemen rushed to find the holes in Breitbart's account, and this time they did not have to invent them. When the full story of Sherrod's remarks was revealed, the mainstream media pilloried Breitbart, the responsible right scolded him, and a humbled White House offered Sherrod her job back and then some.

As a testament to the media's fixation on the case, when Breitbart died of a heart attack two years later, the *Washington Post* promptly built an article around his relationship with Sherrod. "My prayers go out to Mr. Breitbart's family as they cope during this very difficult time," Sherrod said thoughtfully and left it at that. Despite her unwillingness to pile on, the *Post* ran a lengthy and tasteless recap of the incident on the very day of Breibart's death.[76]

As was true throughout his presidency, the *Post* downplayed Obama's role in a given fiasco. The Breitbart post-mortem was no exception. "President Obama called [Sherrod] to express his regret and try to patch over the mess," wrote reporter Krissah Thompson in this, the article's only reference to the president. Just as predictably, Thompson made no reference at all to the massive scandal this affair prompted Breitbart to investigate, a scandal that deserves a book of its own and a place for Breitbart in a journalism hall of fame.

Oddly, Breitbart had learned of the brewing scandal from his critics. More than a few claimed he had targeted Sherrod "to get Pigford defunded." As Breitbart told the *Daily Caller*, he "had never heard of Pigford" before the Sherrod flap. In the months to follow, he came to own that story. "All I've been doing," he said later, "is eating, breathing, sleeping Pigford, researching Pigford."[77]

Breitbart was referring here to *Pigford v. Glickman*, a multitiered lawsuit that would end up costing taxpayers *billions*, most of it pure scam. The money was originally earmarked as compensation for black farmers allegedly denied USDA loans, but before the Pigford gravy train had left the station, thousands of random blacks and other minorities, many of whom had not seen a farm since CBS canceled *Green Acres*, hopped on board.

Breitbart came to believe that Obama had moved so hastily against Sherrod to keep Pigford out of the news. If true, Obama had good reason to do so. The suit had already netted the Sherrods $13 million and Shirley's job at the USDA. Thanks to Obama, billions more were on their way to people who were equally undeserving.

As late as September 2010, months after Breitbart began exposing the fraud at the heart of the case, Obama and the major media still felt comfortable touting the Pigford settlement. At a September 10 press conference that year, White House correspondent April Ryan, now with CNN, asked Obama pleadingly whether he could assure "those awards are funded" before he left office. Obama answered the way Ryan obviously hoped he would. After explaining the case to "those who aren't familiar," Obama insisted, "It is a fair settlement. It is a just settlement. We think it's important for Congress to fund that settlement. We're going to continue to make it a priority."[78] That Obama had to explain Pigford to White House correspondents testified to the media silence on the subject. True to form, the *Post* did not so much as mention Pigford in its article on Sherrod's reaction to Breitbart's death in March 2012.

In April 2013, however, with the president safely re-elected, the *New York Times* did the unexpected. It ran a major exposé on Pigford, calling the legal action "a runaway train, driven by racial politics, pressure from influential members of Congress and law firms that stand to gain more than $130 million in fees."[79] Just as they did with the voter intimidation case in Philadelphia, Obama's political appointees reportedly overruled career lawyers to appease Obama's base.

This case involved the USDA as well as the DOJ, and the due bill was a good deal higher than in Philadelphia. In fact, the administration committed billions to female and minority farmers who had never even filed a bias claim. "From the start, the claims process prompted allegations of widespread fraud and criticism that its very design encouraged people to lie," wrote *Times* reporter Sharon LaFraniere, "those concerns were played down as the compensation effort grew." The *Times* estimated the total cost of the swindle at about $4.4 billion, in the words of one USDA analyst, "a rip-off of the American taxpayers."

The unusually honest *Times* article tied Obama directly to this race-based boondoggle. Although his name was not mentioned in the article's headline—a grace note President Trump could only envy—LaFraniere did not deny Obama's responsibility. As a senator, Obama had supported expanding Pigford compensation. As president, he pressed for an additional billion or so to make this happen. Obama's billion-dollar demand maddened the career attorneys involved in the case given that the courts, including the Supreme Court, had already ruled against compensating the various female, Hispanic, Native American, and additional black "farmers" who clamored for a slice of the Pigford pie.

Politics drove much of the decision-making. According to LaFraniere, President Bill Clinton had recruited a politico "known for his expertise in black voter turnout" to help launch the program. Obama likewise viewed the Pigford payouts as government-issued walking around money. LaFraniere paraphrased a black farm leader as saying Obama's support for Pigford "led him to throw the backing of his 109,000-member black farmers' association behind the Obama presidential primary campaign." The political courtship of Native Americans was even more flagrant. A Berkeley professor who had prepared a 340-page report on the case told LaFraniere, "It was just a joke. I was so disgusted. It was simply buying the support of the Native-Americans."

LaFraniere concluded her deeply troubling report with a focus on Thomas Burrell, head of an entity called the Black Farmers and Agriculturalists Association. She recounted his rollicking speech to a group of several hundred African Americans at a Little Rock church. "The judge has said since you all look alike, whichever one says he came into the office, that's the one to pay—hint, hint. There is no limit to the amount of money, and there is no limit to the amount of folks who can file." Such was racial justice in the age of Obama.

Among the very few in the major media to follow up on the *Times* article was the self-described "right leaning" Conor Friedersdorf of the *Atlantic*. His article—"How Did Progressive Journalists Get Pigford So Wrong?"—illustrates the way the responsible right could and occasionally did undermine the efforts of the samizdat in the age of Obama.

Yes, many progressives did get Pigford wrong. Among those Friedersdorf profiled was Adam Serwer of *American Prospect*. Last heard from on these pages trivializing the New Black Panthers case, Serwer put his race-baiting skills to work this time trivializing Pigford. As Serwer saw things in 2010, three years before the *Times* weighed in, Pigford represented "a new low for conservative anti-anti-racism." Indifferent to the evidence, Serwer insisted that the claims of the farmers had been "exhaustively documented." A champion of reparations before his time,

Serwer could imagine no motive for the right's objection to "the transfer of income from whites to nonwhites" other than racism.

Had Friedersdorf honored the proposition in the article's title, he might have helped keep the Pigford story alive, but that was not his intention. Although admitting Serwer's post was "uncharitable," Friedersdorf listed him among the writers he found to be "careful, accurate and valuable." Like many on the timid right, the self-described "civil libertarian" showed himself much too eager to earn the left's fabled "grudging respect."

To earn that respect, Friedersdorf targeted the samizdat's MVP, Andrew Breitbart. He argued that the "polemicist" Breitbart neutralized "smart, honest" journalists on the right. "I can't blame journalists for ignoring Breitbart's claims," sniffed Friedersdorf. "He'd already proved himself unreliable at that point in his career for reasons that everyone outside the conservative movement already understands." Incredibly, Friedersdorf dedicated the final eight hundred words of an article supposedly about progressive malfeasance to Breitbart's imagined failings.

To prove Breitbart's unreliability, Friedersdorf referred the reader to two articles, one posted on Breitbart.com that Breitbart might not even have read, and another that Friedersdorf did not know well enough to critique. The first article was silly and irrelevant. The second story involved what Friedersdorf called "the most indefensible thing that happened when Andrew Breitbart worked with James O'Keefe."[80] He referred here to O'Keefe's sting of the San Diego ACORN office, a sting that led to the firing of the worker who freely offered real housing advice for O'Keefe's imagined crew of underage sex slaves.

Friedersdorf seems to have taken his account of that incident from "careful, accurate and valuable" journalists such as Adam Serwer. He could not have watched the raw videos of the sting in question or read the depositions that ensued. If he had done either, he would have understood why ACORN fired the fellow and why O'Keefe settled the civil suit against him. The $100,000 settlement—chump change by contemporary standards—had nothing to do with the man's innocence and everything to do with California's restrictive laws on recording conversations. Breitbart had been dead for a year when Friedersdorf slammed him and O'Keefe. I cannot imagine Friedersdorf would have had the nerve to take on Breitbart when he was alive. Years later, Friedersdorf and the *Atlantic* were forced to retract the claim that the subject of O'Keefe's sting was portrayed untruthfully. This represented the 306th retraction posted on Project Veritas's Wall of Shame.[81]

For all its thunder, the exhaustive *New York Times* Pigford exposé failed to resonate in the media echo chamber. The samizdat tried to keep it alive, but a story of this scope needed nurturing by the mainstream. That support was not forthcoming. As far as I can tell, no one in the media ever asked Obama about Pigford once the *Times* story broke. The story came and went, and the administration continued on its unblemished way.

On the last full day of Obama's eight years in the White House, *Washington Post* fact checker Glenn Kessler assessed Obama's claim that his was "the first administration in modern history that hasn't had a major scandal." White House spokesman Eric Schultz offered a qualified defense of his boss's statement. Said Schultz, "There's been no scandals over the past eight years the likes of which we've seen plague previous Administrations—as reaffirmed by journalists from across the spectrum." In that no one in the major media "reaffirmed" LaFraniere's excellent reporting, Pigford was thus not a scandal. Kessler proved the point by not so much as mentioning Pigford in his review of White House missteps. In fact, he designated Obama's scandal-free boast "largely correct."[82] This is meaningless. As Sharyl Attkisson observed of America's major newsrooms, "Anything short of a signed confession from the president himself is deemed a phony Republican scandal, and those who dare to ask questions are crazies, partisans, or conspiracy theorists."[83]

Obama got away with paying his dues to the liberal black establishment when he did it quietly. The Philadelphia and Pigford cases suggest as much. Neither one put Obama's appeasement strategy on display. On two memorable occasions during the presidency, however, Obama went public with his biases. The first one, a relatively trivial incident, cost Obama politically. The second incident helped Obama politically, but, indirectly at least, would cost thousands of black Americans their lives.

On July 16, 2009, Harvard University professor Henry Louis Gates Jr. returned home late from a trip abroad, found his Cambridge house locked and himself keyless, and broke in with the help of his driver. A neighbor witnessed the break-in and called the police. The police responded. In his carefully worded report, Sergeant James Crowley told how he saw Gates through the glass-paned front door, identified himself, and asked Gates to step out on the front porch. Gates answered, "No, I will not." Crowley explained he was investigating a report of a break-in in progress. Gates shot back, "Why, because I am a black man in America?" Gates continued to rant at Crowley, calling him a racist and refusing all requests to cease his "tumultuous behavior." When Crowley asked Gates to speak with him outside, Gates shot back, "I'll speak with your mama outside." As a crowd gathered and additional police officers arrived, at least one of them black, Crowley warned Gates several times he would be arrested if he did not desist. Gates kept at it and was arrested for disorderly conduct.[84]

The media love stories, real or contrived, in which a rogue white cop abuses a black person. The *New York Times* ran multiple articles on the incident even before Barack Obama got involved. The first of these articles—"Harvard Professor Jailed; Officer Is Accused of Bias"—concluded with a narrative-setting comment from one of Gates's fellow professors, "My colleagues and I have asked the question of whether this kind of egregious act would have happened had Professor Gates been a white professor."[85] Journalists routinely give the last, unchallenged word to a person whose testimony best reflects the reporter's bias. This trick helps preserve at least the illusion of objectivity.

Under ordinary circumstances, the media would have been happy to move on after a day or two of cop bashing and chest thumping, the officer's career ruined, the neighbor's reputation besmirched. With a black president in the White House, however, a reporter thought it important that Obama address the racial implications of the incident. The occasion was a press conference on health care, but any occasion would have sufficed.

Still needing to anchor his identity as an authentic African American, Obama forgot for a moment his assigned role as the nation's "healer-in-chief." After admitting he did not know all the facts, he did know "that the Cambridge police acted stupidly." If he read the *Times* account of his impromptu remarks, Obama would have known he said more than he should have. Sergeant Crowley refused to apologize.[86] More troubling still, police across the nation came to Crowley's defense. As Obama knew, America has a lot of cops, some 790,000 of one sort or another, and most of them vote. As Obama quickly learned, Crowley was one of the best of them. An Obama supporter, he had been hand-picked by his black police commissioner to teach recruits on how to avoid racial profiling.

The president who was elected in no small part to cool racial tensions had inflamed them. To restore calm and his reputation as a healer, Obama invited Gates and Crowley to the White House. For racial balance, Obama also invited Vice President Joe Biden, who doesn't drink, to the instantly famous "beer summit." On this occasion, the *Times* gave the last meaningful quote to Gates. Said he, "I don't think anybody but Barack Obama would have thought about bringing us together."

If the mainstream media were satisfied with this off-mic racial kabuki, the samizdat was not. Andrew Breitbart, for one, saw through the charade. "The more Sgt. Crowley weighed in, and his brave black co-workers spoke out, the more obvious it became that a national discussion featuring this cast of characters may not end with the results the professor and the president wanted," said Breitbart of the beer summit. "The status quo was at risk, and Mr. Obama used his extraordinary powers to protect it."[87]

In this case, there was little for the samizdat to do but comment. The next time Obama intervened in a local criminal case, citizen journalists on the right would embarrass their mainstream peers with the depth of their reporting and, in the process, help prevent a terrible injustice. What they could not prevent, however, was the media-fueled carnage that followed.

To this day, George Zimmerman cannot believe what happened to him that rainy Sunday night in Sanford, Florida. The then twenty-eight-year-old neighborhood watch captain headed out to Target to do his food shopping for the week. While driving through his crime-ridden townhouse community, he spotted "a male approximately 5' 11" to 6' 2" casually walking in the rain and looking into homes." Zimmerman did as the Sanford Police had previously asked and called the non-emergency number he had been given.

After circling Zimmerman's truck menacingly, the man took off running. When the dispatcher asked in which direction the man was heading, Zimmerman left his truck to see. "Are you following him?" the dispatcher asked. When Zimmerman answered in the affirmative, the dispatcher said, "We don't need you to do that." Zimmerman responded, "Okay," and stopped.

In a report Zimmerman wrote for the police that evening, he told of walking back to the truck and being surprised by the man. "You got a problem?" the man said to him. When Zimmerman answered "No," the suspect said, "You do now." He did indeed. The man was half a foot taller and an experienced fighter. "As I looked and tried to find my phone to dial 9-1-1 the suspect punched me in the face. I fell backwards onto my back. The suspect got on top of me. I yelled 'Help' several times."

Zimmerman continued, "As I tried to sit upright, the suspect grabbed my head and slammed it into the concrete sidewalk several times. I continued to yell 'Help.' Each time I attempted to sit up, the suspect slammed my head into the sidewalk. My head felt like it was going to explode." When the man ignored a neighbor's threat to call the police, Zimmerman felt he had no option but to pull his gun and shoot. The police arrived a minute later to find seventeen-year-old Trayvon Martin dead with a bullet in his chest. The neighbor confirmed Zimmerman's version of events, and another neighbor's 9-1-1 call picked up at least forty seconds of Zimmerman crying for help. The police did not make an arrest. It was as clear a case of self-defense as they had seen.[88]

The story should never have left Sanford, but it did. For the media, the story had it all: race, guns, an unarmed "black boy," and a shooter, presumably white, named "Zimmerman." As Zimmerman told me, if his parents had not Americanized his first name—he had been named after his Uncle Jorgé—I never would have heard of him. The media, he knew, would have wanted no part of an incident involving a Jorgé and a Trayvon in 2012, especially in Florida, the ultimate battleground state.

The media did, however, like the story the Martin family publicist packaged for them. Within ten days of the shooting, Martin's divorced parents were on ABC's *Good Morning America* sharing pre-adolescent photos of their innocent son, the son who wanted to be a pilot or a football player, the son who, in the words of Congresswoman Frederica Wilson, "was hunted down like a rabid dog."[89]

"This clearly was murder. It was not an accident," Trayvon's mom, Sybrina Fulton, told the millions who watched.[90] She did not tell them how she and her husband split when Trayvon was three, how his step-mother raised the boy until the boy's father abandoned her when Trayvon was fifteen, how Sybrina herself had kicked Trayvon out of her home for fighting months earlier, or how Trayvon's life devolved into a maelstrom of street fighting, burglary, guns, sex, and drugs.

To reinforce their standard narrative, the media slighted or suppressed information about George Zimmerman. Most Americans never learned his mother was from Peru, his great grandfather was black, and his first language was Spanish. Just a year earlier, he had successfully and publicly led a campaign to get justice for a homeless black man beaten by a police lieutenant's son. He mentored two black teens. He was an Obama supporter. Incredibly, in her book on the case, *Suspicion Nation*, NBC's Lisa Bloom mentions none of the above, not even Zimmerman's Hispanic roots.

To make their story line work, the media had to turn Zimmerman into a reckless, gun-toting racist, even a white supremacist. The tragedy was that they succeeded. For weeks, the major media and the firemen prodded the Sanford Police to arrest Zimmerman. Al Sharpton and Jesse Jackson descended on Sanford. Petitions were signed. Marches were held. The New Black Panthers put a $10,000 bounty on Zimmerman's head, and again the DOJ chose not to see. Black politicians and pundits leaned on Obama to say something, anything.

Sensing his point of greatest vulnerability, any number of black pundits zeroed in on Obama's Achilles' heel, his fear of seeming inauthentic. Blogger Yvette Carnell's post hit the target. "Obama is perfectly willing to give a sermon to black men on Father's Day about what they need to be doing," she commented, "but totally incapable of advocating for a black boy who was murdered in the street while carrying only Skittles and iced tea."[91]

Obama held out for nearly four weeks. Finally, on the morning of March 23, after introducing the new head of the World Bank in the White House Rose Garden, Obama took just one question, likely pre-arranged. It was on the shooting. Said Obama for the ages, "My main message is to the parents of Trayvon—If I had a son, he would look like Trayvon."[92] In projecting Trayvon as a "son," Obama strongly suggested that all black children were equally vulnerable to the predations of white men. Four weeks after the shooting, Obama had no excuse for not knowing the facts of the case. As shall be seen, this would prove to be the most destructive moment of his presidency.

On this same March day, the samizdat kicked into gear. Leading the way was a fellow who prefers to be known only as "Sundance." Just a year earlier, he and a handful of like-minded citizens, most of them female, banded together to form a blogging collective called the "Conservative Treehouse." Like most citizen journalists in the samizdat, Sundance and his fellow "Treepers" worked without compensation.

"Look, I'm as concerned at Trayvon Martin's shooting as anyone,"[93] Sundance observed in the headline of his March 23 post, but the presence of Al Sharpton and the ubiquitous Pee Wee football photos of Trayvon made him suspicious. "I remember the Tawana Brawley fiasco," he wrote, "and even more recently I well remember the Duke Lacrosse players rape case fraud. Optics are not always reality."

On March 31, Al Sharpton led thousands through the streets of Sanford demanding Zimmerman's arrest. On that same day, Sundance posted a lengthy deconstruction of the case based on the input of his fellow Treepers. His headline—"Trayvon Martin was apparently a 17 year old undisciplined punk thug, drug dealing, thief and wanna be gangsta"—summed up the unfortunate reality of Martin's life, a reality the national media studiously suppressed.[94] The Treepers presented a precise map and timeline, offered links to information sources, assessed the motives of those involved, and carefully distinguished between what they knew for a fact and what they suspected.

In that I was writing a book about the Zimmerman case while it was moving through the courts, I communicated regularly with Sundance. A supermarket executive who retired early, he did a fair amount of gumshoe reporting in the Miami area, Trayvon's home base. One day, he called to tell me that the valve stems had been surgically removed from two of his now terminally flat tires. The culprit left on his windshield a Miami-Dade Police business card with the name sliced off. On the back of the card was written one word—"STOP!!" Sundance then sent me his own full name, his address, and his Social Security number "just in case something happens to me." There was a reason he blogged under a pseudonym.

One thing Sundance did suspect, but could not prove, was that the Florida state attorneys had enabled, if not orchestrated, a shocking legal fraud. He believed the young woman that prosecutors claimed was on the phone with Trayvon prior to his death was a fraud. Without this "phone witness," the state could not have arrested Zimmerman. The affidavit of probable cause was based largely on her testimony. Five years after the trial, samizdat filmmaker Joel Gilbert called seeking my advice on a proposed film about the Zimmerman case. I had met Gilbert a few years earlier when he interviewed me for a documentary he was doing on socialism, *No Place Like Utopia.*

Like just about every player in the samizdat, Gilbert defied the outsider's image of what a putative right-wing activist should look and act like. For years, the Los Angeles-based Gilbert fronted a Bob Dylan tribute band. He made a documentary about Dylan along the way and, even today, wears his mop of dark hair much as the early Dylan did. In an odd twist of fate, his documentary about the Trayvon Martin shooting represented his second film about a man named "Zimmerman."

Gilbert knew something about the Soviet samizdat. As a nineteen-year-old in 1984, he visited "refuseniks" in the Soviet Union as part of a discreet program run by Jewish organizations. The goal was to encourage these dissidents and keep them informed until the Soviet Union allowed them to leave the country. Gilbert knew a good deal about Obama as well. In 2012, he produced a documentary on Frank Marshall Davis that raised the question of whether "Pop" was Obama's real father. His thesis was plausible if impossible to confirm short of a DNA test. According to the *Atlantic*, the Davis film appealed only to "the looniest of the right wing,"[95] but if nothing else, it forced the media to acknowledge Davis's existence. I had enough confidence in Gilbert's work to introduce him to George Zimmerman, who was still living in the shadows five years after his acquittal.

In September 2019, Gilbert debuted his documentary, *The Trayvon Hoax*, at the National Press Club. In a dazzling bit of investigative journalism, he confirmed Sundance's suspicions about the state's star witness, Rachel Jeantel. To prove Jeantel an impostor, Gilbert enlisted private investigator Susan Daniels, as well as two prominent handwriting analysts, an audio expert, and a forensic DNA lab. After poring through page after page of text messages, phone calls, tweets, Facebook messages, high school yearbooks, and crime reports, Gilbert was able to find the real girlfriend, a then sixteen-year-old Haitian American hottie Trayvon knew as "Diamond."

Gilbert discovered that when Diamond refused to perjure herself about what she knew, Trayvon's support team allowed the mentally challenged Jeantel, Diamond's half-sister, to pose as a witness. This was the most consequential bit of judicial malpractice in memory.

At the time of the film's release, Trayvon's mother, Sybrina Fulton, was running for office in what the *Miami Herald* called "the most high-profile race in the history of commission politics." Hillary Clinton had publicly endorsed Fulton, as had Cory Booker.

As Gilbert proved beyond doubt, however, Fulton was the one adult who inarguably knew about the witness switch. A Pulitzer awaited the intrepid reporter who followed Gilbert's leads. Not a one could be bothered, not in New York, not in Orlando, not even in Miami. Only twelve minutes elapsed from the time Gilbert sent an email to the *Herald*'s managing editor asking for his help to the time Gilbert was told, "Thanks for reaching out. We are going to pass." The ensuing email flurry from the *Herald* newsroom quickly built to Category 5 level contempt, and this was *Miami*.

Only after Judicial Watch founder Larry Klayman filed a $100 million suit on Zimmerman's behalf in December 2019 did the *Herald* pay any attention to Gilbert's evidence, and even then its editors got everything wrong. In the *Herald* version of reality, Zimmerman "approached the teen" and "a struggle ensued." Worse, the *Herald* claimed that Zimmerman's attorneys "used the Stand Your Ground defense." If they had watched the film, the editors would have known each of these claims was false. They didn't care. They unapologetically set "the merits of the case aside" in making one final request of Zimmerman: "Please, go away and leave Trayvon's parents alone."[96]

In a court of law, the merits of the case could not be set aside. Fake witness or not, the evidence that Zimmerman had acted in self-defense was overwhelming. Any suspense about the trial's outcome ended when witness Jonathan Good confirmed his initial account to the police:

> So I open my door. It was a black man with a black hoodie on top of the other, either a white guy or now I found out I think it was a Hispanic guy with a red sweatshirt on the ground yelling out help! And I tried to tell them, get out of here, you know, stop or whatever, and then one guy on top in the black hoodie was pretty much just throwing down blows on the guy kind of MMA [mixed martial arts]-style.

Those who followed the case through the samizdat knew Good's testimony would sink the prosecution. Those who took their news from the major media had to be surprised, certainly those who took their cues from NBC's Lisa Bloom. Although Bloom claims to have covered the trial from "gavel to gavel," in *Suspicion Nation* she imagines Trayvon as the one yelling out for help and, unforgivably, omits Good's pivotal testimony altogether.[97]

Zimmerman would go on to sue NBC for libel. The judge threw out the suit. She argued that Zimmerman had made himself a public figure by "voluntarily injecting his views into the public controversy surrounding race relations and public safety in Sanford."[98] The judge was referring to Zimmerman's quest to seek justice for a black homeless man beaten by a white policeman's son. The irony of her ruling had to make

Zimmerman's head spin. To protect their narrative, the media had will-fully kept the public ignorant of this "public controversy." Yes, CNN did serve up one online article—"Tape showed Zimmerman's anger over black man's beating"[99]—but there was no echo in the media echo cham-ber. None. Indeed, NBC's Lisa Bloom wrote a book on the Zimmerman case without a single mention of Zimmerman's audiotaped pleading on the black homeless man's behalf.

One feature of the samizdat that the major media refuse to acknowl-edge is its willingness to self-correct. On a productive blog like the *Conservative Treehouse*, the volunteer "administrators" made sure that those posting stayed on topic and that inaccurate information was checked and countered. This does not always happen in the samizdat, but it almost never happens in the major media.

At one point, for instance, CNN decided that a garbled mystery word on the dispatcher call was "coons." To CNN, it seemed more believ-able for a young, Hispanic civil rights activist to say on a rainy February night, "It's fucking coons," than to say, "It's fucking cold," syntax and common sense be damned. If the samizdat—and Comedy Central's Jon Stewart—found CNN's conclusion ludicrous, the larger media did not. "When I listened, I heard [coons] immediately and in this CNN account, I hear it clear as day," insisted the overly praised Ta-Nehisi Coates in the *Atlantic*.[100] One expected no less from Mr. Coates.

Coates emphasized the "importance" of deciphering Zimmerman's words. "If Zimmerman actually did use a racial slur before he killed Martin," he said, "then you have the makings of a federal case." To find that elusive slur, Obama's Department of Justice promptly sent teams of FBI agents to Sanford, where they interviewed thirty-five of Zimmerman's friends, neighbors, and co-workers. Despite their best efforts, the federal thought police came up empty.

The Justice Department's Community Relations Service (CRS) had better luck in making Zimmerman's life miserable. CRS serves, accord-ing to its own delusional lights, as "America's Peacemaker." CRS allegedly "works with all parties to develop solutions to conflict and serves as a neutral party." In the Obama years, however, there was nothing "neutral" about CRS.[101] Attorney General Eric Holder sent these would-be community organizers to Sanford to help the locals orchestrate protests, the desired "solution" being the arrest and prosecution of an innocent man.

The pressure applied proved irresistible. State authorities yielded swiftly to the federal power, and Zimmerman went to jail. Those in Obama's circle who were paying attention saw just how easy it was to frame anyone who challenged their messaging, including, down the road, a president-elect. As was the norm during the Obama years, the media watched approvingly. The DOJ pulled off this unholy coup without protest from a single mainstream journalist. Concerned citizens learned about the CRS intervention only through the dogged research of Judicial Watch, the samizdat DOJ.[102]

As a result of the hopelessly skewed MSM reporting, few on the left expected Zimmerman's acquittal in July 2013. Outrage followed along predictable lines. Obama had one more opportunity to quell the furor. Six days after the verdict, he appeared unexpectedly at a routine White House press conference, specifically to address the "Trayvon Martin ruling." Obama began by sending his "thoughts and prayers" to the family of Trayvon Martin. For Zimmerman and his family, still in hiding, there was not a word. Much as he had a year earlier, Obama identified himself with Martin, this time even more directly. "Trayvon Martin could have been me thirty-five years ago," said Obama, ignoring the fact that the lads at his elite Punahou School did not make a habit of attacking armed strangers.

David Maraniss took a shot at assessing Obama's thinking in the *Washington Post*. Wrote Maraniss, "Obama was speaking not so much as a president addressing the populace but as a black man addressing white society."[103] This was true as far as it went, but what Maraniss failed to say is that Obama was not speaking honestly to any of his audiences. "There is a lot of pain around what happened here," Obama said of the black response to the verdict, but he dared not address the reasons for the pain: the collapse of the family in black America, the ensuing epidemic of crime, the understandable wariness of vulnerable non-blacks when around young black males, and the media's chronic dishonesty about all of the above.

To be fair, Obama conceded that young black men were "disproportionately both victims and perpetrators of violence," but he encouraged the mob's media-fueled belief that Martin was a victim of violence, not a perpetrator. Obama's DOJ had spent more than a year in Florida. Obama had to know about Martin's troubled background and the nature of the attack. "As a black man addressing white society," however, he knew he could deceive his audience with impunity.

If I dwell overlong on this incident, it is for two reasons, one personal. In getting to know Zimmerman and his family, I have seen up close the irrevocable damage that has been done to them. Zimmerman cannot have a fixed address or hold a job. In 2015, a gunshot from a would-be assassin missed hitting him by inches. Three years later, when he proposed writing a memoir, agents and publishers responded to him as if he had proposed writing a sex comedy about the Prophet Muhammad. "Now that the publishers I know have passed on it, I just want to move on," wrote an agent brave enough to try tackling the project. "My wife (and I) want to be sure that, should you ever do anything with this project, it is never mentioned that I was ever associated with it in any way."

Without a hint of regret, the most powerful institutions of the nation—the Department of Justice, the leading civil rights groups, the White House—conspired to send him, an innocent man, to prison for the rest of his life. Without any meaningful exceptions, the mainstream media enabled this dark turn in American history. There have been no apologies, no revisions, no lessons learned. The monster must be fed.

The second reason for my concern is societal. The citizen journalists of the samizdat helped Zimmerman's attorneys prepare their defense and kept the open-minded half of America informed, but they could not prevent the division that followed. Only Obama could have done that, and he chose not to. Instead, he concluded his feckless press conference with a nod once again to America becoming "a more perfect union," as if those words had any more meaning than they did in his equally empty Philadelphia speech.

America certainly was not becoming a more harmonious union. An NBC News and *Wall Street Journal* poll taken in the week after the verdict showed Obama failing in the one area in which even Republicans hoped he would succeed. In January 2009, 79 percent of whites and 64 percent of blacks held a favorable view of race relations in America. By July 2013, those figures had fallen to 52 percent among whites and 38 percent among blacks. In the way of explanation, the *Wall Street Journal* quoted a black New Jersey Democrat. "Things aren't going to change," she told the reporters. "You can't change ignorance." The woman, the reader was told, "pointed to the Zimmerman verdict as proof that racism in the U.S. still exists."[104] Propaganda works.

Getting neither satisfaction nor any corrective truth from Obama, militants transformed their anger into action. The most radical of these activists formed Black Lives Matter (BLM), a group whose website traces its founding "to the acquittal of Trayvon Martin's murderer, George Zimmerman." In August 2014, a year and a month after Zimmerman's acquittal, protesters chanting "black lives matter" turned the St. Louis suburb of Ferguson upside down and left much of it in ruins.

With a huge assist from the major media, BLM activists and their camp followers were quickly able to replicate the Trayvon tragedy, this time as farce. Three days after the shooting of Michael Brown by Police Officer Darren Wilson, the *Washington Post* featured a large photo of Brown in cap and gown under the headline, "Mike Brown notched a hard-fought victory just days before he was shot: A diploma." The *Post* informed its readers that Brown was "unarmed," a "gentle giant," "too timid" for football, and a devoted student, in attendance "every dog-gone day." Readers also learned some actual facts: within just three days of the shooting, Al Sharpton descended on the town; protestors settled on "Hands up, don't shoot" as a mantra; President Obama "offered his 'deepest condolences' to Brown's family"; and Brown's family was now represented "by the same attorney used by the family of Trayvon Martin, the Florida teenager gunned down by a neighborhood watch volunteer in 2012." Readers take note. "Teenager" Trayvon was not shot in self-defense. He was "gunned down."[105]

Sundance and his fellow Treepers knew a media con when they saw one. They promptly began "crowdsourcing" the evidence—the videos, the photos, the interviews, the maps, the time frame, the police reports. Within three weeks of the shooting, Sundance was able to post a lengthy and prescient deconstruction of the crime scene. At its center was one Anthony Shahid, a self-admitted "cop hater and grievance producer" kicked out of the St. Louis NAACP for being too radical. Wrote Sundance, "Quick as a jackrabbit, and totally understanding the value of the moment in front of a watching media, Anthony Shahid knew just what to do with the surrounding crowd." While Brown's body lay in the street, Shahid instructed those around him to raise their hands in unison and chant, "Hands up, don't shoot." The Treepers also unearthed a critical witness interview that the major media ignored lest it contradict the many hours of Shahid-coached interviews already aired.[106]

A day after the *Treehouse* piece, the *Times* reported how Shahid, "a civil rights activist," was organizing a rally and demanding "that Officer Wilson be fired and arrested on charges of murder." That the civil rights movement had descended into lynch mob justice seemed to trouble no one in the *Times* newsroom. In this same August 30 article about "the killing of an unarmed black teenager," the reporters interviewed "a top aide to Louis Farrakhan" as though his "top aide" status made him a voice worth heeding. That aide, Akbar Muhammad, compared the police response in Ferguson to "an army going to war in Iraq." To the reporters, this apparently sounded reasonable. They did not challenge Muhammad even indirectly.[107]

Within twenty-four hours of the shooting, organizers from the Justice Department's Community Relations Service arrived in Ferguson. "To reduce and counter the spread of dangerous speculation with timely and factual information," boasted its website, "CRS worked with law enforcement to institute rumor control measures."[108] If this was truly CRS's mission, it failed miserably. From hour one, the media feasted on rumors. The day after the shooting, the *Washington Post's* Jonathan Capehart set the table for what was to follow during an appearance on MSNBC. Although conceding he did not have all the facts, Capehart tied Brown's shooting to Trayvon Martin's, accepted the testimony of the one "hands up" witness at face value, and claimed that he and all other black men in America were living "under siege."[109] None of this made Capehart unusual. He had simply nailed the media narrative before his peers.

What did make Capehart unusual was his public admission that he had been duped. In March 2015, seven months after the incident, the *Washington Post* ran a Capehart column under the headline, "'Hands up, don't shoot' was built on a lie." A recently released Justice Department report forced Capehart to concede, "Brown never surrendered with his hands up, and Wilson was justified in shooting Brown."[110]

In this instance, regrettably, it is hard to give Capehart much credit. He had earlier discounted the "poisoned opinion" of a St. Louis County grand jury, pilloried Wilson for his "broad-brush" description of crime in Ferguson, and fully ignored the reporting from sites such as the *Conservative Treehouse*, *Legal Insurrection*, and the journals on the responsible right.[111]

Those tuned in to the samizdat knew the truth six months before Capehart did. In the Ferguson case, those six months would be crucial. In the age of Twitter, a lie can "trend" before the truth can get a single retweet. No previous hashtag had ever been tweeted more than "#Ferguson." The damage that Capehart and his MSM colleagues did in the first weeks and months following the shooting could not be undone. A week *after* the St. Louis County prosecutor cleared Wilson, for instance, five black players on the then St. Louis Rams ran onto the field with their hands in the air in an undisguised anti-police gesture. Five years after the incident, miscellaneous protestors were still chanting at cops, "Hands up, don't shoot."

Throughout it all, Barack Obama played to his base. Five days after the shooting, he spoke of Michael Brown, much as he had of Trayvon, as a victim. "We lost a young man, Michael Brown, in heartbreaking and tragic circumstances," said Obama at a press conference. "He was 18 years old, and his family will never hold Michael in their arms again."[112] In truth, Brown's family had not held the gentle giant in their arms in a long time, if ever.

Like Trayvon, Brown's parents separated when he was three, but they had never married. After the split, Michael stayed with his mother, but he often called his father asking to be "rescued." Both his parents hooked up with new partners, and Brown fell between the cracks. When Brown was sixteen, his mother threw him out of the house, forcing him to live with his father and his father's newest partner. For three months, Brown stayed in his room and refused to go to school. Unwanted by either parent, alienated from both, Brown spent the last year of his life living with his grandmother. Like so many abandoned young black men, Trayvon included, Brown projected the anger he felt towards his parents on to the non-black authority figures in his orbit: the Asian merchant he roughed up in the minutes before his demise, and the cop he recklessly assaulted in his own patrol car. Being high at the time did not improve his judgment.

After Father's Day 2008, Obama would never again address the collapse of the black family in any meaningful way. Instead, he reverted to what he had done throughout his career to assert his authenticity. He would "darken the canvas." Friendly biographer David Remnick used that phrase to explain the many "novelistic contrivances" in *Dreams from My Father*.[113] Biographer David Maraniss made the same point as Remnick, claiming Obama portrayed himself in *Dreams* as "blacker and more disaffected" than he really was.[114]

When he met with Ferguson protestors, Obama did some serious canvas darkening. Falling back on his own experiences, he assured them that the problem went much deeper than Ferguson. A few days later, he summed up his reaction to Ferguson for a Black Entertainment Television (BET) audience. Said Obama, now fully identifying with Michael Brown, "My mind went back to what it was like for me when I was 17, 18, 20."[115] He noted too that America had a "systemic problem,"[116] the police being the most obvious symptom.

Obama asked that any protests be peaceful, but the crazies had other plans. A week after his BET appearance, marchers took to the streets of New York City chanting, "What do we want? Dead cops. When do we want it? Now."[117] Inspired by the anti-police fervor in the air, Ismaaiyl Brinsley of Baltimore took a train to Brooklyn and shot a pair of defenseless cops, killing them both. In July 2016, Micah Xavier Johnson ambushed police officers in Dallas, killing five, injuring nine more. A week later, Gavin Long shot six police officers in Baton Rouge, killing three.

In embracing Michael Brown and endorsing the media's Ferguson narrative, Obama gave a green light to activists hoping to stage their own Ferguson-style morality plays. This they proceeded to do in Baltimore,

New York, Chicago, and lesser cities across the nation. In each staging, a black man played the role of victim; a police officer, preferably white and male, played the heavy.

Officer Darren Wilson never felt the need to darken his canvas. "There are death threats against him, there are bounties on his head," Wilson's lawyer told CNN.[118] Wilson, his wife, and their two children, one a newborn, moved from safe house to safe house for months after the shooting. In late November 2014, after the grand jury decision, Wilson was forced out of his job. "I have been told that my continued employment may put the residents and police officers of the City of Ferguson at risk, which is a circumstance that I cannot allow," Wilson said in a statement. He received no severance from the Ferguson PD.

Not long after his resignation, I spent an afternoon with Wilson in a modest new home he and his police officer wife bought through a proxy. For safety's sake, he could not be the named owner. Although six-foot-four, Wilson gave away eighty pounds to the equally tall and considerably more violent Brown. In real life, the crew-cut, baby-faced Wilson seemed as guileless as his photos made him appear. He was as unprepared for the crush of opprobrium as was George Zimmerman, also twenty-eight and married at the time of his undoing.

Wilson and I spent the afternoon pushing his infant daughter in her swing, reviewing his past, and assessing his future. Wilson had willed his way through a hardscrabble working-class childhood and emerged as something of a model police officer, only to have it all snatched away from him to sustain a lie. He had no job and no prospect of getting a job, certainly not in the St. Louis area, at least not as a police officer. Were it not for the courage of St. Louis County prosecutor Bob McCulloch, a Democrat, Wilson suspected he would be in prison. McCulloch's grand jury introduced too much legitimate eyewitness testimony for the DOJ to ignore.

Wilson had something going for him that Zimmerman did not: a community of fellow police officers. The cops got the picture. They knew they too could face termination, lawsuits, criminal charges, and death threats, all driven by the mandates of mob justice. They knew, as well, that the political class, from the president on down, would gladly throw them to the wolves to preserve the peace. Nationwide, but especially in cities where rioting followed lethal police-citizen encounters, cops instinctively began to pull back from actively policing black neighborhoods. Sensing opportunity, criminals moved into the void.

Attorney and Manhattan Institute fellow Heather Mac Donald has dubbed this phenomenon the "Ferguson Effect." Observed Mac Donald in a 2016 *Washington Post* column, "Arrests, summonses and pedestrian stops were dropping in many cities, where data on such police activity were available. Arrests in St. Louis City and County, for example, fell by a third after the shooting of Michael Brown. Misdemeanor drug arrests fell by two-thirds in Baltimore through November 2015."[119] At an emergency session of police chiefs held a year after the Ferguson incident, Chicago Mayor Rahm Emanuel explained the phenomenon to Attorney General Loretta Lynch. "[Cops] don't want to be a news story themselves," said Emanuel, "they don't want their career ended early, and it's having an impact."[120]

The impact was deadly and undeniable. According to FBI data, the murder rate in the United States declined steadily from 2006 to 2014 except for a minor blip in 2012. As a result, there were three thousand or so fewer murders in 2014 than in 2006.

After Brown's death in August 2014, the trend sharply reversed itself. In 2015, the murder rate rose nearly 11 percent, its greatest one-year jump in a half century. In 2016, the trend continued with an 8.5 percent increase over the year before. What this means is that nearly three thousand more Americans were murdered in 2016 than in 2014, an estimated eighteen hundred of them black.

Missouri proved particularly vulnerable. There, the spike began almost immediately after the August 2014 shooting in Ferguson. As a result, St. Louis had the highest murder rate in the nation in 2014, a dubious honor it held through 2017. Statewide, the murder rate nearly doubled from 2014 to 2017, and there was no good explanation for the surge in Missouri or nationwide other than the "Ferguson effect."[121]

If the catastrophe of Obama's racial leadership had a face, it was that of former San Francisco 49er quarterback Colin Kaepernick, the biracial adopted son of a white Christian family. "I am not going to stand up to show pride in a flag for a country that oppresses black people and people of color," said Kaepernick, explaining why he chose to sit out the national anthem. "There are bodies in the street," he added, "and people getting paid leave and getting away with murder."[122]

Yes, there were bodies in the street, but Kaepernick had no idea how they got there. Misled by his president and the media, he somehow concluded that America "oppresses black people" and leaves them to die in the streets. He reached this conclusion, it should be noted, in the eighth year of the Obama presidency while making $12 million a year, nearly $12 million a year more than his fellow twenty-eight-year-olds, Zimmerman and Wilson.

For all of those years, an African American headed the Department of Justice, and Democrats headed every major city in America save New York, the one city that defied the murderous post-Ferguson trend. It was hard to know who Kaepernick thought could fix the problems that troubled him. It certainly was not Barack Obama.

Through his passive acquiescence, Obama allowed this division to fester and the mayhem to explode. It was not necessarily coincidental that the murder rate started to decline as soon as Obama left the White House, and dropped substantially in 2018 under the "racist" President Trump. Until January 2017, black activists had a cheerleader in the White House. After that date, the police did.

Although Obama was not strategist enough to foment unrest, his allies were. From the progressive perspective, an angry base was a motivated one. In 2018, still stoking the rage generated by the false reporting around the Trayvon Martin shooting, black underdog Andrew Gillum upset his moderate opponents in the Florida Democratic primary and very nearly won the Florida governorship. The long march continued.

The Rainbow Front

I f the Obama era was a disaster for black America, it was something of a golden age for gay America. Although concocted to explain America's role in the misbegotten invasion of Libya, the phrase "leading from behind"—no pun intended—makes even more sense in describing Obama's role in advancing the LGBT agenda. In this instance, Obama led from way behind.

In August 2008, at Rick Warren's Saddleback Church in California, Obama staked out what seemed like a politically savvy position on gay marriage. "I believe that marriage is the union between a man and a woman," said Obama to widespread applause from the congregation. "Now, for me as a Christian," he added, "it's also a sacred union. God's in the mix."[1] Those paying any attention at all, God most certainly, knew Obama was playing games at Saddleback. As early as 1996, in filling out a questionnaire for a state senate seat in his liberal Chicago district, Obama endorsed same-sex marriage. In the intervening twelve years, he blew this way and that depending on the politics of the moment.

Not surprisingly, the *New York Times* made no allusion to Obama's vacillation in its lengthy article on the Saddleback forum. The reporters did note, however, "Mr. Obama also has an extensive religious outreach program, and polls show that he leads Mr. McCain among many religious denominations, with the notable exception of evangelical Christians."[2] In short, Obama was hustling Christian voters. This was not unusual. They get hustled all the time. But by putting "God in the mix," Obama put a little blasphemy into the hustle.

If the media gave Obama a pass, the LGBT lobby did not. Activists fumed when Obama came down on the side of tradition. That he chose to stake his claim in California, where a same-sex marriage proposition was on the ballot, peeved them even more. Seven years later, in his book, *Believer: My Forty Years in Politics,* campaign strategist David Axelrod tried to rehabilitate Obama's reputation among gays. Axelrod did so with an unorthodox twist. He claimed Obama actually had a "heartfelt belief" in gay marriage but lied at Saddleback to appease the realists in his campaign. "Opposition to gay marriage was particularly strong in the black church," writes Axelrod, "and as [Obama] ran for higher office, he grudgingly accepted the counsel of more pragmatic folks like me, and modified his position to support civil unions rather than marriage, which he would term a 'sacred union.'"[3] This is an astonishing admission. Lying and blasphemy struck Axelrod as less of a moral failing than questioning, even for a moment, same-sex marriage.

Understandably, the fear of offending the "black church" made Obama cautious about championing the LGBT cause, but there may have been another reason for his restraint. Obama faced rumors that he himself was gay. No subject made those close to Obama more nervous. Girlfriend Alex McNear, for instance, redacted a section of a letter she shared with biographer David Garrow, thinking Obama's reflections on homosexuality "too explosive."[4] Her concern was understandable.

In his early twenties, Obama had written to McNear that he viewed gay sex as "an attempt to remove oneself from the present, a refusal perhaps to perpetuate the endless farce of earthly life." Obama continued, "You see, I make love to men daily, but in the imagination. My mind is androgynous to a great extent and I hope to make it more so."[5] Only after McNear sold the Barack Obama letters to Emory University in 2016 was Garrow able to access the original and even then with some difficulty. Garrow included the passage in the paperback version of his book.

Given Frank Marshall Davis's admitted bisexuality and Obama's mental indulgence in the same, the honest critic has to think hard about this excerpt from "Pop," a poem Obama wrote while at Occidental: "Pop takes another shot, neat / Points out the same amber / Stain on his shorts that I've got on mine / and / Makes me smell his smell, coming / From me."[6] A samizdat therapist who blogged under the label "Neo-Neocon" hesitated to call the interaction "outright sexual abuse," but she imagined it at the very least "a boundary violation." She explained, "This child feels invaded—perhaps even taken over—by this man, and is fighting against that sensation."[7]

In January 2008, a fellow named Larry Sinclair fueled rumors about Obama's sexuality when he went up on YouTube with his allegations of a two-day coke and sex romp with Obama in 1999. Fearless, if nothing else, Sinclair then booked space at the National Press Club in Washington to detail his reputed relationship with Obama. From the beginning, the media, including the responsible right, pretended Sinclair did not exist. The actual work of extinguishing Sinclair's credibility was left to the firemen. As soon as he announced plans for the press conference, they launched an internet petition drive demanding the Press Club deny Sinclair its stage.

To its credit, the National Press Club refused to buckle. Sinclair held his conference.[8] In watching it years later, I am impressed by how well Sinclair understood Obama's hold on the media. If you asked a question about a black man who chose to run for president, he observed, "All of a sudden you're called a racist, a bigot." A genuine character, Sinclair acknowledged up front the various crimes he had committed in years past. He wanted to take that cudgel away from the media. Sinclair then explained in exquisite detail the nature of his alleged 1999 interaction with then state senator Obama. He provided dates, the name of the hotel, the name of the Muslim limo driver who arranged the assignation, the specifics of their sexual interlude, as well as insights into his more recent phone conversations with Donald Young, a member of Reverend Wright's church and an alleged lover of Obama's.

More than once during the question and answer period, reporters asked Sinclair, given his "tremendous credibility problem," why they should take him seriously. In turn, Sinclair asked the reporters "to do your jobs and find facts." He provided them several useful leads and challenged them to follow up. Sinclair specifically asked the reporters to check Young's phone records. He believed Obama to be complicit in the choir member's December 2007 murder, a crime that remains unsolved to this day.

If Obama's fire brigade had an MVP, it was surely Ben Smith, then with *Politico*. No one erased more evidence more reliably than did this well-connected young journalist. Smith, thirty-one at the time, began writing for *Politico*, an influential political journal launched by two *Washington Post* alumni, soon after it was launched in 2007. During the 2008 campaign, those who read *Politico* could be forgiven for thinking that Smith's primary assignment was to debunk the many "conspiracy theories" surrounding Obama.

In February 2008, for instance, Smith gave Obama's chief strategist David Axelrod the opportunity to bury rumors about Obama's connection with Bill Ayers. Axelrod readily obliged him. "Bill Ayers lives in his neighborhood. Their kids attend the same school," he said. "They're certainly friendly, they know each other, as anyone whose kids go to school together." For Smith, Axelrod's word was evidence enough, but it was not enough for those in the samizdat who actually tracked the Ayers-Obama connection. They knew what Smith should have known, namely that Ayers's *youngest* child was eighteen years older than Obama's oldest. Smith added this thesis-killing correction as an "update."[9]

True to form, Smith quickly moved to discredit Sinclair. *Politico* editors headlined Smith's article from the day of the press conference, "Obama accuser has long rap sheet." In an aside that President Trump might find amusing, *Politico* refused to publish Sinclair's "outlandish" allegations because they were "unsubstantiated." *Wired*, meanwhile, ran an article celebrating those leftist bloggers who succeeded in getting Sinclair arrested on an outstanding Delaware warrant just as he was leaving the Press Club.[10]

As should be obvious, the media had stunningly different standards for Sinclair and, say, Stormy Daniels or Christine Blasey Ford. The same media that insisted we "believe the women" were not at all inclined to believe the men, at least not this man. The same media that insisted "love is love" saw something inherently distasteful in Sinclair's tale of consensual gay sex. The messenger in this case had to be attacked, exposed, eliminated as a threat, and that he was. To this day, few have ever heard of Sinclair. Fewer still have heard of the late Donald Young. In fact, so quickly were Sinclair's allegations trashed and burned, John Heilemann and Mark Halperin did not even mention Sinclair in their comprehensive look at the 2008 campaign, *Game Change*.

Obama, as the world knows, won the presidential election in November 2008. He did particularly well in California, where Hispanic and black voters came out in record numbers to support him. Unfortunately for LGBT activists, a majority of these same voters supported traditional marriage and voted accordingly. As a result of their votes, Proposition 8, the ballot measure that embedded traditional marriage in the state constitution, also passed. Although the American media were reluctant to say so, the UK *Guardian* spoke to the rift Obama's calculations had created between him and his gay base. "Many in the gay and lesbian community hoped to celebrate the victory of Barack Obama," wrote the *Guardian*'s Matthew Weaver a day after the 2008 election, "but instead of partying they have taken to the streets in fury after California voted to reverse gay marriage."[11]

A month after the election, gay activists found an opportunity to direct their easily provoked anger at the president they helped elect. What irked them this time was Obama's outreach to Saddleback's Rick Warren. Obama asked Warren, a Proposition 8 supporter, to give the invocation at his upcoming inauguration. The Human Rights Campaign sent what the *Washington Post* called a "blistering" letter to Obama. "By inviting Rick Warren to your inauguration," read the letter, "you have tarnished the view that gay, lesbian, bisexual and transgender Americans have a place at your table."[12]

The trio of *Post* reporters covering this story imagined only two moral positions in the gay marriage debate: Obama's cautious support on one side, the activists' righteous fervor on the other. This kind of dialectic would dominate major media coverage for the next four years. As of December 2008, the major media were backing Obama. The *Post* article reflected the general trend. It was structured to give Obama's position—an emphasis on dialogue and diversity of opinion—the greater weight. Opponents of gay marriage, the majority of even California voters in 2008, would increasingly be treated as backwards, if not bigoted. The *Post* article ignored them altogether.

If the conservative media had any role in the drive towards same-sex marriage, it was to highlight the plight of those who got run over. As it happens, the samizdat found its most prominent champion in an entertainment mogul no sane person has ever accused of being a social conservative; yes, Donald Trump. At the time, Trump was a co-owner of the Miss USA pageant. A favorite to win the 2009 pageant was a tall, twenty-one-year-old blond from California named Carrie Prejean.

One of five finalists, Prejean readied herself for the question and answer portion of the contest. As in most such pageants, the questions were typically benign and open ended. "World peace" or "animal rights" made for good answers to at least half the questions ever asked. Not this time. Still smarting from the Prop 8 rebuke, the flamboyantly gay celebrity judge Perez Hilton had dropped a rhetorical IED into the question bowl, and the unlucky Prejean set if off. Hilton's question read, "Vermont recently became the 4th state to legalize same-sex marriage. Do you think every state should follow suit. Why or why not?"

"Well I think it's great that Americans are able to choose one way or the other," answered Prejean uncertainly. "We live in a land where you can choose same-sex marriage or opposite marriage." The nervous Prejean seems to have coined the term "opposite marriage," but her answer was otherwise generous and rational. She continued, "You know what, in my country, in my family, I think I believe that marriage should be between a man and a woman, no offense to anybody out there. But that's how I was raised and I believe that it should be between a man and a woman."[13]

Ignoring Prejean's caveat, "gossip gangsta" Hilton took offense. Did he ever. "If that girl would have won Miss USA I would have gone up on stage, I shit you not," he boasted on his blog, "and snatched that tiara off her head." Hilton reportedly gave her a zero for her answer, likely costing her the Miss USA title. It did not take long for Prejean to understand how she had transgressed the ascendant progressive orthodoxy. Her gay manager promptly discouraged her from attending the coronation ball. "A lot of people are mad at you," he texted her. "I'm afraid of what might happen to you. You really shouldn't come."[14]

Not satisfied with denying her the Miss USA title, a vindictive Hollywood community worked to make Prejean's life hell. This culminated with the surfacing of a semi-nude modeling photo Prejean had shot in the past, a violation of contest rules that could have cost her Miss California crown. This is where Trump stepped in. At a heavily attended press conference at Trump Tower, he allowed Prejean to keep her crown, which was news enough for the entertainment media. Of greater real news value was Trump's comment, "It's the same answer that the president of the United States gave. She gave an honorable answer. She gave an answer from her heart."[15] Trump was right. Prejean echoed in tone and content Obama's remarks from Saddleback just eight months prior. Obama's answer helped make him president. Prejean's answer made her a pariah among the same people who voted for Obama.

The *New York Times* was just one of many media outlets that covered the press conference but failed to mention Trump's comparison of Prejean's answer to Obama's. The *Times* article did note, however, that Trump was a Republican, as if to explain his defense of Prejean. When asked his own take on same-sex marriage, Trump ducked the question, answering, "This isn't about me." The reporters in attendance laughed.[16] I suspect Trump did too. He understood there was no future in the entertainment business for anyone fool enough, or faithful enough, to resist the progressive advance on the rainbow front.

As Obama's first term moved forward, and LGBT activists pressed him to endorse the cause of "marriage equality," Obama kept a watch on the polls. If other presidents "flip-flopped," Obama was said to "evolve." Other than his most besotted acolytes, no one took the "evolve" line seriously. The calculations behind it were too obvious. Newsrooms that were evolving more quickly than Obama felt increasingly free to point out just how sluggish his evolution was. Emboldened activists confronted Obama to his face. Among them was Hollywood fundraiser Chad Griffin, who famously asked the president, "How can we help you evolve more quickly?"[17]

Unlike Obama, Chad Griffin was not giving talks in black churches. By a greater than two-to-one margin, black voters in California supported Proposition 8. Asking black Christians to change their position on same-sex marriage came with greater risk than asking them to change their position, say, on minimum wage or gun control. Marriage was not peripheral to Christianity. Jesus Christ himself laid down the law, and he did so in a way that defied easy criticism, even from the left. In Mark 10:7–12, Jesus cites Genesis as the basis of his argument. "But from the beginning of the creation God made them male and female," he told the Pharisees then testing him on the subject of divorce. "For this cause shall a man leave his father and mother, and cleave to his wife; And they twain shall be one flesh: so then they are no more twain, but one flesh. What therefore God hath joined together, let not man put asunder."[18]

In the era of intersectionality, African Americans were expected to put asunder their own traditions and cleave to the most current LGBT orthodoxy. Gays may have been fewer in number than blacks, but they were louder and wealthier. Black pastors, in particular, failed to anticipate their diminished status in the multicultural synod. As late as 2004, for instance, the *New York Times* reported uncritically on a rally organized by several hundred black ministers in Atlanta to press for a state constitutional ban on gay marriage.

"This is neither a hate nor a fear issue," read the carefully crafted statement. "People are free in our nation to pursue relationships as they choose. To redefine marriage, however, to suit the preference of those choosing alternative lifestyles is wrong." The *Times* even acknowledged as legitimate the pastors' outrage at having the civil rights template co-opted. Reported the *Times*, "Many of the pastors said they were offended by the gay rights movement's argument that their struggle is the same as the fight for equal rights for all races."[19]

As Obama evolved, however, the black pastors were expected to evolve along with him. Pushing them hard down the evolutionary trail were the media. In its 2007 "Power" edition, the editors of the gay publication *Out* boasted, "Yes, there really is a queer cabal in the Eastern elite media." They cited by name seven openly gay *Times* reporters and joked, sort of, "This is one group you don't want to run into in a dark alley."[20] In 2011, to keep the cabal at bay, Obama ended Bill Clinton's "don't ask, don't tell" policy in the military and unilaterally decided to not enforce DOMA, the Defense of Marriage Act, a bill signed into law by Clinton in September 1996.

The *Times* headlined its article, "In Shift, U.S. Says Marriage Act Blocks Gay Rights."[21] In fact, however, the "U.S." said nothing. Obama and Attorney General Eric Holder "determined" by their own lights that the law, a law they had been enforcing for the previous two years, was suddenly "unconstitutional." The Senate had voted 85–14 to enact DOMA just fifteen years earlier. A Democratic president signed it, and Obama decided to ignore it. The editors at the *Washington Post* were pleased. The president declared he "would no longer be an advocate for the indefensible," they wrote smugly. This was the "correct" position. "Simple decency" demanded it, but it was "risky" nonetheless. They worried that a conservative Republican administration in the future, using Obama's move as precedent, might try to "sabotage" some law passed under Obama. In fact, nothing Donald Trump has done as president approached Obama's DOMA decision in sheer lawlessness.

Like the *Post* editors, the *Times* reporters welcomed Obama's move. Conceding that "conservatives" were upset, they weighted the article unblushingly in the president's defense. In a later article, the *Times* framed Obama's DOMA reversal as still another "manifestation of the Obama administration's evolving position on gay rights."[22] Pity those who did not evolve quite as swiftly. Authorities in more progressive states such as Oregon, Colorado, and New York manufactured new ways to make their lives hell. Muslims were off limits, but it was open season on Christian bakers and florists and event planners. Even in states that had not yet legalized same-sex marriage, orthodox Christians faced huge fines and even jail terms for honoring a faith tradition that Obama endorsed in 2008. The samizdat rallied to the side of the oppressed, but the Obama White House and the major media, when they bothered to notice, cheered on their oppressors.

By 2012, the media had prodded enough people to accept the seeming inevitability of same-sex marriage—or scared them from saying otherwise—that Obama advisers thought it safe for their man to declare his open support. The question that remained was where and how Obama would announce the culmination of his evolution. For maximum impact, they chose the left-leaning, female-oriented daytime TV show, *The View*.

Then Joe Biden went and spoiled it all. On *Meet the Press* in May 2012, Biden said without much thought, not unusual for Joe, "I am absolutely comfortable with the fact that men marrying men, women marrying women, and heterosexual men and women marrying another are entitled to the same exact rights, all the civil rights, all the civil liberties." In green rooms across the fruited plain, Obama advisers raged, but they could not express their disgust on air. Said Axelrod, "It was galling." Axelrod tried to spin the news Obama's way but without success.[23] The pushback here was coming from his left flank, not his right. Whatever Obama now said would seem weak and anti-climactic. It would prove to be both.

In 2015, the Supreme Court narrowly endorsed same-sex marriage, in the process stripping states of the power to make their own marriage laws. With the issue now popular enough for Obama to take credit, he ordered the White House lit up in rainbow colors. "Equality for the LGBTQ community was a victory for all historically marginalized groups," writes Valerie Jarrett in her memoir, *Finding My Voice*, "from women to black people to Latinos to those with disabilities. The broader progressive movement understood that we were all linked together."[24] I cannot imagine that black pastors got the linkage part. As many had come to see, the intersectional steamroller almost inevitably ground down their culture and trivialized their struggles.

Even after the Supreme Court decision, the media would not ease up on Christian traditionalists. When beleaguered Colorado baker Jack Phillips finally prevailed in the U.S. Supreme Court in 2018 by a 7–2 vote, a *Washington Post* editorial railed against Phillips and the decision. Op-ed writer Jim Downs called the Trump administration's support for Phillips "homophobic" and scolded the Supreme Court for elevating "the individual experience of a heterosexual baker over the collective hostility that LGBT people historically confront."[25] Heterosexual baker? At the heart of the issue was not Phillips's heterosexuality but his Christianity, and only the latter, the media once understood, is protected by the First Amendment.

The Brown Front

On a late September morning in 2003, I ventured down to Kansas City's Union Station to watch a radio show recorded live called *Under the Clock*, a reference to the station's landmark clock. Hosting the show was Rev. Emanuel Cleaver II, former mayor of Kansas City and future congressman. That morning's subject was the so-called "Immigrant Workers Freedom Ride," which was then passing through Kansas City.

A future chair of the Congressional Black Caucus, Cleaver could not hide his dismay that the riders had so casually pilfered the symbols and language of the black civil rights movement. As he knew firsthand, the original freedom riders risked savage beatings, even death, to assert their rights as citizens. These wannabe freedom riders were not citizens, not even legal residents, and risked nothing worse than tepid coffee and motion sickness.

That day at Union Station, organizers spoke of America's need for hard-working immigrants to keep the economy humming. In a moment of exasperation, Cleaver said, and I paraphrase from memory, "For years I was told there were not enough jobs, but now you are telling me there are too many?" Cleaver can be forgiven his confusion. Just eight years earlier, as the chair of the U.S. Commission on Immigration Reform, former Texas Congresswoman Barbara Jordan laid out what was then the nation's consensual position.

"For immigration to continue to serve our national interest, it must be lawful," said the strikingly eloquent black Democrat. "There are people who argue that some illegal aliens contribute to our community because they may work, pay taxes, send their children to our schools, and in all respects except one, obey the law. Let me be clear: that is not enough."[1]

In his 1995 State of the Union address, President Bill Clinton cited Jordan's work and endorsed it. He argued that all Americans were "rightly disturbed" by the influx of "illegal aliens" entering the country, taking away jobs from citizens, and imposing burdens on taxpayers. "That's why our administration has moved aggressively to secure our borders," he insisted.[2] In between government gigs at the time, Cleaver had apparently not gotten the memo that the Democrats' game plan was evolving. Positions that were very recently universal were on the way to becoming immoral.

The *New York Times* traced the idea for the 2003 freedom ride to leaders of the Hotel Employees and Restaurant Employees International Union. According to the *Times*, these union leaders had convinced the AFL-CIO to reverse its historic position against illegal immigration.[3] At the time, there was a whole lot of reversing going on. The media played a major role. The sympathetic *Times* article referred to the bus riders as either "immigrants" or "illegal immigrants." The phrase "illegal aliens" was just too twentieth century for *Times* editors. Soon they would switch to "undocumented immigrant." In New York City, it would one day become illegal to call an illegal alien an "illegal alien."

If any black leaders objected to the hijacking of civil rights symbolism, *Times* readers did not get to read those objections.

By 2003, progressive activists were not overly worried about black leaders. They presumed they could count on their support in any case. What they cared about was expanding their base by importing new voters. No other rationale explains the Democratic Party's dramatic, comprehensive shift on an issue that benefitted almost no Americans other than the owners of packing houses and swimming pools.

For movement leaders, Barack Obama came along at just the right time. As a self-identified black man, he could sell Democrats on the position shift with less risk of alienating black voters. And that is what he set out to do. Much as he did on the subject of gay marriage, Obama initially feinted to the center. "We simply cannot allow people to pour into the United States undetected, undocumented, unchecked and circumventing the line of people who are waiting patiently, diligently and lawfully to become immigrants into this country," said Senator Obama in 2005.

So forceful was Obama that in 2018, President Trump tweeted a video of this excerpt under the message, "I agree with President Obama 100%!"[4] The firemen rushed to the scene of this post-presidential flare-up and assured the Obama faithful that Obama did not really mean what he said in 2005, and in this case, they were right.

In an October 2010 conversation on Univision radio, Obama gave away the deeper progressive strategy. In Washington, they call it a "Kinsley gaffe": a politician accidentally says what he means. For the past two years, Democrats had controlled the presidency and both chambers of Congress. Unwilling to take responsibility for "comprehensive immigration reform," Democrats did nothing. Rather than admit failure, Obama blamed the Republicans, and he did so with uncharacteristic bite. Said Obama, "If Latinos sit out the election instead of saying, 'We're gonna punish our enemies, and we're gonna reward our friends who stand with us on issues that are important to us'—if they don't see that kind of upsurge in voting in this election—then I think it's going to be harder."[5] In shepherding Latinos into the progressive fold, Obama added the caution that outside the fold lurked "enemies" who deserved to be "punished."

Progressives hoped to frighten Hispanics, much as they had been frightening African Americans for decades. If fear mongering worked with one ethnic group, they figured, why not with another? In the *New York Times* initial article on the president's remarks, reporter Ashley Southall noted Obama's comparison of the black "struggle to gain civil rights" with the illegal lobby's struggle to gain free entry, but she missed the edge in Obama's warning. The "enemies" comment passed unnoted. Southall conveyed no sense of the political wound Obama had just self-inflicted.[6]

The samizdat caught what the *Times* missed. Throughout the blogosphere, one post after another poured salt on the wound. "Obama's Turnout Pitch To Latinos: Get Out There And Punish Your 'Enemies,'" read one typical headline.[7] "Shades of Richard Nixon: Obama to Latinos—'Punish Our Enemies'" read a more mischievous one.[8] In fact, the samizdat made noise enough to awaken the Republicans in Congress and ultimately force Obama to at least "explain" his remarks. His explanation fell flat. Three days after attempting it, voters handed Obama a catastrophic loss in the midterms.

A month after the midterm blow-out, Obama's border policy, such as it was, took another hit with the murder of Border Patrol Agent Brian Terry. It was problem enough that Mexican bandits killed Terry in Arizona. More problematic still was that they used two AR-15-style weapons purchased in Arizona courtesy of an Obama boondoggle whose logic continues to defy easy explanation ten years after Terry's murder.

Although he would try valiantly to distance himself from this mindless operation, President Obama's fingerprints were all over it. Three months after his inauguration, Obama flew to Mexico to meet with Mexican President Felipe Calderón. In laying out areas of shared interest, Obama cited the issue "of gun tracing, the tracing of bullets and ballistics and gun information that have been used in major crimes."[9]

In 2009, the Bureau of Alcohol, Tobacco, and Firearms (ATF) reported to Eric Holder's Department of Justice (DOJ). Six months after Obama's Mexico visit, Deputy Atty. Gen. David W. Ogden, Holder's number-two man, produced a lengthy memo called the "Department of Justice Strategy for Combating the Mexican Cartels." The memo directed relevant ATF offices to focus their efforts on eliminating Mexican drug cartels but left operational details to the field offices. To sex things up, the Phoenix office at the center of the controversy branded its operation "Fast and Furious" after the movie franchise of the same name.

As some agents would later report, the ATF under Obama's DOJ had begun to see gun control as part of its larger political mission. Fast and Furious may well have been conceived to advance that cause. For sure, gun control advocates manned every link in the chain of command from ATF Phoenix honcho Bill Newell to senior U.S. Attorney for Arizona Dennis Burke to Deputy AG David Ogden to Holder to White House Chief of Staff Rahm Emanuel to President Obama. It seems unlikely Holder or Obama knew the details of the operation in advance. Burke certainly did. His public lament that Arizona had become "the gun locker of the Mexican drug cartels" suggests a motive other than busting cartels.[10]

In retrospect, the operation made little sense. ATF agents pressured licensed gun dealers in Arizona to sell weapons to buyers they suspected of being straw purchasers for the cartels. The stated goal was to track the guns to their ultimate buyer, Mexico's powerful Sinaloa cartel, and make high level arrests for crimes such as drug trafficking, money laundering, and conspiracy. The dealers heeded the ATF dictate, many of them reluctantly. The straw men made their purchases, but, inexplicably, the ATF made no arrests in the program's first year.[11] During that time, as many as two thousand guns streamed into the hands of the cartels. One ATF deputy attaché would aptly call the operation a "perfect storm of idiocy."[12]

If nothing else, the ATF and DOJ proved much more successful in suppressing the news than they did in busting the cartels. The major media did not report on Fast and Furious for months after Terry's December 2010 murder and only then with a major assist from the samizdat. The information flowed initially from within the Phoenix ATF office, where many agents felt a deep sense of guilt over Terry's death. Seven days after his murder, agents Jay Dobyns and Vince Cefalu reported that Terry's killers used guns bought through the Fast and Furious program. Their initial accounts went out on their own blog, *cleanupatf.org*. To help spread the word, the agents began communicating with two prominent Second Amendment bloggers, David Codrea, a field editor for *GUNS* magazine, and Mike Vanderboegh, the majordomo of a hard-core gun rights website, *Sipsey Street Irregulars*. Codrea and Vanderboegh quickly enlisted other bloggers and interested parties. It was Vanderboegh who coined the phrase "a coalition of willing Lilliputians," as smart a description of the samizdat as I've heard.[13]

In the absence of any official explanation that made sense, Vanderboegh offered one that gained currency in the samizdat. He cited as the source of this theory an unnamed veteran intelligence operative. As the source saw it, the anti-gun White House knew that past attempts to exploit mass shootings, even school shootings, proved counterproductive at the ballot box. The White House needed a "game changer." Were there a steady stream of news about Mexican mayhem in which American-bought weapons were used, the source imagined the kind of message that would follow: "We've got to tighten up on American gun owners, gun stores and gun shows because they are feeding the slaughter." With the ATF controlling the statistics and the major media controlling the news, an ill-informed American public might well be swayed to support a crackdown on guns.[14]

If planners counted on the complacency of the ATF agents, they didn't get it. With the help of the samizdat, a few outraged agents were put in touch with Republican Senator Charles Grassley, the ranking minority member of the Committee on the Judiciary. In late January 2011, Grassley asked the DOJ if, in fact, the Phoenix ATF office had allowed guns to "walk" into Mexico. On February 4, 2011, Assistant Attorney General Ronald Weich responded, "At the outset, the allegation described in your January 27 letter—that ATF 'sanctioned' or otherwise knowingly allowed the sale of assault weapons to a straw purchaser who then transported them into Mexico—is false."[15] The DOJ would spend months, years, explaining away this deception.

About this time, an anonymous source sent Sharyl Attkisson's producer at CBS News a copy of Grassley's letter outlining the case. When Grassley's office would not share any additional information with Attkisson, she did something few of her peers would condescend to do: she dove into the samizdat, posting a public notice on relevant gun blogs asking for information. She got it. On February 22, 2011, CBS News ran Attkisson's five-minute report. It made an "instant splash," writes Attkisson in her book *Stonewalled*. As was routine during the age of Obama, adds Attkisson, "The media don't pick up on the story. They're steering clear."[16] To Eric Holder's delight, the reporters on his beat did not press him for answers. The few reporters who did the research could not get their stories published. "The bosses don't want them," laments Attkisson.

One reporter who could and did get her stories published had a natural edge on her mainstream peers: she knew something about guns and Arizona. Katie Pavlich grew up in the Grand Canyon State hunting with her father. Pavlich had another advantage. Her boss at the samizdat publication, *Townhall*, encouraged her to pursue the story. Mainstream reporters made it easier for Pavlich by ceding the turf, and this twenty-two-year-old whirlwind seized the opportunity. In April 2012, the conservative publisher Regnery released Pavlich's book, *Fast and Furious: Barack Obama's Bloodiest Scandal and the Shameless Cover-Up.* In the book, Pavlich gives a deserved shout-out to Attkisson. "Without you," writes Pavlich, "this story would never have received the attention it has so far."[17] The book remains to this day the definitive account of this misbegotten adventure.

As an all too telling aside, when *Free Beacon* reporter C.J. Ciaramella asked the DOJ a specific question about Fast and Furious, a DOJ spokeswoman referred Ciaramella to a review of Pavlich's book in Media Matters for America (MMFA). This struck Ciaramella as odd as he had not even asked about the book. In referring a reporter to this partisan propaganda factory, the DOJ seemed to have forgotten that this ill-conceived program had already resulted in the death of two American agents and an ever-increasing number of Mexican citizens, many of them innocent. MMFA articles titled "Fast and Fallacious" and "Fast and Spurious"[18] answered no question a serious reporter might have asked.

Mike Vanderboegh, the blogger who first started reporting about Terry's death, caught it even harder than Pavlich. Matt Gertz, the apparent MMFA case officer on the Fast and Furious beat, dug deep into Vanderboegh's background. In a period stretching over months, Gertz wrote an unseemly series of articles about the "extremist" blogger that had nothing to do with the quality of Vanderboegh's information and even less to do with finding justice for Brian Terry.[19]

In March 2011, three months after Terry's death, Obama made his first public comments about Fast and Furious. His interrogator was Univision's Jorge Ramos. Obama conceded "a serious mistake may have been made," but as to whose mistake, a squirming Obama told Ramos, "Well, we don't have all the facts." Certainly, at least according to the president, neither he nor AG Eric Holder authorized it. In fact, as happened far too often during his presidency, Obama claimed he first heard about the looming scandal "on the news." "Who authorized it then?" Ramos prodded. "This is a pretty big government, the United States government," said Obama lamely. "I have got a lot of moving parts."[20]

One of those moving parts was John Brennan, then Obama's Homeland Security Advisor. In June 2010, Brennan traveled to Phoenix to discuss border security with Arizona Gov. Jan Brewer. In September 2010, the ATF's Newell briefed Brennan's office on the agency's "ambitious efforts to stop weapons trafficking" in advance of Brennan's meeting with the Mexican president. It is hard to believe that someone as savvy as Brennan did not know about Fast and Furious.[21]

On May 2, 2011, either unaware or indifferent to what Obama told Ramos, the DOJ's Weich refused to admit that "mistakes" had been made. "It remains our understanding," Weich wrote Grassley, "that ATF's Operation Fast and Furious did not knowingly permit straw buyers to take guns into Mexico." On that same May 2, Holder and Department of Homeland Security (DHS) head Janet Napolitano met with Obama at the White House. Contrary to custom, no reason for the meeting was listed on the White House log, but it was a good bet the co-conspirators discussed Holder's scheduled rendezvous the following day with the House Judiciary Committee. When the Committee asked when he first knew about the program, Holder replied to its wide-eyed members, "I probably heard about Fast and Furious over the last few weeks." The only major media outlet to report this astonishing quote was NBC News, but the network did so in a grossly misleading story headlined, "AP sources—Bush era probe involved guns 'walking.'"[22]

Shielded by the media, Holder did not seem to worry about being called out in public. Mexican bandits had killed Brian Terry five months prior. CBS had begun running Attkisson's reports three months prior. Obama told a Mexican audience that Holder had launched an investigation six weeks prior. And yet Holder claimed to have learned of the operation a few weeks *after* he allegedly started investigating it. It got worse. When asked whether the head of DOJ criminal division, Lanny Breuer, authorized the operation, Holder answered blankly, "I'm not sure whether Mr. Breuer authorized it."[23]

In fact, as Breuer would later admit to the Senate Judiciary Committee, he learned of this gun walking madness as early as April 2010, eight months before Terry was killed. Breuer's testimony revealed all subsequent DOJ denials to be the lies they were. "The Justice Department had publicly denied to Congress that ATF would ever walk guns," said Grassley. "Yet the head of the Criminal Division, Mr. Breuer, knew otherwise and said nothing."[24] By December 2011, enough facts had surfaced to force the DOJ into at least a mimicry of candor. On December 2, the DOJ informed Grassley that the February 4, 2011, letter sent by Weich "contains inaccuracies" and, as a result, the DOJ "now formally withdraws the February 4 letter."[25]

As with so many scandals during his administration, Obama got away with this. Yes, the Republicans in Congress pressed the White House for answers and even cited Holder for contempt, the first attorney general ever to suffer that fate. Yes, Obama had to invoke executive privilege for the first and only time in his presidency. Yes, Breuer was forced to apologize. Yes, the ATF head resigned, as did a U.S. attorney, and any number of lesser figures were reassigned. The public, however, scarcely noticed. To some who did notice, it was a joke. On Comedy Central, for instance, comedian Stephen Colbert laughed off Fast and Furious as "the biggest scandal in history I have ever forgotten to talk about."[26] During the Obama era, the media had any number of "phony" scandals to laugh off.

Not everyone in the major media fell into line. Honorable exceptions include Jake Tapper, then with ABC, and even Jorge Ramos. Easily the most dogged of the mainstream journalists was Sharyl Attkisson, and she paid for her persistence. The DOJ would not let her into its building. MMFA and other firemen smeared her. CBS cut back on her air time the closer she got to the scandal's source. And the White House gave her holy hell.

"Goddammit it, Sharyl!" Obama flack Eric Schultz shouted at her. "The Washington Post is reasonable, the L.A. Times is reasonable, the New York Times is reasonable, you're the only one who's not reasonable!"[27]

In 2012, Attkisson was not surprised to see a familiar name emerge in a WikiLeaks dump pilfered from the global intelligence company, Stratfor. The memo read, "Brennan is behind the witch hunts of investigative journalists learning information from inside the beltway sources. There is a specific tasker from the [White House] to go after anyone printing materials negative to the Obama agenda (oh my). Even the FBI is shocked."[28]

If an award were given to the most "reasonable" mainstream journal-ist—category: Fast and Furious—the winner had to be CNN's Candy Crowley. She earned the prize "moderating" the second of the three presidential debates in 2012. Reeling after Mitt Romney pummeled him in the first of the three, Obama hoped to regain his footing in the town hall-style debate. Unknown to Romney, Obama had an advantage. The ref was in his pocket.

When an audience member asked what each candidate would do to keep "assault weapons" away from criminals, Obama gave a banal, evasive answer straight out of the Democratic playbook. Romney, by contrast, ripped his answer right from the news, and it had everything to do with putting "assault weapons" in criminal hands. He introduced the subject of Fast and Furious. "I'd like to understand who it was that did this," said Romney, "what the idea was behind it, why it led to the violence—thousands of guns going to Mexican drug lords."

Obama then looked pleadingly to the ref. "Candy!" he said.

"Governor, Governor," Crowley interjected, "if I could, the question was about these assault weapons that once were banned and are no longer banned." In fact, the questioner never mentioned a ban. Romney's answer was totally on point. Crowley, however, wanted to shove the whole subject of Fast and Furious, if not down the memory hole, certainly off the damn debate stage. She also hoped to score points for the home team.

"Now, I know that you signed an assault weapons ban when you were in Massachusetts," Crowley continued. "Obviously with this question, you no longer do support that. Why is that? Given the kind of violence that we see sometimes with these mass killings, why is it that you've changed your mind?"[29] Obama took it all in stride. He had spent the first four years with the referee in his corner. He was looking forward to four more.

Four months before the debate, however, Obama did something so flagrantly unconstitutional, it worried the major media. With the stroke of a pen, Obama chose to "mend" the nation's immigration policies. He would make the system "more fair, more efficient, and more just"—at least by his own lights. With Congress unable to pass a law giving relief to the so-called "Dreamers"—young people brought to this country illegally by their parents—Obama unilaterally decided to give as many as a million people relief from deportation proceedings, as well as the right to apply for work authorization.[30]

Obama knew he was subverting the rule of law. As late as March 2011, he was telling the audience at a Univision town hall, "America is a nation of laws, which means I, as the President, am obligated to enforce the law. I don't have a choice about that." Obama was very specific about which laws had to be enforced. "With respect to the notion that I can just suspend deportations through executive order, that's just not the case, because there are laws on the books that Congress has passed."[31] At the time of the executive order, as was customary, the mainstream media chose not to recall Obama's constitutional opposition to executive orders just a year prior.

Confident of media support, Obama's political people did not even bother disguising their motives. The very same day Obama issued the executive order, his national campaign director sent out a fundraising email under the subject heading, "wonderful news."[32] The politics were so flagrant, they stirred even Candy Crowley to take a stab at journalism. In an interview with senior White House adviser David Plouffe, Crowley asked if Obama's solo decision to grant something very much like amnesty to nearly a million aliens was "political."

"It was not, Candy," Plouffe lied shamelessly.

"Five months before the election?" Crowley persisted. She even quoted constitutional law professor Jonathan Turley to the effect that "Obama fulfilled the dream of an imperial presidency that Richard Nixon strived for."[33] Plouffe stuck to his lie. When he continued to stonewall, Crowley surrendered meekly, saying, "Well, let me ask you quick questions about some other issues." Plouffe knew she would surrender. For the previous four years, all the "reasonable" journalists had made a habit of doing just that.

The Green Front

It just so happened that on November 4, 2008, the day Barack Obama was elected president, Michael Crichton died. His death further unbalanced the debate on the one subject that would drive environmental policy throughout the Obama years, global warming, aka "climate change." A successful author and film producer and a Harvard-educated MD, Crichton was the rare climate skeptic that had the means and the moxie to take on the White House.

In September 2003, Crichton gave a memorable speech at the famed Commonwealth Club in San Francisco. Asked to address the greatest challenge facing mankind, he settled on the "challenge of distinguishing reality from fantasy, truth from propaganda."[1] The challenge had become more daunting of late, said Crichton, as environmentalism had morphed from the pragmatic boosterism of a Teddy Roosevelt to something very much like a faith. "The religion of choice for urban atheists," Crichton nervily called it.

Crichton walked his audience through the doomsday scenarios environmentalists had laid out in the previous half-century from overpopulation to DDT to global warming. "If we allow science to become politicized," he concluded, "then we are lost." It is perhaps just as well that Crichton died the day he did. He would not have to watch Obama and his allies impose an orthodoxy on the land that made "truth" and "reality" endangered species.

Resisting the new orthodoxy was the samizdat, aided tentatively by the responsible right, as well as some stalwart international dissidents. Crichton had the wherewithal to lead the resistance. With his death, the movement lacked a high-profile leader. Doing his best to fill the void was samizdat truth warrior Steve Milloy. Through his books and his popular blog, *JunkScience.com*, Milloy has been giving the left fits for a quarter of a century. The impeccably credentialed scholar and attorney has been single-handedly covering the whole waterfront of "eco-idiocy" from secondhand smoke hysteria to global warming alarmism to unwittingly destructive forest mismanagement.

If proof were needed of his effectiveness, one need only read Milloy's Wikipedia entry.[2] So thoroughly have the firemen taken over his page that only the naïve would think they are doing their job pro bono. No clumsy accusations of "conspiracy theory" here. No, this well-edited entry avoids the rhetorical overkill of the amateur and gives the illusion of balance.

That said, the editors have established their thesis by the second sentence, namely that Milloy's "close financial and organizational ties to tobacco and oil companies have been the subject of criticism from a number of sources." As proof of Milloy's motives, the editors mention Fox News fourteen times, the Philip Morris tobacco company fifteen times, and some variation of the word "lobby" sixteen times. The unknowing reader comes away thinking that Milloy, despite his Master's in Health Sciences from Johns Hopkins and his Master of Laws from Georgetown, is just another corporate whore, a money changer in the temple of Gaia.

If the right lacked a prominent figurehead, the left did not. In Obama, the eco-faithful had their new "messiah," a word freely used to describe Obama during his ascendancy. "It's a question that the entire nation is asking—is he the one?" said Oprah Winfrey at a Sunday Obama rally in December 2007. "South Carolina—I do believe he's the one." At the same rally, Michelle Obama laid on the biblical imagery as well. "We need a leader who's going to touch our souls. Who's going to make us feel differently about one another," she insisted.[3]

Although Obama remained an all-purpose messiah throughout most of the campaign, he applied his messianic potential to the climate in an unforgettable June 2008 speech. Having just wrapped up the Democratic nomination, Obama saw his selection to lead the party as a turning point in American history, particularly environmental history. "This was the moment," he told his audience, "when the rise of the oceans began to slow and our planet began to heal."[4]

As Obama's audience understood, or thought they did, the oceans were rising due to a human-caused increase in global temperatures. Like other progressives, Obama would pretend he welcomed open discussion on this and any other subject. In his 2006 book, *The Audacity of Hope*, he boldly declared, "I believe in free speech, whether politically correct or politically incorrect." This sentence, however, followed immediately after one that read, "I believe in evolution, scientific inquiry, and global warming." Like free speech, scientific inquiry is a value one holds dear. Global warming and evolution are theories to be proven or disproven. For Obama to lump them all together was to define environmentalism as his religion of choice. To challenge his beliefs was to run the risk of heresy.

If global warming were the "existential threat" the progressive punditry insisted it was, President Obama should have welcomed scientific inquiry. He should have staged open forums in which climate skeptics could air their dissent on the nature of the problem and on proposed solutions. By addressing the skeptics openly, he might have succeeded in enlisting Americans in the fight to control climate much the way FDR enlisted Americans in the fight to subdue our enemies in World War II, a comparable threat to mankind at least in the eyes of the cliché hounds on the left.

None of the above happened. As Angelo Codevilla observed at the end of Obama's tenure, "Power is insecure as long as others are able to question the truth of what the progressives say about themselves and the world."[5] Obama and his allies were insufficiently secure in their knowledge to risk it in an open forum. Among those allies was CBS News. Her bosses, said Sharyl Attkisson, were so fearful that critical stories would discourage the move to green energy, they hoped "to prevent the public from seeing them at all."[6]

Even before Obama's election, progressives had begun the move away from editorial suppression and towards defamation. As a case in point, two days before Obama announced his candidacy for the presidency in February 2007, syndicated columnist Ellen Goodman spoke for many on the left in declaring debate on this subject taboo. To show her seriousness, Goodman evoked the most powerful of metaphors from her own Jewish heritage. "I would like to say we're at a point where global warming is impossible to deny," she wrote. "Let's just say that global warming deniers are now on a par with Holocaust deniers, though one denies the past and the other denies the present and future."[7]

In February 2008, I got an up-close look at the way the left dealt with dissent on this subject. A college near my Kansas City home invited me to participate in a three-person panel titled "Science, Politics and Policy." The panel included a biologist from the college, myself, and the star of the proceedings, Chris Mooney, an elfin young journalist who had wowed the Democratic-media complex with his 2005 book, *The Republican War on Science.* The college had flown Mooney from Los Angeles at no small expense, built a day around his presence on campus, and served me up to the masses as the Christian to his lion. I got carfare for my troubles.

On the subject of global warming, I cited the Roman warming and the Medieval warming as evidence of increased temperatures over vast areas before the era of mass carbon output. Incredibly, neither Mooney nor the biologist seemed aware of either era. "How do we know there was warming?" the biologist scoffed.

I asked the two whether they thought the Vikings named the island "Greenland" just to sell real estate. I told the students about the settlements in Greenland, the vineyards that stretched into the north of England, the historical artifacts, the memoirs, and the core samples taken beyond Europe that suggested the warming was not just local. The best response either of my debate partners could come up with was the biologist's rejoinder, "But then it got cold again."[8]

It was to prevent embarrassing moments like this that the word "denier" proved so useful. Before long, Obama himself was throwing the word around. With his assist, "denier" joined "racist," "sexist," "homophobe" and other one-word smears so useful in suppressing dissent and dehumanizing dissenters. In fact, "denier" seems to have sneaked into popular usage before the phrase "climate change" did. Goodman did not use "climate change" when she introduced "denier" in 2007. Nor did Crichton use it in his 2003 speech in San Francisco. Nor did Chris

Mooney in 2008. The reason they did not use the phrase was because it had yet to enter the everyday lexicon.

At some point during Obama's White House years, green activists changed the name of the phenomenon they were exploiting. It is difficult to be more specific on the timing. The media will not report when the semantic shift occurred or who was responsible for it. Hell, they will not even concede there was a shift. In fact, the change in language was due to a very real but seldom discussed phenomenon, the dreaded "hiatus." As the climate change-friendly *Economist* revealed in May 2013, "Over the past 15 years air temperatures at the Earth's surface have been flat while greenhouse-gas emissions have continued to soar."[9] The *Economist* titled the article "A sensitive matter." That matter was "sensitive" for one reason: if citizens knew about the pause in warming, the political class would be hard pressed to sell them on the sacrifices needed to slay the climate dragon. Later, of course, scientists would be found to discredit the hiatus, but during the Obama presidency even the alarmists believed it.

It seems likely that Obama was hip to the hiatus early. In his 2006 book, *The Audacity of Hope*, he uses "climate change" as a term of art. He warns his readers not just of a warming but of a Pandora's box of evils sprung on the world as a result of climate change: "melting ice caps, rising sea levels, changing weather patterns, more frequent hurricanes, more violent tornadoes, endless dust storms, decaying forests, dying coral reefs, and increases in respiratory illness and insect-borne diseases." The source of the evil was "our fossil fuel-based economy," and "just about every scientist" confirmed the problem was real.[10] As it happened, the fear of rising sea levels and frequent hurricanes did not dissuade Obama from buying an $11.75 million beachfront property on Martha's Vineyard, but then again, none of his professed "faiths" ran very deep.

Throughout Obama's presidency urban planners across America used the threat of climate change to argue for increased population density and more public transportation. In 2009, just months after Obama took office, the H1N1 epidemic swept the country, infecting more than sixty million people and killing a CDC-estimated 12,469 Americans, the first victim a ten-year-old California girl.[11] Honest reporting would have dimmed the public's enthusiasm for public transportation. Both to protect the president and the green agenda, the media raised next to no alarm about the disease's spread. In retrospect, the difference between media coverage of H1N1 and COVID-19 is astonishing.

From his Alinsky days, Obama understood that to have real teeth, a cause needed victims, the more "marginalized" the better. Fortunately, he knew just the man to find them. Less than two months into his presidency, Obama made Anthony "Van" Jones his "green jobs czar," a revealing shorthand for "special advisor for green jobs, enterprise and innovation." The Jones story deserves special attention as his hire reflected how radical the transformation of America might have been had the samizdat not resisted.

In addition to helping Obama create jobs, Jones was expected to help "shape and advance the Administration's energy and climate initiatives with a specific interest in improvements and opportunities for vulnerable communities."[12] Obama saw Jones as a pioneer in a brave new world, the fusion of black and green with labor union input, intersectionality at its purest. A year before his appointment, Jones crudely spelled out the basic understanding of the so-called "environmental justice" movement. Said Jones, "The white polluters and white environmentalists are essentially steering poison into the people-of-color communities." By putting the unequaled moral force of the black front behind the green, Jones and Obama hoped to strengthen both.

Van Jones's appointment passed largely unnoticed in the mainstream media. On the right, the Manhattan Institute's Max Schulz paid heed, but he did not go deep in his criticism. From Schulz's perspective, Jones was a "green hustler," someone more concerned with self-promotion than with creating jobs, an activist whose most marketable skill was "melding racial grievance and claims of economic injustice with the increasingly faddish orthodoxy of environmentalism."[13] Yes, Jones was all of that, but he was more vulnerable than Schulz knew.

New Zealand's Trevor Loudon went deeper. In true samizdat fashion, Loudon was doing the job the major media should have done. Even before the election, Jones had shown up on Loudon's sensitive anti-communist radar. As Loudon could see, Jones *was* the radical black activist that many on the right presumed Barack Obama to be. A Yale

Law School grad, Jones made no effort to disguise his radicalism. He got himself arrested twice while protesting. Obama never did. As a young man, Jones had been active with Standing Together to Organize a Revolutionary Movement (STORM), a group with Maoist affectations, and had advocated on behalf of the conspicuously guilty cop-killer Mumia Abu-Jamal.

"I met all these young radical people of color—I mean really radical: communists and anarchists," Jones told the *East Bay Express* about his experiences while still a Yale Law Student, "And it was, like, 'This is what I need to be a part of.' I spent the next ten years of my life working with a lot of those people I met in jail, trying to be a revolutionary."[14] The lengthy and well-written *East Bay Express* article laid out the full scope of Jones's self-avowed "communist" roots. There should have been no mystery about his ambitions. By his own calculation, Jones continued to play revolutionary until at least 2002. He started dressing better about that time but never really changed course. In 2005, he made his intentions clear, telling the *East Bay Express*, "I'm willing to forgo the cheap satisfaction of the radical pose for the deep satisfaction of radical ends."

What caught the attention of the ever-observant Loudon was a September 26, 2008, article in a publication called *In These Times.* Founded by the openly socialist James Weinstein, the publication asked its editors and writers to share their ideas of what a truly progressive cabinet would look like. Credit here goes to Chuck Collins, a senior scholar at the left-wing Institute for Policy Studies (IPS). The prescient Collins picked Van Jones "to direct the Commerce Department's new 'green jobs initiative.'"[15]

Collins was not just guessing. According to Loudon, the IPS was the "ideas bank" for the Obama administration. For Loudon, the White House strategy was coming into focus. In November 2008, he found a blog post from progressive activist Mark Rudd that confirmed his suspicions. "Look to the second level appointments," wrote Rudd. "There's a whole govt. in waiting that [John] Podesta has at the Center for American Progress. They're mostly progressives."[16] Podesta, as Loudon pointed out, was co-chair of the Obama-Biden Transition Team.[17] Rudd was an old Weather Underground running mate of Bill Ayers. These people talked to each other.

Obama had to know about Jones's background. He and Jones inhabited overlapping circles, and a quick Google search—or a chat with Podesta—could have told Obama what he did not know. The Jones hire was clearly not a mistake. Jones was actively doing what Obama could do only passively. Said Jones, all but defining the intersectional urge, "I care about the progressive movements as they are, but I mainly care about all of our movements becoming a lot bigger and a lot stronger."[18] For the hard left, the environment, like gay rights or civil rights or immigration, was always a means to an end.

Within weeks of Jones's appointment in March 2009, Loudon began blogging about Jones's background and sharing his research with others in the samizdat.[19] Phil Kerpen, then the policy director of Americans for Prosperity (AFP), was among those most interested. Fireman blogger Kevin Grandia described AFP as "a fringe group of free-marketeers" in an article tellingly titled, "The Right Wing Attack Machine Behind the Van Jones Affair."[20] In the Obama era, a "right wing attack" was unwitting code for "journalism." The Brooklyn-born, public school educated Kerpen amplified his material by feeding it to radio talk show host Glenn Beck, then also host of a program on Fox News.

Jones would have survived his openly Marxist past and his covertly Marxist present, but just a month before he took office, he made the mistake of calling Republicans "assholes." Jones had also signed a petition in 2004 demanding an investigation into the Bush crowd's alleged orchestration of the 9/11 attacks. When the samizdat surfaced proof of both miscues, congressional Republicans joined the fight, and even the mainstream media knew that Jones was toast.[21] Hard to believe, but just a decade or so ago, the Democratic-media complex still expected a certain level of civility from those it would deign to protect.

With the White House signaling its unease, Jones resigned on September 5, 2009. As was often the case, the media held Obama blameless or nearly so and shifted the agency of Jones's demise to the Republicans. "White House Official Resigns After G.O.P. Criticism," read the *New York Times* headline.[22] With some precision, Jones blamed not the GOP, but the samizdat. Said the deposed czar upon resigning, "On the eve of historic fights for health care and clean energy, opponents of reform have mounted a vicious smear campaign against me. They are using lies and distortions to distract and divide."[23]

The "smear" included nothing more damning than Jones's own words. His critics did not have to take those words out of context. Jones spoke freely about his ambitions until he sensed he might have a future in government. Even the MSM could not defend him. The firemen, of course, tried to. They accused the samizdat of exaggerating Jones's radicalism, but Jones's 2005 comment—"I'm willing to forgo the cheap satisfaction of the radical pose for the deep satisfaction of radical ends"— suggested only a change in style from his days on the barricades.

An exchange on *Meet the Press* following Jones's resignation perfectly captured the creeping cluelessness of mainstream journalism. At the time, no two journalists more fully embodied the concept of "media elite" than host David Gregory's guests, Pulitzer Prize-winning *Times* columnist Tom Friedman and NBC's anchor emeritus Tom Brokaw. Gregory initiated the exchange with his observation that in the age of the internet, "You can be a target real fast." Friedman agreed. The takeaway from the attack on Jones, he argued, was to "really keep yourself tight, don't say anything controversial, don't think anything—don't put anything in print." Friedman did not exactly defend Jones. That would have taken a dollop of courage. Instead, he chastised the right. That took none.

Just five years removed from his anchor desk, Brokaw showed just what a dinosaur sounds like when he has no idea he has become a dinosaur. "One of the things I've been saying to audiences," he pontificated, "is this question comes up a lot, and a lot of people will repeat back to me and take it as face value something that they read on the internet. And my line to them is you have to vet information."

No piker himself when it came to condescension, Friedman added, "I just want to say one thing to pick up on Tom's point, which is the Internet is an open sewer of untreated, unfiltered information, left, right, center, up, down, and requires that kind of filtering by anyone." Friedman so admired his "open sewer" chestnut, he would repeatedly pull it out of the fire for others to marvel at anew.

Irony abounds here. In his *Times* article on the Jones resignation, reporter John Broder questioned the "vetting process" that allowed Jones to be appointed. For a Republican appointee, "the paper of record" would have done the vetting itself. During the Obama era, the *Times* repeatedly abdicated that responsibility. As a result, mainstream mandarins knew no more about Jones's radical background than did their audiences. If they knew, they did not find it newsworthy that a self-declared communist was driving the president's energy policy.

The samizdat had the real dope on Jones and shared it widely long before his fall. Like so many in the major media, Brokaw and Friedman refused to see it, let alone believe it. *Real Clear Politics* columnist Jack Kelly explained the consequences: "The first time that readers of The New York Times or The Washington Post, or viewers of CBS News or NBC News, were made aware there was a controversy about Mr. Jones was when they reported his resignation."[24] During the Obama years, everyday conservatives often knew about looming issues well before major newsrooms did. Rarely, however, did establishment nabobs such as Brokaw and Friedman put their ignorance on such proud display.

The same month that President Obama hired Van Jones, he offered up a $535 million loan guarantee to a green energy start-up, the very first distribution from the president's overly ambitious $862 billion (or so) stimulus package. Caught up in the spirit of magical thinking, Obama's new energy secretary, Steven Chu, planned to "create millions of new, good-paying jobs that can't be outsourced." And where better to start than with this California-based company with the enviro-friendly name "Solyndra." As Solyndra founder Chris Gronet noted at the time, Solyndra would not only create jobs, but it would also heal the planet by "meaningfully impacting global warming."[25] Apparently, Gronet had yet to receive the "climate change" memo.

At roughly the same time Gronet was cashing his check, former Senate aide Marc Morano "set up shop as the Matt Drudge of climate denial." So wrote *Rolling Stone's* Tim Dickinson. In that Dickinson titled his article, "The Climate Killers," the Drudge comparison was not intended to flatter. In subtitling his article, "Meet the 17 polluters and *deniers* who are derailing efforts to curb *global warming*" (italics added),

Dickinson provided further evidence that "denier" entered the lexicon before "climate change."[26]

Morano, a weather junkie from childhood and a political junkie from his college days, calls his shop "Climate Depot." Like so many underfunded communicators in the samizdat, Morano only wishes that the companies accused of donating to him—no, not a dime from ExxonMobil—actually did. Ten or so years after its founding in April 2009, Climate Depot remains a one-man operation, but a surprisingly influential one. The influence derives from the fact that Morano knows his stuff. He has attended nearly every United Nations environmental summit since 2002, including the ones in Johannesburg and Rio de Janeiro, and has consumed everything about climate worth consuming.

Like many skeptics, Morano fully distrusts the motives of climate alarmists. He believes, as Crichton did, that environmental activists will use any plausible scare to demand more government control, global and national. This is not mere theory. Morano has a catalogue of quotes from world leaders making the argument themselves. Testifying before a congressional committee in 2019, for example, one UN environmental honcho said proudly, "Global warming is my religion." Another announced, "One must say clearly that we redistribute de facto the world's wealth by climate policy."[27] Quotes of this variety routinely circle throughout the samizdat but rarely surface in the mainstream media.

In 2009, the mischievous Morano, then forty, had to be saying to himself, "So much fraud, so little time." While he was regularly reporting on what he calls the "green jobs scam," Solyndra included, he found himself the lead reporter on perhaps the boldest intellectual hoax since the Piltdown Man. It began with the hacking of a server at the Climate Research Unit at the University of East Anglia in the UK. The emails exchanged among several high-profile climate scientists showed their unmistakable urge to suppress or modify data to better amp up the hysteria around global warming.

British irregular James Delingpole gets credit for giving the scandal the seemingly inevitable name, "Climategate." Morano, however, was the one who pushed news of the scandal through the samizdat and into a predictably sluggish mainstream. "His only weapon," wrote John

Richardson in an ironically flattering *Esquire* feature on Morano, was "the Web site called ClimateDepot.com." Always a far piece ahead of the mainstream, Morano helped expose what Richardson conceded was a "major scandal."[28] "I thank the media for ignoring Climategate," Morano told me. "It gave us the chance to establish the narrative."[29]

Obama had to live with its consequences. The Climategate story broke just before the president headed to Copenhagen, there to pledge major cuts in U.S. carbon emissions and to persuade other nations to follow suit. Nothing the major media said could undo the reporting done by citizen journalists such as Delingpole and Morano. Armed only with the truth and their frequently crashing websites, they reversed whatever climate momentum the Obama administration had seized.

On December 6, 2009, more than two weeks after the story broke, the *New York Times* tried to cauterize the emotional wounds of the faithful. In the very first sentence of a lengthy article, reporters Andrew Revkin and John Broder reminded anxious readers of the "unequivocal" evidence for "global warming." To further reassure them, the reporters refused to use the word "scandal" to describe the scandal at hand.[30] Try as they might, though, the *Times* reporters could not disinfect the proceedings at Copenhagen. The whiff of scandal lingered, empowering critics eager "to question the scientific basis for the Copenhagen talks" and demoralizing the true believers. It would have taken a leader of some conviction to rally the troops, but as the Martha's Vineyard purchase proved, that's not who Obama was. "Copenhagen's failure belongs to Obama," wrote "climate justice" activist Naomi Klein in the progressive British journal, the *Guardian*. "The American president has been uniquely placed to lead the world on climate change and squandered every opportunity."[31] Ouch!

While Climategate was exploding, Solyndra was imploding. It is just that no one beyond the walls of the company knew it, not the samizdat, not the major media, not even President Obama. In late May 2010, Obama visited the "expanding" Solyndra plant in Fremont, California. *New York Times* reporter Jackie Calmes sensed nothing amiss. Through Calmes's eyes, the plant seemed to offer proof, if any were needed, of the wisdom of Obama's stimulus package. "It really gives you a sense of what the future of manufacturing looks like," Obama told plant workers. "The promise of clean energy isn't an article of faith, not anymore. The future is here."[32]

Fifteen months later, that future was somewhere else. "Solar Firm Aided by Federal Loans Shuts Doors," the *Times* reported in late August 2011.[33] According to the *Times*, competition from China contributed to the downfall not just of Solyndra, but of two other American solar companies. Nine days later, *Times* readers learned that Solyndra had problems well beyond foreign competition. To see just how severe those problems were, readers had to look no further than the photo of FBI workers carting boxes away from the besieged company offices. The raid resulted from an investigation into the loans "guaranteed by the Department of Energy under a highly promoted federal stimulus program."[34] Maybe the stimulus wasn't working that well after all.

As might be expected, Morano and other skeptics enjoyed the Solyndra implosion immensely. In the weeks that followed, they made hay with its many ironies, among them the disparity in the White House response to Solyndra and that of the 2010 BP mess in the Gulf of Mexico. "When we had the oil spill, we immediately had a moratorium on off shore drilling. The oil industry was demonized and literally shut down," Morano told Fox News's Neil Cavuto. "But after the green energy debacle, they are being feted and rewarded."[35] By "they" Morano meant the other solar power companies in which Obama continued to invest heavily. Nor were the skeptics alone in their criticism of the administration. The *Washington Post*, the *Atlantic*, and the *Guardian* all cautiously used the word "scandal" to describe the reckless way politics drove the Obama White House decision to fund Solyndra.

The old saw bears repeating that a scandal is only a scandal if the *New York Times* calls it a scandal on its front page, and that wasn't going to happen. On September 23, 2011, two weeks after the FBI raid on Solyndra, *Times* columnist Joe Nocera shifted the readers' discontent from the Obama White House to the Republicans in Congress. "That's how Washington works in the modern age," Nocera assured them, "the party out of power gins up phony scandals aimed at hurting the party in power." Lest anyone miss his point, the editors headlined the column, "The Phony Solyndra Scandal."[36] Once again, with the help of the *Times*, Obama deftly dodged a "scandal" and would continue dodging them for the next five years of his celebrated "scandal free" presidency.

The Pink Front

On January 20, 2017, women and their male feminist allies massed in major cities across America to protest the inauguration of Donald Trump. My suspicion is that thousands of these people had already booked hotel rooms in Washington in anticipation of Hillary Clinton's inauguration and launched the protest lest their room deposits go to waste. In any case, women across the nation mimicked their sisters in DC, and so a movement was born.

Two female reporters for the *New York Times*—one, natch, a woman of color—breathlessly chronicled the "sea of pink hats" at one venue and "the river of pink hats" at another. For the left, pink was the new red, "all shades of pink." Unwary readers could not have missed the color scheme—the lengthy article overflowed with photos—but they could easily have missed the strong leftist tilt of the march. The reporters did not once use the words "progressive," "liberal," "left-wing," or "leftist," let alone "pinko." To the *Times*, these were just a bunch of understandably angry, everyday women in pink. [1]

This was a routine deception on the part of the *Times*. It was well enough known that an estimated 53 percent of white women voted for the man these pink ladies were protesting. Well known too was the fact that march organizers had specifically excluded pro-life groups. Lest anyone miss the point, the march's official platform made access to "safe, legal, affordable abortion and birth control for all people" a defining principle of the movement.[2] In reality, it was *the* defining principle.

Seven months before Trump's inauguration, President Obama addressed a gathering called the "United States of Women Summit." Although he pretended otherwise, Obama was not speaking to all women or even to all feminists. He was speaking to the advance guard of the pink front. "For the first time in history," Obama told his audience, "a woman is a major party's presumptive presidential nominee."[3] Much depended here on how one defined "presumptive." In January 2007, Hillary Clinton was the presumptive nominee of her party, and then Barack Obama exerted his half-white male privilege. Some women never forgave him. From the beginning, he had to win back their affection. There would be no faulting his effort. As to his accomplishments, that is another story.

In the age of Trump, we forget how grandiose Obama could be. The 2016 summit found him at his most self-important. The man who could make the oceans subside reminded his audience that he had "significantly improved the lives of women and girls not just here at home, but around the world." Unsaid was that many of those imagined "improvements" came at the expense of the average woman. More women were "choosing to be single," said Obama as though the "choosing" part was both real and good. In the black community, it was conspicuously neither. He boasted too that women were now receiving almost 50 percent more college degrees than men, not pausing to reflect how those numbers were sapping male ambition and unbalancing the marriage market. Unsurprisingly, his only reference to marriage was of the gay variety. Indeed, virtually all of Obama's improvements destabilized the nuclear family and opened the door to widespread government intervention at the micro level.

From the beginning, Obama had no more pressing goal than to appease the pink front. Their issues were his issues. This explains why he called thirty-year-old Georgetown law student Sandra Fluke to console her after radio giant Rush Limbaugh called her a "slut." Fluke's testimony about her birth control needs had prompted the dig from Limbaugh. "He encouraged me and supported me and thanked me for speaking out about the concerns of American women," said Fluke of Obama, who seems to have conflated her concerns with those of American women writ large. As it happens, Obama made the call on March 1, 2012, four days after the shooting of Trayvon Martin. As the days passed and Obama remained silent on the Martin case, black leaders began to question publicly why the president called Fluke, but not Martin's parents. Under pressure as a result of the Fluke call, Obama threw his full support behind the Trayvon movement. As Obama was learning, intersectionality could be a bitch to manage.

To keep the pink front's support, Obama set out to solve three seemingly major problems, all of them illusory: unequal pay for men and women, the "rape culture" on America's campuses, and the denial of "reproductive rights." To advance these agenda items, Obama depended on a complicit, relentlessly dishonest mainstream media. Thwarting him at every step were the conservative media, both samizdat and responsible right, as well as a few liberal allies. The right's weapon of choice was the truth. The left's weapon of choice was the word "sexist."

On January 29, 2016, the White House celebrated the seventh anniversary of the Lilly Ledbetter Fair Pay Act. To keep his female supporters happy and to reward the trial lawyers, Obama had made Ledbetter the first very act he signed into law. True, equal pay for equal work had been federal law for forty-three years prior, but Ledbetter boosters preferred the off-the-shelf gripe that nothing much had changed. For all the fanfare, Ledbetter simply extended the time frame within which a woman could sue for back pay. Nothing much would change.

Sure enough, at the act's seventh anniversary in 2016, Obama was still lamenting that the median wage of a woman working full-time year-round was "only 79 percent of a man's median earnings."[4] To remedy the presumed pay gap, Obama proposed several cosmetic solutions designed less to solve the "problem" than to give the illusion of doing the same. Among the solutions was a new federal rule requiring companies of more than one hundred employees to submit salary data for employees by gender, race, and ethnicity.

The data, the *Washington Post* told its readers, would somehow "help close the gap between salaries of men and women."[5] The reporting by the *Times* on this measure was, if possible, even more naïve and uncritical than the *Post*'s. Reporter Julie Hirschfeld Davis imagined the effort as part of Obama's push "to crack down on firms that pay women less for doing the same work as men."[6] More than fifty years after the passage of the original Equal Pay Act, seven years into the Obama presidency, Davis and her editors seemed to believe there were still large employers whose lawless, sexist behavior merited a crackdown. The *Times* newsroom was hardly unique. Throughout the mainstream media, the drumbeat was incessant: women were getting shortchanged.

Beyond the mainstream, truth tellers of all stripes had been challenging the orthodoxy for years, but there had been no unified resistance to the pink front since Phyllis Schlafly almost single-handedly derailed the Equal Rights Amendment in the early 1970s. In recent years, the most effective resistance has come from individual women, two most prominently, Camille Paglia and Christina Hoff Sommers. Although both are championed by the samizdat, neither fits any known right-wing stereotype: Paglia is a lesbian and registered Democrat; Sommers, a Democrat-leaning, one-time flower child. Both are or have been academics.

Other commentators, some of them in the mainstream, have questioned the notion that women are systematically underpaid, but few have had the moxie to defy Obama as has Sommers. In January 2014, the president did his dissembling in prime time. The occasion was the optic-rich State of the Union address. Among his many bromides and half-truths, Obama served up one very conscious deception.

"Today," he said, "women make up about half our workforce, but they still make 77 cents for every dollar a man earns." Obama said this quizzically, as though he had a hard time believing such an injustice could still exist. Then he switched gears. "That is wrong," he thundered in faux black preacher mode, "and in 2014, it's an embarrassment. A woman deserves equal pay for equal work."[7]

On the last comment, the control room switched to an image of a smiling and applauding Nancy Pelosi. Then Pelosi stood and applauded, as did all the other Democrats. After hesitating a moment, the Republicans stood and applauded as well. Their president had just accused America's employers of a sexist conspiracy to suppress women's wages, an accusation they knew to be false. Yet the feckless lot of them joined in the hoopla. If there really was a "war on women," the pink front need not fear the Vichy Republicans. They had unilaterally disarmed.

Washington Post fact checker Glenn Kessler approached the wage issue more honestly than most in the mainstream, but he did so cautiously. "There is clearly a wage gap," he wrote in response to Obama's speech, "but differences in the life choices of men and women—such as women tending to leave the workforce when they have children—make it difficult to make simple comparisons." Kessler introduced enough facts to suggest he knew Obama had deceived his audience, but he came nowhere close to saying so.[8]

This was not the first time Kessler nudged the president for his deceptive use of statistics. In June 2012, on a well-promoted conference call dealing with equal pay, Obama said, "Women still earn just 70 cents for every dollar a man earns. It's worse for African American women and Latinas." The anodyne title of Kessler's response—"The White House's use of data on the gender wage gap"—reflected the pains the *Post* took to avoid criticizing the president. Kessler began with the overly generous assumption that Obama "meant to say 77 cents," and so he dismissed the "70 cent" number as an irrelevant slip. Still, as he acknowledged ever so gingerly, there were problems even with the "77 cent" figure. Obama relied too heavily, thought Kessler, on "broad comparisons."[9] That was as rough as it got for Obama at the *Post*.

As a female, and one not dependent on an editor's approval, Sommers had no need to mince about as Kessler did. "What is wrong and embarrassing," she wrote, mimicking Obama's 2014 rhetoric, "is the President of the United States reciting a massively discredited factoid." Sommers noted that the "spurious" twenty-three-cent gender pay gap did not account for the most basic variables: occupational differences, educational levels, age, job tenure, or even hours worked per week. With the known variables controlled, the wage gap narrowed to five cents on the dollar, but even that, Sommers argued, may have been due to a "subtle, hard-to-measure difference between male and female workers."[10]

If Kessler understood Obama's larger strategy, he did not say so. Sommers did understand and scolded Obama for employing it. "The White House should stop using women's choices to construct a false claim about social inequality that is poisoning our gender debates," she wrote. As Sommers noted, the documentation on this subject was abundant. The mainstream media knew the president was trolling for votes with phony numbers. Sommers even cited Kessler's two fact checks on the issue, but hers, alas, was a voice in the wilderness. So fearful were Republicans of weaponized feminism, they dared not come to her defense.

Once again, Obama invested a ton of rhetoric in a problem he had to know was imaginary. And so, just as he failed to prevent the oceans from rising, he failed to equalize pay between men and women. If anything, the climate would have been an easier fix than rewiring the sexes. Obama could commit himself to this Sisyphean task because no one of consequence would remind him the task was futile.

Ever resourceful, Obama proved himself capable of addressing several imaginary problems at the same time. To secure the female vote in 2012, he would have to. On April 4, 2011, in launching his re-election campaign, Obama promised, "The work of laying the foundation for our campaign must start today." Apparently, he meant "today" literally. On that very same day, his administration sent a "Dear Colleague" letter to the seven thousand or so higher education institutions that received federal funds. The "letter" ran a dense nineteen pages and was signed by Russlynn Ali, the assistant secretary of civil rights in the Department of Education.[11] Like Van Jones, Ali was one of those edgy secondary level appointments eager to advance the progressive agenda. The announcement was as subtle as a Kmart blue light special. It served as a suspiciously well-timed reminder to the pink front that it had a friend in the White House.

Citing the untested trope that "1 in 5 women" on campus are the victims of sexual assault, Ali set up the Office of Civil Rights (OCR) as something of a superagency overseeing student-on-student sexual altercations. The OCR derived the authority to impose its will, she claimed, from the already much abused Title IX, the 1972 law that outlawed sexual discrimination by academic institutions receiving federal aid.

Given the many years she taught at the university level, Paglia well understood the academic mind. Unlike ordinary Americans, the advance guard among the professoriate had come to think of sex differences as "malleable fictions." This was more fashion than science, but the fashionistas had lots of clout and little tolerance. To win their hearts, Obama ordered up nineteen pages of funding threats. Paglia mocked the logic behind the letter: "The assumption is that complaints and protests, enforced by sympathetic campus bureaucrats and government regulators, can and will fundamentally alter all men."[12]

For all its faults, Title IX was actually passed by Congress as part of a larger bill and signed into law by President Nixon. In dictating changes to this law by a "letter," Obama circumvented congressional oversight and public comment. Given academia's hard-left skew, Obama expected minimal pushback and received less. The major media proved equally pliable. *Times* reporter Sam Dillon did not even hint that this "effort by the Obama administration to draw attention to sexual violence" might be controversial.[13]

Controversial it was. On the right, the *National Review*, the *Washington Examiner*, the *Wall Street Journal*, the *Daily Caller*, and the *New York Post* promptly raised the alarm. As might be expected, the *Post* won for best headline: "The feds mad assault on campus sex."[14] For most effective analysis, the award went again to Sommers. She was just mainstream enough to get the unfriendly but influential *Chronicle of Higher Education* to publish her bluntly titled article, "In Making Campuses Safe for Women, a Travesty of Justice for Men."[15]

The *Chronicle's* few open-minded readers would have had to wonder how the Obama White House could have indulged such madness. Campus disciplinary committees designed to adjudicate cases of cheating and plagiarism and such things were now being tasked to investigate potential sex crimes between legally adult students. If the committees did not do so to the satisfaction of Ali's OCR, their institutions risked losing federal funding—lights out for most, literally.

More perversely still, these disciplinary committees were expected to use the "preponderance of the evidence" standard to rule on the guilt or innocence of the accused. The fact that many academics, perhaps most, cared more for social justice or sexual justice than for actual justice did not bode well for males on campus.

As a case in point, just five years prior, scores of prominent Duke professors demanded punishment for the school's lacrosse team even after the three accused players had been cleared of the outlandish rape charges against them. "To be found guilty of rape by a campus tribunal can mean both expulsion and a career-destroying black mark on your permanent record," wrote Sommers. "Such occurrences could become routine under the Ali dispensation." In fact, such occurrences would become shamefully routine. As with Robespierre's Committee on Public Safety, seemingly good intentions quickly paved the way to a reign of terror.

Sommers addressed the rationale for the ruling, namely the belief that one-in-five coeds would be sexually assaulted during their stay on campus. As Sommers explained, that figure had a dubious provenance. It derived from a DOJ-funded online survey that let the young women decide for themselves whether they had been assaulted. To jack up the numbers, the survey designers defined such ambiguous misadventures as attempted forced kissing or sex while drunk as "assault."

The Obama Department of Education issued this fiat at a time when roughly 44 percent of college males and 32 percent of college females admitted to binge drinking, when one-third of all college students smoked marijuana regularly, and when at least half of all students were sexually active.[16] Change was in store for this heretofore judgment-free, drink- and drug-saturated campus culture. Now, thousands of blundering young men faced humiliation, expulsion, and possible criminal action as a result of what Paglia called "oafish hookup melodramas, arising from mixed signals and imprudence on both sides."[17] The new regulations, Sommers wrote, "are not enlightened new procedures for protecting students from crime. They are a declaration of martial law against men, justified by an imaginary emergency, and a betrayal of the Title IX equity law."

Sommers proved prophetic. That was easy. The likely outcome of OCR regulations should have been obvious to everyone. What was hard was speaking prophecy to power. George Orwell may or may not have said, "In a time of universal deceit, telling the truth is a revolutionary act," but the sentiment holds true regardless of its source. In a time of near universal deceit, especially on America's campuses, Sommers had done something downright revolutionary. She challenged the president of the United States and an unthinking flock of his most pliant sheep.

Telling the truth made Sommers a heroine in the samizdat, but a pariah in academe. Her speaking engagements generated headlines like this one from 2015, "Students Protest Sommers' Lecture,"[18] or this from 2018, "Law-School Students Shout Down 'Known Fascist' Christina Hoff Sommers."[19]

Paglia fared little better. In a January 2019 interview, Paglia ridiculed those universities that accepted at face value complaints from women allegedly assaulted six months or a year prior. "If a real rape was committed," said Paglia, "go friggin' report it to police." As payback, students and alumni at Paglia's own University of the Arts in Philadelphia disrupted a talk she gave on campus. Unsatisfied with mere disruption, they launched a petition drive to have Paglia fired. Scarily, within a day of the protest, more than eight hundred people signed the petition. Fortunately for Paglia, David Yager proved to be the rare university president with a spine. He did not yield to the mob.[20]

The protestors in each of these cases championed an Obama mandate that many journalists were no longer defending. What made the defense difficult was that the OCR star chambers were targeting people such as Northwestern prof Laura Kipnis, a self-avowed socialist who looked and thought very much like an Obama-era journalist. In 2015, Kipnis waded unknowingly into hot water by writing an essay in defense of a colleague accused of rape. Her demand for due process stirred the campus snow globe, and an aroused snowflake accused Kipnis of creating a "hostile environment." That accusation was enough to trigger a Title IX investigation of Kipnis, the aftershocks of which rattled her for years to come. Her 2017 book, *Unwanted Advances*, well describes the "officially sanctioned hysteria" Obama and his minions unleashed on America's campuses.[21]

In April 2015, the pink front took another blow when *Rolling Stone* was forced to retract a sensational article about an alleged gang rape at a University of Virginia frat house. Once a dissident publication, *Rolling Stone* had grown lazy defending progressive dictates, especially those with Obama's imprimatur. In this case, so eager were its journalists to validate campus rape culture, they ignored the basics of their profession.

Reporter Sabrina Rubin Erdely's first mistake was to trust the word of Emily Renda, chief student affairs officer at UVA. Renda introduced her to "Jackie," a UVA student who claimed to have been gang-raped by five fraternity men early in her freshman year. Looking for a case that embodied the "pervasive culture of sexual harassment/rape" on campus, Erdely chose not to question the obvious discrepancies in Jackie's mutating story or interview those accused lest she further "disaffirm" the victim.

On November 19, 2014, *Rolling Stone* published "A Rape on Campus: A Brutal Assault and Struggle for Justice at UVA." The story went wildly viral, netting more than 2.7 million views and damaging any number of lives. Unfortunately for *Rolling Stone* and the campus rape hysterics, Jackie was making stuff up. In its scathing review of the story, the Columbia University Graduate School of Journalism noted that *Rolling Stone*'s failure "encompassed reporting, editing, editorial supervision and fact-checking."[22] These minor failings, alas, did not distinguish the article from much of the other counterfeit journalism in the Obama era.

The media's response to a landmark September 2017 speech by Trump Education Secretary Betsy DeVos showed just how much the ground had shifted. Reporters didn't flip out when DeVos denounced Obama's self-defeating Title IX tyranny. Citing one grotesque example after another, DeVos held little back. "The truth is that the system established by the prior administration has failed too many students," she said. "Survivors, victims of a lack of due process, and campus administrators have all told me that the current approach does a disservice to everyone involved." Given its eagerness to discredit Trump for just about anything, the *Times* response to DeVos's speech had to astonish its readers. The headline of the op-ed by *Times* columnist Bret Stephens read simply, "Betsy DeVos Ends a Campus Witch Hunt."[23] Christina Hoff Sommers could not have said it better herself.

As important as equal pay and campus rape culture were to Obama, these were not hills on which he and his allies were prepared to die. "Reproductive rights" *was* that hill. For all the help from savvy feminists in the other two campaigns, on this one, conservatives were on their own. With no allies on the left or center, they would have to counter a relentless stream of disinformation from very nearly every major media outpost and the many firehouses as well.

The disinformation begins with the organizational name "Planned Parenthood." As popular black comedian Dave Chappelle pointed out to the left's discomfort, "This is the age of spin, the age where nobody knows what the f— they're even looking at. Did you know that Planned Parenthood was for abortions? It's for people that don't plan things out at all."[24]

A corollary euphemism is "reproductive rights." From the beginning, American progressives, led by Planned Parenthood's eugenicist founding mother Margaret Sanger, did all in their power to discourage women from reproducing. In the early part of this century, that discouragement took the form of state laws denying reproductive rights to women considered "unfit." In the notorious 1927 *Buck v. Bell* case, heartily endorsed by Sanger, progressive Supreme Court Justice Oliver Wendell Holmes wrote the majority decision affirming a state's right to deny certain women the right to reproduce. This has always been a progressive thing.

Within five years of *Buck v. Bell*, the Nazis marched in and left eugenicists with a whole lot of explaining to do. Choosing to switch rather than fight, progressives erased their eugenics past and shifted their energy to the cause of abortion. The more radical among them argued that a woman's right to terminate a pregnancy extended to the very moment a baby entered the world and, in some cases, even beyond. Obama was one of those radicals. Weak of knee on several fronts, in defense of abortion he was a warrior.

In 2008, however, Obama did not want the general electorate to know what a warrior he was. With the media's ready assistance, he positioned himself as a moderate, someone who hoped to "find common ground" with pro-lifers on how to "reduce the number of abortions." Obama made this claim during the widely viewed presidential forum at Pastor Rick Warren's Saddleback Church in California. Cutting though Obama's obfuscations, Warren asked a simple question, one that a constitutional lawyer like Obama should have welcomed: when do infants acquire "human rights"? Obama memorably responded, "Answering that question with specificity, you know, is above my pay grade."[25]

Obama was playing word games here. As a student at Harvard Law, he had addressed that very issue in some depth. In fact, the only item he personally contributed to the *Harvard Law Review* dealt with the civil rights of an unborn child, or, more specifically, the lack of rights. As Obama chillingly explained in this unsigned editor's note, a "fetus" has no civil rights. The government, he insisted, had more compelling interests than "ensuring that any particular fetus is born."[26] *Politico*, which unearthed the article, made note of the fact that Obama had never mentioned his law review piece, "a demurral that's part of his campaign's broader pattern of rarely volunteering information or documents about the candidate, even when relatively innocuous."[27] This legal article was not innocuous. *Politico* just liked to pretend it was.

In the run-up to the 2012 election, the editors of the *Washington Post* employed the always reliable "fact checker" gambit to ease Obama's way out of an abortion-related jam. The trouble started when pro-life activists surfaced Obama's committee votes as an Illinois state senator against a series of infant protection bills. These bills would have established that a child born alive after an unsuccessful abortion would be "fully recognized as a human person and accorded immediate protection under the law." With some notable exceptions, the responsible right, like many Republican lawmakers, shied from confronting Obama on his seeming indifference to infanticide.

The samizdat had no such qualms. The most compelling voice on the born alive issue belonged to Melissa Ohden, a survivor of a botched abortion. In a more just world, film producers would be clamoring for a story in which a baby girl survives her abortion, grows up to become an attractive and eloquent pro-life activist, and reunites with a mother who did not even know she was alive. Unfortunately for Ohden, the Queen of Hearts had a keener sense of justice than the average Hollywood producer.

With Hollywood abdicating, the pro-life movement saw an opportunity and seized it. In 2012, the Susan B. Anthony List ran an ad featuring Ohden, who had this to say about Obama, "When he was in the Illinois state Senate, Barack Obama voted to deny basic Constitutional protections for babies born alive from an abortion—not once, but four times." The *Post* could not let this stand.

In an article headlined, "Did Obama deny rights to infants who survive abortion?" Josh Hicks handed out "Pinocchios" to several offenders.

Obama was not among them. Ohden got two for claiming she was "'discarded' at birth." Hicks could not identify any witnesses to that event thirty-five years prior. Ohden got one other Pinocchio for saying Obama "voted to deny basic Constitutional protections for babies born alive from an abortion." According to Hicks, this was technically true, but Ohden's claim was "slanted" and lacked "context." Obama's votes, you see, were intended not to deny newborns their rights but rather to "block any legislation that could erode the premise of the *Roe v. Wade* decision."[28] If Pulitzer gave out a "distinction without a difference" award, Hicks would have been a contender.

In the same article, Hicks gave three Pinocchios to former Arkansas governor Mike Huckabee for his claim that Obama "believes that human life is disposable and expendable...even beyond the womb." True, Hicks admitted, Obama voted against the Born-Alive Infants Protection legislation in Illinois. That said, wrote Hicks, "We find it hard to fathom that the former senator expressed a belief that human life is disposable outside the womb." Of course, no politician in the post-Hitler era would ever "express" such a thought out loud. Huckabee never said he did.

Casual *Post* readers could not miss the large colorful Pinocchios slapped on Ohden and Huckabee. They could miss, however, Hicks's concession deep in the article that Obama "misrepresented the facts." So flagrant was the misrepresentation, Hicks admitted, he "could have awarded Four Pinocchios to Obama." Four Pinocchios means a "whopper." He withheld the Pinocchios because Obama's comments, despite the headline, were not "the focus of this particular column." Yes, it was that easy being Obama. The media allowed him to signal his unswerving support for abortion rights to his left without alarming America's soccer moms in the middle.

Even his fellow Democrats failed to see how committed Obama was to promoting the abortion rights agenda. This became obvious in March 2010 as Obama's proposed Affordable Care Act was worming its way through Congress. Upon reading the bill the Senate sent to the House, Michigan Rep. Bart Stupak and his caucus of pro-life House Democrats balked. Although small, Stupak's caucus was just large enough to block the bill's passage. Despite Obama's earlier promises, the bill contained no language to protect the conscience of religious pro-lifers or prevent the federal funding of abortion.

To secure Stupak's support, Obama proposed an executive order to assure that no federal funds would be used to pay for abortion except in the case of rape, incest, or endangerment of the mother. That gesture provided cover enough for Stupak and his colleagues to support the bill, and their votes gave Obama the margin of victory. Stupak's capitulation, however, won him no friends on the left or the right. Three weeks later, after a storm of criticism from all sides, the nine-term congressman announced he would not seek re-election.

Nearly two years later, the Obama White House showed Stupak just how badly he had been played. A Health and Human Services (HHS) mandate forced virtually all health plans, including those of religious institutions, to cover surgical sterilizations and abortion-inducing drugs. Stupak was appalled. "Not only does the HHS mandate violate the Executive Order," he said at the time, "but it also violates statutory law."[29] The major media completely ignored Stupak's lament. Only the samizdat kept it alive.

The samizdat, however, could not win a war of words on this subject. The mainstream media controlled the very terms of debate. They avoided whenever possible the use of the words "pro-life" or "unborn" or "baby." They deceived their publics on the reasons why women had abortions, especially late term abortions. And, at all costs, they suppressed information about the inner workings of the abortion industry.

If the samizdat could not compete in words, it could compete in images. James O'Keefe certainly thought so. In 2006, when O'Keefe was just twenty-two, he met the pro-life prodigy, Lila Rose, then just eighteen. In his 2013 book, *Breakthrough,* O'Keefe describes Rose as "poised, beautiful, outspoken, fearless, godly." Having spent some time with Rose, I would confirm O'Keefe's description. At age fifteen, the homeschooled Rose founded a pro-life organization called Live Action in her family's California living room. Since then, Live Action has grown to become one of the largest and most effective organizations in the pro-life movement.

As a freshman at UCLA, Rose helped O'Keefe pioneer the "pimp and prostitute" undercover strategy he would employ three years later to bring down ACORN. Young enough to ignore the power differential, the pair set their sights high. They went after Planned Parenthood. The youthful Rose posed as a fifteen-year-old. O'Keefe posed as her adult pimp. In the first clinic they infiltrated, a staffer said on hidden camera, "If you're fifteen, we have to report that. If not, if you're older than that, we don't need to." Rose replied, "But if I just say that I'm *not* fifteen, then it's different?" Taking the hint, Rose claimed to be sixteen. Said the staffer, "Figure out a birthday that works, and I don't know anything."[30]

O'Keefe edited the video MTV-style, and it went quickly viral. Planned Parenthood then sent Rose a ham-handed cease and desist letter threatening prosecution. Writes O'Keefe, "This billion-dollar corporation was trying to take down an eighteen-year-old girl for exposing its own law breaking. It was poetry in motion."[31] The letter moved quickly through the samizdat, finally landing on the desk of Fox News rating king, Bill O'Reilly. Fox News's Sean Hannity ran with the story as well. Working on their own dime, the young activists had shown just how vulnerable was this unholy leviathan.

In 2006, seventeen-year-old David Daleiden, then with Live Action, watched this all go down and took notes. Seven years later, the steely Daleiden was ready to launch what would prove to be the most sustained and effective undercover journalism project since the *Chicago Sun-Times's* famed political sting of 1977. That year, the *Sun-Times* purchased a rundown bar, renamed it "The Mirage," staffed it with its reporters, and captured on camera the shakedowns, payoffs, and sundry criminal mischief of Chicago's political underclass.

Daleiden's "Mirage" was a sham biomedical research company called "Biomax Procurement Services." Over time, he had become aware that Planned Parenthood was engaged in the trafficking of "fetal tissue," a double-edged euphemism for "baby parts." Working through a journalistic entity of his own creation, the Center for Medical Progress (CMP), Daleiden and his partner, Sandra Merritt, learned the language and the mechanics of the fetal tissue procurement business and went to work.

Planned Parenthood was no ACORN. To penetrate its many and sophisticated defenses, Daleiden and Merritt would have to hit hard and deep. This they did. Over a period lasting more than two years, the highly disciplined twosome worked their way into the good graces of Planned Parenthood clinicians in several states and captured on camera the chilling words and deeds of the practitioners in the nation's least regulated major industry.

In July 2015, Daleiden started dropping the videos O'Keefe-style. The combination of callow words and cruel images, repeated in one video after another, rocked Washington. The timing was good. The 2016 presidential campaigns were revving up, and many Republicans spoke out about what they saw. "The out-of-sight, out-of-mind mantra that propelled the pro-choice movement for decades is forever gone," Kellyanne Conway, then a Republican pollster, told the *New York Times*. Reeling from the blow, even the *Times* had to wonder whether "the new offensive will succeed in crippling Planned Parenthood."[32]

Obama, the first president to speak at Planned Parenthood's national convention, kept his distance from the hubbub. An indifferent media got no closer to the president than his press secretary, Josh Earnest. On July 30, 2015, a young reporter asked Earnest if Obama had seen the video that was released on that day. The video in question[33] begins with interview footage of harried Planned Parenthood president Cecile Richards insisting, "It's not a fee. It's not a fee. It's just the cost of transmitting this material."[34] The undercover footage that follows undercuts everything Richards said.

A doctor at a mega Planned Parenthood clinic in Colorado is seen explaining the clinic's traffic in body parts. Aware that it is illegal to transfer "human fetal tissue" for "valuable consideration," the doctor plays semantic games with the would-be purchasers. "We don't want to get called on, you know, selling fetal parts across states," she jokes, unaware she is being recorded. This interview is followed by an on-site review of actual body parts with the doctor and a clinician. What is impressive is how well Daleiden and Merritt play their roles as buyers. What is unnerving is how casually the doctor and clinician pick through trays of baby parts—a heart, a brain, a lung—while talking about the commercial viability of the "fetal cadaver."

At the press conference, Earnest appeared to be bored by the whole subject. He did not know if Obama had seen the video in question or any of the videos and did not think it mattered. He airily dismissed CMP's investigative project "as the tried and true tactic that we have seen from extremists on the right: To edit this video and selectively release it so that it grossly distorts the position of the person who is actually speaking on the video."[35] Apparently satisfied with Earnest's explanation, the reporters quickly moved on to a new subject.

Running for president at the time, Hillary Clinton could not afford to be so dismissive. Although her first instinct was to attack the video producers, Clinton herself began to waver as each new video dropped. "I have seen pictures from [the videos] and obviously find them disturbing," Clinton told the *New Hampshire Union Leader* late that July. No one knew better than Clinton, however, what overwhelming force Planned Parenthood and its allies in the Democratic-media complex could bring to bear against a pair of citizen journalists.[36]

For immediate assistance, Planned Parenthood turned to the well-connected fixers at—where else? —Fusion GPS. The beleaguered organization contracted with Fusion to review the unedited footage Daleiden had posted online. O'Keefe started this practice to counter the inevitable claims that he somehow doctored the videos. O'Keefe's transparency went largely unappreciated. The journalists who reviewed his footage knew what they wanted to say even without seeing it. The former journalists at Fusion GPS, now in the employ of Planned Parenthood, did not even have to feign objectivity.

Armed with a ten-page report from Fusion, Richards went on the offensive. Convincing people they did not see what they saw would not be easy, but the networks made the task possible by refusing to show the actual videos. As to the newspapers and online journals, they did their bit by leaving the assessment of the videos to Fusion GPS. Faced with real journalists doing real work, the Obama courtiers reflexively turned stenographer. They welcomed this "forensic study" as heartily as they would Fusion GPS's notorious "Steele dossier" a year later.

According to the *Washington Post*, Fusion's Glenn Simpson "enlisted experts who analyzed both the short, highly produced videos publicized by the antiabortion group, as well as hours of 'full' footage the group posted on YouTube."[37] This took no great effort or skill. Fusion GPS reviewed only the first four videos and supporting footage. The *Post* could and should have done its own analysis, but by 2015, it did not much matter. The *Post* was as deep in the tank for Planned Parenthood as were the paid shills at Fusion GPS.

The *Times* headlined its story, "Planned Parenthood Videos Were Altered, Analysis Finds."[38] Deep in the copy, Fusion admitted they "found no evidence that CMP inserted dialogue not spoken by Planned Parenthood staff," but the headline did the damage. To complete the rout, prosecutorial friends of Planned Parenthood, both in Texas and California, brought utterly bogus criminal charges against Daleiden and Merritt. Mainstream journalists yawned, even cheered.

As the 2016 presidential campaign wound its way to its expected conclusion, Planned Parenthood Action felt confident enough to ridicule CMP for its "fake, criminal videos."[39] Hillary Clinton felt comfortable enough with Planned Parenthood to make her first speech as presumptive nominee at one of its events. Hillary and friends were on a winning streak until, alas, they weren't. Thanks to the samizdat, millions of Americans had seen those pesky videos, even if Obama refused to.

The Crescent Front

On September 7, 2008, Barack Obama appeared on ABC's *This Week with George Stephanopoulos*. When Stephanopoulos challenged Obama on his prior claims that the McCain campaign was spreading rumors about him, Obama admitted, "You are absolutely right about that. John McCain has not talked about my Muslim faith, and that..." Before Obama could go any further, Stephanopoulos intervened with a *sotto voce* "Christian faith," and Obama was spared once again any serious questioning about his religious beliefs.[1]

Although many in the samizdat posed Obama's choice of faith as an *either/or* question, a more realistic proposition would have been *either*, *or*, or *neither*. Although he postured as a Christian, Obama appears to have chosen that faith as he did his wife: to make himself more politically viable in the black community. Yes, he had Muslim roots and was exposed to Islam as a boy, but he had no real commitment to that faith either. In truth, Obama was a secular humanist, much as his mother was. Marx meant more to him than either Jesus or Muhammad, and Marx did not mean all that much to him either.

Obama did, however, have some extended flirtations with Islam, Islamic nations, individual Muslims, and radical Palestinians of all faiths that, had the public known, might have kept him out of the White House or limited him to a single term. That Obama survived is a tribute to the mainstream media's ability to keep his secret life secret.

Obama, in fact, may owe his presidency to the *Los Angeles Times*. In 2008, the *Times* secured a copy of a video recorded at a dinner held in Chicago in 2003 on behalf of Obama's close friend, Rashid Khalidi. The occasion was Khalidi's imminent departure from Chicago for

Columbia University in New York. In 2008, his friendship with Obama posed obvious problems for the candidate. Khalidi would deny he was a spokesman for the lethal Palestinian Liberation Organization, but he was close enough to the PLO to give the rumors merit.

In his April 2008 account of the dinner, Peter Wallsten of the *Times* reported a few of the provocative toasts offered to the departing Khalidi. One of the dinner guests compared "Zionist settlers on the West Bank" to Osama bin Laden. Another guest recited a poem accusing Israel of terrorism. For his part, Obama was quoted as thanking Khalidi for offering "consistent reminders to me of my own blind spots and my own biases."[2] That much admitted, the *Times* absolutely refused to air the videotape it had in its possession or let any other party see it.

Not until late October 2008 did the conservative media become aware that the *Times* was withholding the tape. Breaking the story was the *Gateway Pundit*, founded as a one-man samizdat enterprise in 2004 by St. Louis resident Jim Hoft. Hoft contacted Wallsten, who insisted he would not release the video, nor share the name of his source.[3] In the *National Review*, Andy McCarthy asked rhetorically how the *Times* would have responded had John McCain sat quietly while "racists and terror mongers gave speeches that reeked of hatred for an American ally and rationalizations of terror attacks."[4] If anyone doubts the answer to that question, consider the media firestorms that erupted after the release of Mitt Romney's "47 percent" tape in 2012 or Donald Trump's *Access Hollywood* tape in 2012.

Predictably, as soon as McCain raised the issue of the videotape, the *New York Times* rushed to Khalidi's defense. In an article published less than a week before the election, the *Times* found an admittedly liberal rabbi to tell readers that the charges of anti-Semitism leveled against Khalidi were "completely absurd and uncalled for and malicious." Meanwhile, liberal historian and Khalidi backer Alan Brinkley assured those same readers that the controversy was "trumped-up."[5]

The controversy was far from absurd or trumped up. In fact, Khalidi's vicious verbal attacks against Israel got him banned in 2005 from lecturing to teachers at New York City's public schools. As the *New York Times* knew, too, McCain was directing his attack not at Khalidi but at the *Los Angeles Times*. The real controversy was implicit in the headline of a *New York Times* article from the day before its profile article on Khalidi, "McCain Attacks Los Angeles Times Over Its Refusal to Release '03 Obama Video."[6]

Obama's reaction to the virulent Israel hatred was lost for the ages. That was unfortunate. Among the anti-Israel guests in attendance were Bill Ayers and Bernardine Dohrn. Wallsten did not acknowledge Ayers's presence. He told Hoft he did not know Ayers was there. This omission, intentional or not, mattered. Six days after Wallsten's article appeared, Obama would notoriously refer to Ayers in a Democratic debate as just some "guy" who lived in the neighborhood. If the tape showed more than that, the truth was locked inside the *Los Angeles Times* newsroom. The major media shrugged. Beyond the conservative media, regular and irregular, no one expressed much of an interest in seeing the video. As McCarthy quipped, "The press doesn't think it's quite as newsworthy as Sarah Palin's wardrobe."

Another journalist who came to Obama's aid, unapologetically at that, was photographer and occasional National Public Radio (NPR) commentator Askia Muhammad. In January 2018, as a way of promoting his new book, Muhammad shared with the world a photo he had taken in 2005 at a Black Congressional Caucus event. In the center of the photo is a smiling Barack Obama. Standing right next to him, also smiling broadly, is Nation of Islam honcho Louis Farrakhan. Sensing what might generously be called "bad optics," a Black Caucus member stopped Muhammad even before he left the building.

"I gave the picture up at the time and basically swore secrecy," Muhammad admitted thirteen years later. "But after the nomination was secured and all the way up until the inauguration; then for eight years after he was President, it was kept under cover." When asked whether he thought the photo, if revealed, would have made a difference in the 2008 campaign, Muhammad said emphatically, "It absolutely would have made a difference."[7] He was right. Even the firemen would have had a hard time explaining Obama's cozy relationship with a man who casually referred to Jews as "termites" and to Judaism as "the synagogue of

Satan."[8] The fact that Obama participated in Farrakhan's 1995 "Million Man March" would not have made that explanation any easier.

The photo emerged on the left side of the blogosphere and caused a stir on the right, but for the most part, the mainstream media chose not to notice its emergence or question the journalistic ethics involved. The *New York Times* first reported on the photo nearly two months after it surfaced and then only as a side note in a larger article on the "religious fundamentalist" Farrakhan.[9]

In their dutiful effort to protect Obama, journalists had learned to kneecap critics with a single word. "Racist" had been around forever, "sexist" for nearly as long, but "Islamophobe" arrived on the scene not too long before "denier." In September 2010, at a forum on Capitol Hill, moderate Muslim Abdur-Rahman Muhammad traced the coinage of "Islamophobia" to a meeting he attended some years prior in Northern Virginia. Envious of the success homosexuals enjoyed with "homophobia," Muslim activists improvised their own one-click slander with "Islamophobia." According to Muhammad, they planned to use the word "to beat up their critics."[10] Ironically, the word first appeared in the *New York Times* on September 9, 2001.[11] By the time Obama declared his candidacy in 2007, "Islamophobia" had found its rightful place in the left's defamatory arsenal.

A month before Muhammad testified on Capitol Hill, President Obama used the occasion of a White House dinner celebrating Ramadan to defend the proposed community center and mosque near Ground Zero in lower Manhattan. "This is America, and our commitment to religious freedom must be unshakable," said Obama in words that had to ring a bit hollow to the bakers and florists hectored for their Christian beliefs about marriage, let alone those Christian institutions forced into subsidizing abortive drugs. Sheryl Gay Stolberg, reporting for the *New York Times*, failed to note the irony. In a conspicuous bit of deck-stacking, Stolberg concluded her article with five quotes favoring Obama's position, including one from an Arab-American journalist who urged Obama "to stand up to Islamophobia."[12]

For all the strategic stonewalling by the *Los Angeles Times*, no journalist deep-sixed more damaging information about Obama than Ben

Smith, then with *Politico*. On September 4, 2008, Smith reported on a story that the major media fully ignored but that, in his words, had been "lighting up the conservative blogs for the last week." Actually, the story had been lighting up the samizdat for considerably longer. I reported on it a week before Smith, and others had been reporting on it before me. The story involved a recently surfaced March 2008 NY1 interview with venerable black New York politico Percy Sutton.[13]

During this interview, on a show called *Inside City Hall*, Sutton matter-of-factly told host Dominic Carter how he first became aware of Barack Obama. According to Sutton, he had been "introduced to [Obama] by a friend." Sutton described the friend, Dr. Khalid al-Mansour, as "the principal adviser to one of the world's richest men." Sutton was referring here to Saudi Prince Al-Waleed bin Talal. Reportedly, al-Mansour asked that Sutton "please write a letter in support of [Obama]...a young man that has applied to Harvard." The well-connected Sutton obliged him.

There were many reasons to take this story seriously. For one, although an octogenarian, Sutton was still a figure of some prominence in New York. For another, he spoke lucidly and specifically about his intervention only after Carter asked his opinion on the Obama candidacy. He had no reason to make this story up.

In a competitive media environment, mainstream reporters would have swarmed all over this story, much as the citizen journalists of the samizdat did. Al-Mansour made great copy. He was openly anti-Semitic. So was his patron, bin Talal. In October 2001, New York City Mayor Rudy Giuliani refused a $10 million check from the Saudi billionaire to help rebuild New York. Giuliani did not want favors from a man who argued publicly, "Our Palestinian brethren continue to be slaughtered at the hands of Israelis while the world turns the other cheek."[14] If Sutton remembered events correctly, his account would have seriously dimmed Obama's chances in November. Lest its readers find out, the *New York Times* reported not a single word on the story, not even to discredit it.

The discrediting job fell to fire captain Smith. In his September 4 article, before he explained the nature of the controversy, he trivialized it. First, according to Smith, the Obama camp "flatly" denied the story. In fact, however, Obama spokesman Ben LaBolt did not "flatly" deny anything of consequence. He noted only that Obama did not know al-Mansour and that Obama was in Chicago in 1988, not New York. Nothing Sutton said made these points worth denying. He implied no face-to-face meetings among any of the parties. On the question of the letter itself, the most important question, LaBolt cagily built in an escape clause, saying, "*To our knowledge*, no such letter was written" (italics added).

Smith also insisted that the letter seemed "off in at least one key detail." Sutton claimed al-Mansour was "raising money" for Obama, but, as Smith noted, Obama took out more than $40,000 in student loans at Harvard. Tuition and fees at Harvard ran more than $25,000 a year during Obama's three-year stint. Room and board and car would have run another $20,000 per annum. That's a differential of roughly $100,000. This was bad math on Smith's part and even worse journalism.

This whole story would have gone up in smoke had it not been for one intrepid reporter, Ken Timmerman. During the Obama presidency, Timmerman served as a one-man truth squad on all things Islamic. He knew his stuff. As a young reporter in 1982, he was taken hostage by Palestinian guerrillas in Beirut, and he had been tracking the Middle East ever since. For the first dozen or so years of his career, Timmerman worked fully within the mainstream—*Newsweek*, CBS News, *Time Magazine*. He helped pioneer what he calls "fact based, data based reporting." In 1994, he followed the facts on the China trade to the doors of the Oval Office. Unwilling to see him go further, *Time* fired him. Yes, Virginia, that happens. For Timmerman, a Clinton supporter in 1992, that was "the day the media died."[15]

By 2008, Timmerman had gone full samizdat, a much tougher way to make a living, he acknowledges, but a more satisfying one. Writing for the online publication *Newsmax*, he badly scooped Smith on the Sutton story. He spoke to al-Mansour at some length before Smith knew who al-Mansour was. "I never discuss Barack Obama," al-Mansour told him. As Timmerman noted, "Al-Mansour deflected several attempts to get him to answer direct questions about his relationship with Obama and the Percy Sutton revelations."[16]

By the time Smith did reach al-Mansour, someone had gotten to al-Mansour. He told Smith he initially declined to refute Sutton's account only out of respect for Sutton, "a dear friend" whose health was "not good." Added al-Mansour, "I'm sure he's written a letter [to someone else] and he got it confused somehow."[17] Two days later, on September 6, Smith poured some lighter fluid on the story and struck a match. "To put the story to rest for good," he reproduced an email from "a spokesman for Sutton's family" named Kevin Wardally. Wrote Wardally:

> The information Mr. Percy Sutton imparted on March 25 in a NY1 News interview regarding his connection to Barack Obama is inaccurate. As best as our family and the Chairman's closest friends can tell, Mr. Sutton, now 86 years of age, misspoke in describing certain details and events in that television interview.[18]

The opening sentence of the September 6 article gave away more than Smith intended. He wrote, "Conservative bloggers have, understandably, spent some time in recent days chasing suggestive comments made by the former Manhattan borough president Percy Sutton earlier this year." For starters, there was nothing "suggestive" about Sutton's comments. More to the point, if conservative bloggers were "understandably" keen on the story, why weren't Smith's colleagues in the mainstream media at least a little bit interested?

Timmerman, in fact, did the journalism his better-paid peers chose not to. He followed up with all the principals, contacted the Obama campaign, spoke to the people at Harvard, and reached out to numerous people who knew Sutton. On September 23, 2008, *Newsmax* published the results of his efforts. The story had not been put "to rest" after all. According to Smith, al-Mansour said, "He'd never met Obama," but a "meeting" was never at issue. According to Timmerman, al-Mansour strongly implied he and Obama had spoken.

More problematic for Smith, no one at the Sutton family business knew who Wardally was. In his email to Smith, Wardally even got Sutton's age wrong. When Timmerman asked him to explain the family's response, Wardally claimed a nephew of Sutton's retained him, but that nephew no longer worked with his uncle. As a prominent black entrepreneur told Timmerman, "Percy Sutton doesn't go out idly on television saying things he doesn't mean."[19]

For all of Timmerman's good work, the ashes of the Sutton story had been buried too deep to retrieve. In *Game Change*, Heilemann and Halperin neglected to mention this potential game-changing development. The three relevant Davids—Remnick, Maraniss, Garrow—were equally mute in their respective biographies. The story had one more chance at life. In September 2012, during the home stretch of the presidential campaign, al-Mansour appeared on an internet-based radio show, *The National and International Roundtable*.[20]

In his introduction, the host, Arif Khatib, acknowledged that al-Mansour "made news in 2008 when it was revealed that he had been a patron of President Barack Obama and had recommended him for admission to Harvard Law School." In truth, al-Mansour made no news beyond the samizdat, but in his own circles the story lived on. Unfortunately for history's sake, the host never asked al-Mansour about his relationship with Obama, and al-Mansour volunteered nothing.

Four days later, writing from the furthest reaches of the samizdat— the *Daily Inter Lake* in northern Montana—conservative columnist Frank Miele unearthed an eye-popping column from November 1979 written by one Vernon Jarrett, a widely syndicated black columnist then with the *Chicago Tribune*. As the reader may recall, Jarrett was a protégé of Obama mentor Frank Marshall Davis and the father-in-law of Obama's closest adviser, Valerie Jarrett.

Jarrett opened the column with this provocative question: "What about those rumored billions of dollars the oil-rich Arab nations are supposed to unload on American black leaders and minority institutions?" Assuring Jarrett that this was "not just a rumor" was none other than Khalid al-Mansour. According to Jarrett, al-Mansour had been encouraging Arab leaders to take a more active role in black America. This effort would include "giving financial help to disadvantaged students."[21]

In the column explaining his find, Miele showed just how tuned in he was to the samizdat. He knew about the Frank Marshall Davis connection to Vernon Jarrett, the Valerie Jarrett connection to Obama, and finally the Sutton revelation from 2008 about al-Mansour. The salons in America's newsrooms knew next to nothing about Davis, Sutton, or al-Mansour.

"It is also at least suggestive that Obama began that college educa-tion as a member of the highly international student body of Occidental College in 1979," added Miele. That was the year Jarrett interviewed al-Mansour about his plan to finance promising black students, and Obama would have needed help. Occidental is one of America's pricier colleges.[22]

Once again, Ben Smith rushed into the breach. Now the editor of *BuzzFeed News*, Smith had one of his staffers locate al-Mansour within a day of Miele's posting of the column. In 2008, al-Mansour denied he had anything to do with Percy Sutton. This time, he denied he had any-thing to do with the conveniently deceased Vernon Jarrett. "I've never heard of [the column]," al-Mansour told *BuzzFeed*. "I have no idea what the motivation of Mr. Jarrett was." Smith also repeated the allegation by Wardally that Sutton, suffering from dementia, had "misspoken." In so saying, Smith fully ignored Timmerman's detailed reporting to the contrary.[23] Heading a company with fifteen hundred or so employees and a market value approaching $1 billion, Smith could turn reams of information into ash.

The *Daily Inter Lake*, by contrast, serves as the "newspaper of record" for Flathead and Lake Counties in northern Montana, with a combined population of about 130,000. Undaunted, Miele fired back. Referring to Sutton and Jarrett, he found it newsworthy that al-Mansour would "throw these two distinguished black community leaders under the bus." Unlike Smith, Miele lacked the resources to follow up, but he suggested an obvious motivation for al-Mansour: "Follow the money."[24] Whether money was al-Mansour's motive or not, no real journalist would have taken his word that both Jarrett and Sutton were lying.

As he proved time and again, Smith was not a real journalist. In a 2016 review, the left-leaning Fairness and Accuracy In Reporting (FAIR) lamented that *BuzzFeed*'s coverage of Obama had "turned into little more [than] press releases from the White House social media team." According to FAIR, 99 percent of *BuzzFeed*'s articles were favorable to the president, a state of affairs FAIR called "borderline creepy."[25]

In the 2008 election cycle, the major media had another opportunity to shed light on Obama's Islamic ties but spectacularly failed to do so. Reporters from the *New York Times* or *Washington Post* could have broken it open with a few phone calls. They get their calls answered. Citizen journalists don't. This episode, in fact, showed the limited ability of the samizdat to penetrate the labyrinthine secrets of the deep state.

At the heart of the mystery was a visit Obama made to Pakistan at the end of his sophomore year at Occidental College in 1981. No one knew about this trip until Obama strategically discussed it during a San Francisco fundraiser on April 17, 2008. "I traveled to Pakistan when I was in college," boasted Obama as a way of countering Hillary Clinton's foreign policy experience. "I knew what Sunni and Shia was [Obama has long had problems with noun-verb agreement] before I joined the Senate Foreign Relations Committee."

Jake Tapper, then with ABC, found it curious that he had not heard Obama speak of this adventure, especially "given all the talk of Pakistan during this campaign," but Tapper went no further. He should have. There was much more to this story that needed to be told. Among Obama's biographers, David Remnick provides the most information about what was thought to be a three-week Pakistan sojourn. One friend told Remnick how Obama was "shocked" by what he saw. The subservience of the peasants "blew his mind." A Pakistani friend who accompanied Obama spoke of Obama's "striking" experiences, ones that "stayed in his mind."[26] Yet for all that he witnessed and learned, Obama mentioned not a word about the trip in either *Dreams from My Father* or *The Audacity of Hope*. In the latter book, the omission is particularly noteworthy given that Obama used *Audacity* to establish his foreign policy cred.

This oversight would be of minimal interest were it not for an incident first reported in the *Washington Times* on March 20, 2008, four weeks before the San Francisco fundraiser. The short article detailed how two State Department employees were fired and a third disciplined "for improperly accessing electronic personal data on Democratic presidential candidate Sen. Barack Obama." The *New York Times* weighed in the following day, adding the detail that the passport files of "all three presidential candidates" had been improperly accessed.[27]

The files contained biographical data and passport applications. Reportedly, Obama's file had been breached four times beginning in January 2008, a week after the Iowa primary, a primary Obama won. Stanley, Inc., a major contractor with the State Department, promptly fired the two of its employees who were allegedly involved. A third employee, employer unspecified, was reprimanded but not terminated. State Department spokesman Sean McCormack blamed "imprudent curiosity" for the breach and scolded a Greek reporter who suggested something more sinister.[28]

On the following day, *New York Times* readers learned that the reprimanded employee worked for a DC-area company called The Analysis Corporation (TAC). He was reportedly the only one of the three miscreants to view McCain's file as well as Obama's. The thrust of the day-two article was the Bush State Department's embarrassed apologies to Obama. There was no description of TAC or any reference to its CEO. The article did, however, acknowledge that the files contained "Social Security numbers, addresses, dates of birth and other personal information,"[29] data invaluable to friend or foe.

To its credit, CNN reported on that same March 22 a critical fact the *New York Times* did not find newsworthy. The president and CEO of The Analysis Corporation just happened to be an Obama donor who "advises the Illinois Democrat on foreign policy and intelligence issues." If the name "John Brennan" did not ring a bell in 2008, it certainly does today. After the election, Obama tapped TAC CEO Brennan to be his chief counterterrorism adviser and, in time, the Director of the CIA. Brennan will show up later in this book in regard to the Russia collusion story, but his history should have troubled Obama more than Van Jones's.

In 2016, at a congressional hearing on diversity in the CIA, Brennan told a story about himself that raised eyebrows even among the jaded. In 1980, when Brennan first applied for the CIA, the polygrapher asked a standard question as to whether Brennan had ever worked with a group dedicated to overthrowing the United States. In fact, Brennan had voted for Communist Party candidate for president Gus Hall in 1976 and admitted as much to the CIA polygrapher. "I said I was neither Democratic or Republican," Brennan recounted, "but it was my way, as

I was going to college, of signaling my unhappiness with the system, and the need for change."[30] That answer satisfied Jimmy Carter's CIA brass.[31] In 2016, the unapologetic Brennan shared this anecdote as an illustration of the CIA's embrace of diverse candidates—black, white, or red.

A fluent Arabic speaker, Brennan was rumored to have converted to Islam while CIA chief of station in Saudi Arabia in the late 1990s. His accuser, former FBI agent John Guandolo, claimed to have "direct sources" on the ground in Saudi Arabia with "direct knowledge" of Brennan's conversion.[32] Guandolo made this accusation while the U.S. Senate was considering Obama's nomination of Brennan to head the CIA in February 2013. Whether Guandolo was telling the truth or not will likely never be known. The major media paid zero attention to him or his claim. The firemen rushed in to defame Guandolo as an Islamophobe. Case closed.

The passport story was harder to suppress. According to CNN's source, the unnamed TAC transgressor was considered a "terrific" employee except, of course, for his multiple incursions into Obama's passport file. TAC flacks characterized that behavior as an "aberration," claiming, with the PR equivalent of a straight face, "This individual's actions were taken without the knowledge or direction of anyone at The Analysis Corp. and are wholly inconsistent with our professional and ethical standards." Reportedly, the State Department asked Brennan not to discipline the employee while the investigation was underway. He need not have worried about the investigation's outcome. The State Department's July 2008 report on the incident was redacted to the point of uselessness. If Brennan's employee was ever named, let alone punished, that fact did not make the news or the report.[33]

Although the breach occurred in the *Washington Post's* backyard, the paper remained notably incurious about the Brennan connection. On March 22, 2008, reporter Glenn Kessler did not name Brennan until the thirteenth paragraph of an article whose very headline shifted the blame for the incident to the Bush administration, "Rice Apologizes For Breach of Passport Data."[34] In January 2009, the *Post* ran a thirteen-hundred-word, front-page article on Brennan's appointment as deputy national security advisor, but even then it failed to mention the passport incident.[35]

Once again it fell to Ken Timmerman, then with *Newsmax,* to do the probing the major media refused to do. On January 12, 2009, three days after the *Post's* article on Brennan's appointment, Timmerman reported that Obama had been the main target of the passport breach. According to Timmerman's unnamed source, the purpose of the breach was to "cauterize" Obama's file, meaning to remove or doctor any potentially embarrassing information.[36] If true, this revelation helped make sense of Obama's decision to introduce the subject of his 1981 Pakistan trip a few weeks after his passport file had been properly scrubbed.

In his 2016 book, *Deception,* Timmerman added some additional information. Five days after the passport story broke in March 2008, Washington DC Police arrested, on a marijuana charge, a twenty-four-year old with the unusual name "Leiutenant [*sic*] Quarles Harris Jr." In the versions that bounced around the less reliable corners of the samizdat, this name was often compressed to "Lt. Quarles Harris" without the various commenters bothering to report what exactly Harris was a lieutenant of.

As Timmerman reports, however, the samizdat had reason to take interest in Harris's fate.[37] In addition to the marijuana, police found eight State Department passport applications on the young man when they busted him. According to his charging document, "Harris admitted he obtained the Passport information from a co-conspirator who works for the U.S. Department of State." After he agreed to cooperate in the State Department investigation, the DC Police released Harris on his own recognizance. Less than a month later, DC Police found Harris shot dead in the front seat of his locked car, the shots having penetrated the windshield. Reported the *Washington Times,* "City police said they do not know whether his death was a direct result of his cooperation with federal investigators."[38]

As with the equally suspicious DC murder of DNC staffer Seth Rich eight years later, the *Post* chose to know as little as possible about the motive of the shooter. The fact that an employee of Obama's chief counterterrorism adviser had breached Obama's passport files did not strike its editors as newsworthy. Nor did the subsequent murder of a DC man under investigation for passport fraud. It is altogether possible that Harris's death was unrelated to the breach of Obama's passport files. If so, *Post* readers had no way of knowing. *Post* editors allowed Rich and Harris to die in the darkness while leftist firemen pilloried those who raised questions about either.

If anyone knew about democracy dying in darkness, it was the man who called me unexpectedly on Thanksgiving Day 2013. I was at my daughter's in-laws. We were just about to sit down to dinner when the call came in from a California phone number. As soon as the man identified himself, I begged the indulgence of my hosts. I had to take the call. I had been trying to reach this fellow for nearly a year.

He introduced himself as "Nakoula," short for "Nakoula Basseley Nakoula," one of several names he has used over time. "Why haven't you answered my letters?" he asked me impatiently. "I haven't gotten your letters," I told him. Nakoula had received the one letter I sent in early 2013. He tried repeatedly to contact me after that, but apparently the folks at the La Tuna Federal Correctional Institution were not eager for him to have pen pals. He was a bit desperate. I was among the very few people in the media, maybe the only one, to reach out to him after the feds buried him in the middle of Nowhere, West Texas. Nakoula had a story to tell. I wanted to hear it. During the Obama years, no individual suffered more grievously from White House-media collusion than he had.

Much has been written about the various blunders that led to the attack on the American consulate in Benghazi on September 11, 2012. Not until 2016, however, when the indefatigable Ken Timmerman released his book *Deception*, subtitled *The Making of the Youtube Video Hillary and Obama Blamed for Benghazi*, did anyone write in depth about the filmmaker Obama held responsible for those attacks. That filmmaker would be Nakoula.

Timmerman describes the White House response to Nakoula's video as "disgraceful, un-American, illegal, and a clear violation of Nakoula's constitutional rights."[39] He does not overstate the case. If anything, the major media's treatment of Nakoula was more disgraceful. In the aftermath of Benghazi, journalists shamelessly conspired with the White

House to sell a conspicuously false story that put an innocent man in prison. But then again, as George Zimmerman could attest, in an election year, bad things happened to good people.

The dissembling began while the consulate was in flames and the attack still under way. Needing to draw attention away from the administration's duplicitous meddling in Libyan affairs, then Secretary of State Hillary Clinton released a memo on the night of September 11 blaming the attack on some "inflammatory material posted on the Internet." Obama's role in the creation of this story line has never been explored for the simple reason that no one knows where Obama was that night or what he did.

Incredibly, for eight months after the attack, not a single reporter asked the president or a spokesman the simple question Chris Wallace of Fox News posed on May 19, 2013, "What did the president do the rest of that night to pursue Benghazi?" The man Wallace questioned was Dan Pfeiffer, a senior adviser to the president. A well-schooled flack, Pfeiffer dismissed Obama's whereabouts that night as "irrelevant." Wallace wasn't buying. "No one knows where he was, or how he was involved, or who told him there were no forces," he pressed. Refusing to answer, the defiant Pfeiffer called Wallace's line of questioning "offensive."[40] And that was that, another scandal dodged.

Eager to move on, the major media left it to the samizdat to ask the most basic questions about the "inflammatory" video in question, namely, what did people see and how did they come to see it? The "what" question was not that easily answered. Different people viewed different versions of the video in different languages, but the initial few who had seen anything saw a trailer, short or long, for Nakoula's amateurishly produced movie, *Innocence of Muslims*. The longer version, fourteen minutes, showed what Timmerman calls "a remarkably faithful re-enactment" of a classic scene in Muslim lore, the one in which Muhammad marries the prepubescent Aisha.

In making the film, Nakoula played the very game in which progressives delight: projecting contemporary values on to historical figures. The left routinely presents Christopher Columbus as a genocidal brute and George Washington as a slave owner. In that same spirit, Nakoula presented Muhammad as a child molester.[41]

Timmerman traces the origin of the blame-the-video idea to "a self-appointed watchdog of Islamophobia" named Max Fisher. Fisher took on the procrustean task of shoehorning Islam into the Rainbow Coalition, in this case by presenting Muslims as fellow victims of right-wing bigotry. In an article posted in the *Atlantic* on September 11, but before the attack on the Benghazi consulate began, Fisher focused on an "American film that insults Prophet Mohammed" as the reason for the protests that day at the American embassy in Cairo. There were other more obvious reasons—the detention in the U.S. of the "Blind Sheikh," the drone-strike death of a popular al-Qaeda leader, the very date of September 11—but only the video had a conservative provenance.

Or so Fisher thought. Reckless with his facts, he first reported that Terry Jones, a conservative Christian pastor, produced the film. Fisher made a quick correction upon being informed, misinformed actually, that the producer was an "Israeli-American California real-estate developer." In Fisher's world, an Israeli developer made for almost as rich a target as a Christian pastor. Rather than scrap the whole article as he should have, Fisher kept the focus on Jones but changed his job description, describing him now as "the Florida Koran-burner…helping to promote a movie vilifying Egypt's Muslims." Seemingly oblivious to his own role in this hysteria, Fisher made one unusually honest observation. He noted that an "obsessively outraged media" paid more attention to Jones and the movie than either deserved.[42]

Journalist turned fireman Sidney Blumenthal, a shadow adviser to Hillary Clinton, gets credit for the next step in this disinformation campaign—blaming the Benghazi assault on Nakoula's video. On the night of the consulate attack, Blumenthal shared with Hillary a report he helped prepare. The report claimed that the inspiration for the imagined protests in Benghazi was "a sacrilegious internet video on the prophet Mohammed originating in America."[43] In the memo she released that night, Hillary feigned outrage. "The United States deplores any intentional effort to denigrate the religious beliefs of others," said Clinton.

"Our commitment to religious tolerance goes back to the very beginning of our nation."

Much depends here on the definition of "denigrate." A year earlier, Clinton had been among the hip and tolerant who put aside their scruples to give a standing ovation to the crudely blasphemous Broadway show, *The Book of Mormon*. Creators Trey Parker and Matt Stone had been equally rough on Islam, but for Clinton and Obama, only the Islamic cow was sacred.

Hours after her press release, Blumenthal was feeding Hillary a compound disinformation piece from his son and aspiring fireman, Max. The article's very title suggests the way father and son think: "Meet The Right-Wing Extremist Behind Anti-Muslim Film That Sparked Deadly Riots." Like Fisher, the young Blumenthal found a homegrown Christian activist on whom to pin the video. It was just a different Christian, Steve Klein by name.[44]

As Timmerman explains in convincing detail, the video had nothing to do with the pre-planned assault on the Benghazi compound, and Klein had almost nothing to do with the video. Writes Timmerman, "There were never any demonstrations in front of either U.S. diplomatic facility in Libya. That was just a full-throated lie, invented whole cloth by Sid Blumenthal and his ghost-whisperer, Tyler Drumheller, who had a checkered record at the Central Intelligence Agency."[45]

In the week following the attack, the conservative media produced ample evidence clearing Nakoula's video of any responsibility for that attack. In Obama's world, however, what the conservative media said or showed counted for little, if anything. As a case in point, the memoir by Obama foreign policy adviser Ben Rhodes, *The World As It Is*, reads like a 450-page exercise in denial. Rhodes cannot bring himself to admit that the White House sold the world a conspicuously false story on Benghazi, and he does not even mention Nakoula.

In his retelling, Rhodes merely passed along to National Security Advisor Susan Rice the talking points prepared by the intelligence community (IC) for her to present on the various news programs on the Sunday after the Tuesday attack. Emails extracted from the feds by Judicial Watch, however, show that the CIA had been thoroughly politicized even before John Brennan formally took over. According to Judicial Watch President Tom Fitton, the CIA's role in this mess, like the White House's, "was making sure that President Obama looked good."[46]

On Sunday, September 16, 2012, Rice dutifully played her role in the charade. "Our current best assessment, based on the information that we have at present, is that, in fact, what this began as, it was a spontaneous—not a premeditated—response to what had transpired in Cairo," Rice told Jake Tapper on ABC's *This Week*.[47] She repeated the same obvious lie on four other shows that morning. Understandably, Republicans in Congress and the conservative media objected to such a flagrant falsehood. Their "vitriol" shocked Rhodes. He seemed astonished that anyone would resent being lied to on so critical an issue. "The people attacking [Rice]," he writes, "weren't going to change their minds; reporters would tell you privately that they knew Benghazi was a bogus scandal, but they would still report on the allegations against her in print and on TV."[48] During the Obama years, all scandals were bogus.

Knowing his base, Obama went looking for a reliably clueless audience to hear his take on Benghazi and found one, of all places, at the Ed Sullivan Theater in New York, home of the David Letterman Show.

Letterman had little use for organized religion. A year after Benghazi, for instance, he would say of Pope Francis's appearance at World Youth Day, "I'm telling you, if there's anything the kids can't get enough of, it's a 76-year-old virgin. Come on! World Youth Day. Or as the Vatican calls it, salute to altar boys."[49] Catholicism, like Mormonism or Christian evangelicalism, was fair game for the left. Islam wasn't. Obama knew he could count on Letterman to spare the "Prophet Muhammad" his usual irreverence.

"Here's what happened," Obama told his wide-eyed host a week after the assault. "You had a video that was released by somebody who lives here, sort of a shadowy character who—who made an extremely offensive video directed at Mohammed and Islam." Letterman reeled back in disbelief. "Making fun of the Prophet Mohammed!" he said solemnly. "Making fun of the Prophet Mohammed," confirmed Obama.[50] The same president who defended the First Amendment rights of the

Ground Zero imam showed a shocking indifference to those of Nakoula, a Christian and American citizen of long standing.

Like other progressives, Letterman would be hard pressed to explain how or why Muslims had become part of the Rainbow Coalition. Indeed, their presence in the coalition accounts for the very existence of the "Coexist" bumper sticker. It is not easy to find a middle ground, say, between executing gays and celebrating them. British intellectual Douglas Murray was among those who thought "this whole intersection nonsense [would] fall apart under the weight of its own contradictions," but Murray underestimated the strength of its "Marxist substructure." Marxists aren't bothered by contradictions, he argued, at least not when the various parties agree upon the end game.[51]

The major media helped paper over the contradictions, and by 2012 their cooperation was a given. Obama, in fact, pulled his description of the filmmaker straight from the pages of the *New York Times.* Just one day after the attack concluded in Benghazi, a crew of *ten* reporters did a Joe the Plumber-style hit piece on Nakoula, "a shadowy gas station owner with a record of criminal arrests and bankruptcy." Obama apparently liked the word "shadowy."

More troubling, from the *Times* perspective at least, Nakoula had reportedly "expressed anti-Muslim sentiments as he pushed for the making of the film."[52] These reporters could not have followed the news very closely. In 2011 alone, when Nakoula was making his film, there were at least ten attacks on his fellow Coptic Christians in Egypt, several of them lethal, one resulting in the death of twenty-four Copts. This relentless persecution made "anti-Muslim sentiments" as understandable for Copts as anti-Nazi sentiments were for Jews in pre-war Germany. But Christians weren't part of the progressive coalition in 2012. Muslims were.

The fact that Nakoula and his family had received serious death threats, something of a norm for critics of Islam, did not deter the *Times* from doxing him. The reporters tracked Nakoula to his Southern California home and staked it out. To assure their readers and the world's imams they had found the right suspect, the *Times* reporters inspected the interior of the house "through a window in the door" and pointed out the features that were also seen in the trailer.[53]

With the media cheering on the administration, federal probation officers took Nakoula into custody on September 15 and held him in secret without charge or without access to an attorney, "an extrajudicial prisoner in the United States of America," writes Timmerman.[54] Nakoula was vulnerable. He was on parole for his involvement in a check-kiting scheme. Even more worrisome, he had quietly cooperated with the feds and fingered the scheme's ringleader. Less than forty-eight hours after Clinton first alluded to Nakoula's video, someone in the Obama administration unsealed the indictment and exposed Nakoula to retaliation. "Why did the government release the deal?" Nakoula asked me when I first spoke to him. "Why did they put my life in danger?"[55]

One obvious reason for exposing Nakoula was to prod him into accepting federal protection. The Obama administration followed this short-term strategy with the long-term one of revoking Nakoula's parole. The feds devised a devilish strategy for revoking it and leaked that strategy almost immediately. Just three days after the smoke cleared in Benghazi, the *Times*'s Ian Lovett reported that the feds were inquiring into whether Nakoula "had been the person who uploaded the video to YouTube." If Nakoula had uploaded the video, Lovett continued much too knowingly, he would have violated parole restrictions "against his using the Internet without permission from a probation officer."

Lovett critiqued the "incendiary" fourteen-minute trailer for its depiction of the "Prophet Muhammad" as "a buffoon, a womanizer and a child molester." He also perpetuated the canard that the video "helped set off protests" at the Benghazi consulate.[56] In this otherwise unexceptional article, Lovett captured the spirit of the media in the age of Obama—compliant, complicit, and scarily indifferent to the First Amendment rights of anyone but establishment journalists. That a film-maker was about to spend a year in federal custody for producing a per-fectly legal satire inspired not a single major media journalist to cry foul.

With the November 2012 election looming, some journalists scrapped their vestigial ethics to shorten Obama's odds, and none did it more publicly than CNN's Candy Crowley. The occasion was once again the October 16, 2012, town hall-style debate.[57] If she checked Romney on Fast and Furious, Crowley all but checkmated him on Benghazi.

When an audience member asked, "Who denied enhanced security and why?" Obama responded first. Evading the actual question, he gave a long-winded answer on how he was the very model of a modern major president. For his part, Romney criticized Obama for his squirrelly response to the attack and chastised him for flying to Las Vegas the next day for a fundraiser. Here, Crowley intervened once again. Following Romney's hard-hitting response, Crowley lobbed a softball to Obama, who was then walking towards her, "Does the buck stop with the secretary of state?" Obama had his well-rehearsed answer at the ready. He delivered it flawlessly. "Secretary Clinton has done an extraordinary job, but she works for me," he said. "I'm the president, and I'm always responsible."

Obama then boldly, if mendaciously, rewrote the history of September 12, 2012: "The day after the attack, governor, I stood in the Rose Garden, and I told the American people and the world that we were going to find out exactly what happened, that this was an act of terror, and I also said we are going to hunt down those who committed this crime."

Obama emphasized the "act of terror" line as though daring Romney to contradict him. Again without a hiccup, Obama expressed seeming outrage at any insinuation that his team would "play politics or mislead when we have lost four of our own." As half of America knew, Obama and his team had been playing politics for the previous five weeks, beginning with Hillary's press release the night of September 11. In his Rose Garden speech of September 12, Obama blamed the video, but he did so much more subtly than he would do on Letterman six days later. Less than ninety seconds into the prepared text, he said in reference to the video, "Since our founding, the United States has been a nation that respects all faiths. We reject all efforts to denigrate the religious beliefs of others." It was not until five minutes into the six-minute speech that Obama added, "No acts of terror will ever shake the resolve of this great nation, alter that character, or eclipse the light of the values that we stand for."[58] As the plural "acts" suggest, Obama was speaking generically, and this was his only mention of "terror" in any form. There was no mention of "hunting" anyone.

Romney had listened carefully enough and prepared well enough to understand the gift Obama had just given him. Looking quizzically at Obama, he asked, "You said in the Rose Garden the day after the attack it was an act of terror? It was not a spontaneous demonstration, is that what you are saying?"

Obama answered uncomfortably, "Please proceed. Please proceed, Governor." Romney did, saying to Crowley he just wanted to get Obama's response on record. In the background Obama could be heard saying, "Get the transcript." The camera then showed Crowley waving a piece of paper that could easily have been mistaken for the transcript. Said Crowley to Romney, "He did in fact, sir, call, so let me call it an act of terror."

"Can you say that a little louder, Candy," said Obama, now moving confidently into Romney's space. "He did call it an act of terror," repeated Crowley. Caught off guard, a stuttering Romney cited Ambassador Rice's appearance on five Sunday talk shows, but by now Crowley and Obama were both talking over him. Concluded Crowley, "I want to move you on and people can go to the transcripts." The election may well have been lost at that very moment. The firemen were universally gleeful. Neither they nor the mainstream journalists saw anything amiss with Crowley's intervention.

In re-watching this sequence, and seeing how smoothly Obama handled it, I am convinced he knew the "Hillary" question was coming and maybe knew more than that. In 2012, I would not have suggested a planned tag-teaming, but after CNN contributor Donna Brazile was busted in 2016 for providing the Clinton campaign with actual debate questions, I have had to reconsider. Whether staged or spontaneous, Crowley's rescue of Obama set a new standard for media malpractice.

Challenging the White House narrative on any subject, particularly Benghazi, came with risks. If imprisonment was old school, the cyber gaslighting of CBS News reporter Sharyl Attkisson was new and creepy. "I've been reading your reports online about Benghazi," a prescient friend in the intelligence community told Attkisson in the fall of

2012. "It's pretty incredible. Keep at it. But you'd better watch out."[59] The fellow then explained that the administration had long been monitoring the insufficiently "reasonable" Attkisson. As she continued to report the truth about Benghazi, some agent somewhere in the deep state launched a campaign of electronic harassment against Attkisson. She did not imagine the harassment. An analyst hired by her employer, CBS News, eventually confirmed it. A WikiLeaks document purloined from the global intelligence firm Stratfor in 2010 claimed that Obama's all-purpose fixer John Brennan was "behind the witch hunts of investigative journalists learning information from inside the beltway sources."[60]

Whether Brennan had anything to do with Attkisson's problems remains to be seen. With help from a whistleblower, Attkisson has come to believe that the man guiding her persecution was Rod Rosenstein, a future deputy attorney general and then U.S. Attorney in Baltimore. In January 2020, she named him and four others in a detailed suit that tracked the harassment back to her Fast and Furious reporting in late 2011.[61]

Beyond investigating the cyber invasion of her electronics, CBS did little to support Attkisson. Instead of fighting the power, CBS execs gradually cut back on Attkisson's air time, forcing her out of the major media in 2014 and into the samizdat. At the time, it should be noted, David Rhodes was president of CBS News. His brother, Ben, was Obama's deputy national security adviser. The Democratic-media complex had little tolerance for mainstream reporters who failed to honor the talking points.

Citizen journalists could be ignored. Mainstream journalists had to be contained. If they strayed from the prescribed narrative as Attkisson did, these journalists encountered any number of restraints, including peer pressure. In the way of example, the *Washington Post's* Erik Wemple reviewed Attkisson's book *Stonewalled* with no more urgency than if it were a new Stephen King novel. He did not come out and say her harrowing account of the ordeal was more imagined than real, but he certainly insinuated as much.[62]

As a further way of undermining Attkisson's credibility, Wemple subtly contrasted her story with the well-documented harassment of

James Rosen, then chief Washington correspondent for Fox News. From the White House perspective, Fox News was just mainstream enough to deserve reprisal. For three years beginning in 2010, the Department of Justice had used a search warrant to probe Rosen's personal and professional communications allegedly because of his interaction with a State Department contractor monitoring North Korea's nuclear program. So invasive was the DOJ's surveillance that it moved even the *Washington Post*, if not to condemn the action, at least to report it. "Search warrants like these have a severe chilling effect on the free flow of important information to the public," First Amendment lawyer Charles Tobin told the *Post*, "That's a very dangerous road to go down."[63]

Undaunted, in December 2013, Rosen surfaced as the chief protagonist in the struggle to learn the truth about Obama's impending nuclear deal with Iran. Alone among White House correspondents, he had the effrontery to call out the administration on an obvious lie. So rare were such challenges in the Obama years that several media outposts found the challenge more newsworthy than the lie. The headline of Josh Gerstein's blow-by-blow of Rosen's battle in *Politico* read, "Fox reporter confronts State Department on Iran denial." Although reasonably straightforward in his prose, Gerstein made no attempt to address the issue of why only one reporter found the White House's mendacity troubling.

At a February 2013 press conference, Rosen asked then State Department spokesperson Victoria Nuland about reports of "direct, secret bilateral talks with Iran." Nuland answered, "With regard to the kind of thing you're talking about on a government-to-government level: no." Ten months later, on December 2, 2013, a week after the Obama administration presented the impending nuclear deal to the American people, Rosen alerted the State's new spokesperson, Jen Psaki, to reports that senior U.S. officials had, in fact, been holding meetings in Oman with Iranian officials over the previous two years. "The question today is a simple one," asked Rosen, "when the briefer was asked about those talks and flatly denied them, that was untrue, correct?"

Psaki was cornered, and Rosen was not about to let her escape. He asked her if she stood by Nuland's earlier denials of such meetings. As Psaki ducked and weaved, Rosen jabbed away at the nearly defenseless spokesperson. Was it, he asked, "the policy of the State Department to lie?" Psaki spun her response well enough to provide cover for the non-Fox media: "There are times when diplomacy needs privacy in order to progress. This is a good example of that."[64]

Major Garrett also reported on Rosen's confrontation with Psaki in the *National Journal* but with a bit more nuance than Gerstein. Rosen was right all along, Garrett admitted. The administration was lying. Wrote Garrett, "It has now been revealed that senior U.S. diplomats—Deputy Secretary of State William Burns and Jake Sullivan, Vice President Joe Biden's top foreign policy adviser—conducted at least five secret negotiations with Iranian officials in Oman's capital of Muscat."

So far, so good, but in that the Obama administration was incapable of scandal, Garrett felt obliged to explain why Rosen had to be deceived. You see, Obama's was a "useful lie," a sign he had been "playing the long game" from the get-go. Curiously, the deception seemed to increase Garrett's respect for Obama's team. "The administration can be accused of many things," he wrote, "but naiveté and gullibility cannot be among them." He even praised, with reservations, the "concision and clarity" with which the administration conceded it had been lying.

The nuance of Garrett's article is captured in its headline: "The Allure of the Useful Lie."[65] CBS News shucked all nuance and put a scandal-neutralizing spin on Garrett's reporting. All it took was a new headline. Reposting Garrett's article as written, CBS changed the headline to "The Obama administration's useful lie about Iran Talks."[66] Given that many more people read a headline than a complete article, those who browsed the CBS website would have come away thinking that Obama had done something not duplicitous, but downright clever. The inference implicit in the headline likely reflected the tone of CBS News coverage. Obama's dissembling was not the stuff of scandal. It was the stuff of statesmanship.

Among many others, Israeli Prime Minister Benjamin Netanyahu did not think the lies, or the talks for that matter, were particularly "useful" at all. "What was concluded in Geneva last night is not a historic agreement, it's a historic mistake," said Netanyahu in late November 2013. As proposed, the deal would have Iran "taking only cosmetic steps which it could reverse easily within a few weeks, and in return, sanctions that took years to put in place are going to be eased."[67] For the next two years, as the administration maneuvered to seal the deal, Obama and his aides worked to marginalize those who might agree with Netanyahu.

According to Ben Rhodes, it wasn't all that hard. In the spring of 2016, Rhodes was feeling his oats. As the wordsmith responsible for selling the Iranian nuclear deal, he felt cocky enough to welcome journalist David Samuels to the White House. He and Samuels had much in common. Both were Jewish liberal Democrats from New York City, and both were writers by profession, Samuels a very good one. Although Samuels was not at all a creature of the samizdat, the response to his Rhodes profile in the *New York Times Magazine* gave him a taste of what it was like to be one. In fact, Samuels caught more hell than anyone in the samizdat had since Andrew Breitbart died. Unlike the citizen journalist, the author of a ten-thousand-word *Times* article cannot simply be ignored.

From the left's perspective, Samuels's fatal flaw, in the words of a *Village Voice* critic, was a "creepy lack of bias."[68] Trusting Samuels's liberal credentials, Rhodes threw open all the relevant White House doors. The one that most intrigued Samuels led to what Rhodes's team called the "war room." It was here that Rhodes, by all accounts Obama's most influential foreign policy adviser, ran the "messaging campaign" that led to the successful completion of the Iran deal.

Despite a "startling" lack of real-world experience, Rhodes understood the way the media worked in the realm of foreign policy. Major newspapers used to have foreign bureaus, he said. They no longer did. "They call us to explain to them what's happening in Moscow and Cairo," he told Samuels. "The average reporter we talk to is 27 years old, and their only reporting experience consists of being around political campaigns. That's a sea change. They literally know nothing."[69]

A Rhodes assistant named Ned Price filled in the details. Among the reporters, Price explained, he and Rhodes had their favorites, their "compadres." When Price shied from naming names, the observant Samuels shared his list of likely suspects. It included several "prominent Washington reporters and columnists who often tweet in sync with White House messaging." Price laughed in agreement. "I'll give them some color," he said of the named journalists, "and the next thing I know, lots of these guys are in the dot-com publishing space, and have huge Twitter followings, and they'll be putting this message out on their own." Rhodes handed Samuels even more rope. "We created an echo chamber," he boasted, answering a question as to why so many supportive arms-control experts popped up in the media. "They were saying things that validated what we had given them to say."

What particularly troubled Samuels was that Rhodes routinely put messages into play that were either misleading or completely false. One such story was that Obama and his people began to engage with Iran only after moderates came to power in 2013. According to Samuels, that story was "largely manufactured for the purpose for selling the deal." Even after Rosen blew a hole in the story, Rhodes and Obama continued telling it.

Indifferent to the fact that conservatives knew otherwise, Obama brazenly claimed the deal followed just "two years of negotiations." Obama made this announcement in 2015. As Samuels noted, the "most meaningful part" of the negotiations began in 2012 and the preliminary negotiations a year before that. The Obama White House entered these talks well before the moderates took power, and "power" in this case was an illusion. The Ayatollah Ali Khamenei had "handpicked" these alleged moderates, who did little more than provide cover for the nuclear deal. Rhodes preferred they turned out to be reformers, but, as he admitted, "We are not betting on that." Rhodes made no bones, said Samuels, that his efforts represented "a potentially dangerous distortion of democracy."

The media storm that followed was even more furious than the one that blew through ABC News after George Stephanopoulos challenged Obama during a 2008 primary debate. Given his credentials, critics could not ignore Samuels, but they certainly could smear him. In *New York Magazine*, for instance, Eric Levitz dug deep to produce an article titled, "10 Problems With That *New York Times Magazine* Profile of White House Aide Ben Rhodes." Only ten? The problems ranged from Samuels thinking "Obama's foreign policy is apocalyptically bad" to Samuels quoting "his own knowing chuckle."[70]

Samuels published a lengthy rebuttal in the *Times*. Its editors, he noted, "looked closely at every complaint leveled against the piece and … found absolutely nothing to correct."[71] A good liberal, Samuels took particular offense at the charge that he was a "neocon," an accusation that had been "tweeted and retweeted by thousands of people." Samuels may not have noticed them before, but this time he got to see the firemen at work. They did their job much as Bradbury's firemen did, but with tweets, not flames. "The story itself has vanished," Samuels regretted, "replaced by a digital mash-up of slurs and invective." Such was the state of journalism in the age of Obama.

The Eastern Front

D id I mention I occasionally get phone calls from people wanting information? Sometime during the year 2018, investigative reporter Jerry Corsi reached out to me. This contact occurred after I knew Corsi was in Robert Mueller's crosshairs—I remember wondering whether the call was being monitored—and before Corsi was subpoenaed in early September 2018. Eager to remind samizdat journalists of their lowly status, the *New York Times* headlined its article on Corsi's legal woes, "Jerome Corsi, Conspiracy Theorist, Is Subpoenaed in Mueller Investigation."[1]

The question that Corsi posed cut right to the core of what would prove to be America's most Byzantine political conspiracy since Aaron Burr went rogue and plotted to seize Mexico. He simply asked what I knew about the murder of Seth Rich. In 2004, when Corsi and I first met online, we talked about swiftboats and John Kerry. Here we were, fourteen years later, speaking about another bit of intrigue that had the potential to shake up the presidency and rewrite history. Neither subject aroused the media. In 2004, the media's lack of interest in a major story struck me as odd. In 2018, it struck me as altogether normal.

Although I remained a minor player in the scheme of things, Corsi had become sufficiently visible to attract the conspirators' attention. I use the word "conspirators" throughout this chapter as shorthand for the forces aligned against Trump and his allies. These forces were not necessarily working together, at least not in the beginning. The report by Inspector General Michael Horowitz on FISA abuse—the "IG Report" going forward—strongly suggests that the CIA got involved months before the FBI did.[2] The DNC and the Clinton campaign also got involved before the FBI. By the summer of 2016, as Lee Smith observes in his insider 2019 book, *The Plot Against the President*, the media had signed on to the plot as well, routinely partnering "with the Clinton campaign and intelligence officials." As the election neared, the degree to which these entities worked together was unprecedented and more than a little frightening for the conspiracy's targets.

Unraveling that conspiracy, the Russian version or the Ukrainian one, is beyond the scope of this book. What I can do is show how the eight years of Obama's governance and many more years of media entropy created the conditions for a distinctly modern, media-driven coup. "The press had become a testing ground for operatives, earnest, underpaid, and dense," writes Smith. "Without its absolute commitment to the anti-Trump plot, the coup would never have stood a chance."[3]

Unlike the messy, primitive coups that rattle lesser nation states, this one was clean and bloodless. The conspirators had no need to storm the TV and radio stations when they could simply seize control of the message. The permanent bureaucracy offered no resistance. It welcomed the coup, as did the national security apparatus. To the degree there was resistance, it came from gutsy citizens in front of computer terminals, many of them unpaid, and the elected representatives who heeded them.

One of those citizens was Corsi. Had the *Times* editors been privy to the question he asked me, it would have confirmed their opinion of the man. By that final summer in the age of Obama, to investigate the otherwise inexplicable murder of a young DNC data analyst made the investigator ipso facto a "conspiracy theorist." The firemen had taken over the major newsrooms. It had reached that point.

I told Corsi I knew little more about Rich than any person who closely followed the news. The known facts of the case were largely established within hours by the local media. "A 27-year-old man who worked for the Democratic National Committee was shot and killed as he walked home early Sunday in the Bloomingdale neighborhood of Northwest Washington, D.C.," NBC Washington reported. The shooting occurred at 4:19 a.m. on Sunday, July 10, 2016. Rich was talking to a former girlfriend on the phone when shot. "There had been a struggle," said Seth's mother, Mary Rich. "His hands were bruised, his knees are bruised, his face is bruised, and yet he had two shots to his back, and yet they never took anything." She added, "They took his life for literally no reason."[4]

In the real world, most killers have a reason. Those who fire *two* shots always do. In the major newsrooms, journalists were perversely keen on not knowing what this reason was. In the years since the shooting, they have offered little useful information beyond the account above. What Rich was doing walking the streets of Washington after 4 a.m. remains as much a mystery to them as it did on July 10, 2016.

To this day, much of the plot to unseat Donald Trump remains a mystery to the media. Throughout the last year of the Obama presidency, the major media proved to be even more resistant to facts gathered beyond their sphere than they had been in the previous seven. Confident in their ignorance, and with the full backing of the White House, they gleefully enabled the mother of all messaging campaigns.

The conspirators met more resistance than they might have anticipated. The ensuing battle to control the narrative featured some new combatants. To the surprise of most observers, erstwhile progressive icon Julian Assange threw in on the side of the samizdat and the responsible right. Until this point, progressives had considered Assange one of their own. Now, they had cause to worry. "I know you're a big fan of Julian Assange—he was on our show recently. I feel like he's drifted," HBO host Bill Maher said to fellow progressive Michael Moore in the run-up to the 2016 election. "I really feel like he's lost his way a little, and he *hates* Hillary."[5]

To the even greater surprise of serious progressives, the CIA and FBI threw in on the side of the major media, the social media giants, and the firemen. As the battle progressed, renegade *Rolling Stone* reporter Matt Taibbi said out loud what should have been obvious to everyone on his side of the barricades, "Being on any team is a bad look for the press, but the press being on team FBI/CIA is an atrocity, Trump or no Trump."[6]

Working with Rep. Devin Nunes, the top Republican on the House Permanent Sub-Committee on Intelligence (HPSCI), Lee Smith provides arguably the clearest timeline of when the conspirators first targeted Trump. According to Smith, former British intelligence agent Christopher Steele started speaking with Fusion GPS's Glenn Simpson and the Justice Department's Bruce Ohr on the subject of Trump-Russia in January 2016. In October 2015, Simpson had hired Ohr's wife, Nellie Ohr, a Russian expert, to investigate, in her words, "the relationship of Donald Trump with Russian organized crime figures."[7]

As early as January 2016, certain conspirators—the IG Report suggests the CIA—appear to have activated Stefan Halper, Joseph Mifsud, and their associates in an effort to trap several Trump advisers, most notably George Papadopoulos and Carter Page, the Rosencrantz and Guildenstern of this story.[8] In April 2016, the Clinton campaign and DNC hired Fusion GPS to share its Russian dirt on Trump with the media.

Leading from behind as was his wont, Obama was never so far behind that he could not see what was to come. From time to time he showed his hand, starting with an April 2016 appearance on a Fox News Sunday morning show with Chris Wallace. When asked about Hillary Clinton's nonsecure email system, Obama opined, "She has acknowledged—that there's a carelessness, in terms of managing emails, that she…recognizes." That conceded, he added, "I continue to believe that she has not jeopardized America's national security."[9] Hillary was Obama's chosen successor. He was confident his secrets of state would be safe with her. If she were indicted for her apparent crime, the White House could easily fall into enemy hands. If FBI director James Comey and his colleagues were uncertain of Obama's will before that appearance, they no longer were.

By May, relying on Nellie Ohr's research, Fusion prepared a series of what Nunes called "protodossiers" on Trump-Russia. "It wasn't front-page material," reports Smith. "Still, the protodossiers provided journalists with some leads."[10] In that same month, May 2016, Fusion hired Steele to flesh out the protodossiers. In so doing, Steele, a self-avowed Trump hater, shifted the emphasis of the investigation. Whereas Ohr had been looking into connections between Trump's people and Russian crime lords, Steele's goal was to frame Trump as a tool of the Kremlin.[11]

The DNC made a second hire that spring. In April, the DNC learned that its computers had been hacked. Its staff alerted a DNC attorney at Perkins Coie, and he, in turn, recommended a private cyber security firm called CrowdStrike to clean up the mess. Dmitri Alperovitch, CrowdStrike co-founder and chief technology officer, identified two hacker groups, "both working for the Russian government," as the culprits.

The *Washington Post* did not report the story of the hack until June 14. The *Post* article may well have been prompted by Julian Assange's appearance on a British TV show two days earlier. On that occasion, Assange told the interviewer, "We have upcoming leaks in relation to Hillary Clinton," adding ominously, "We have emails."[12] If Assange released damaging emails, the Clinton campaign needed to establish an alternative story line to offset the pending embarrassment. No doubt it would be more politically useful to portray Hillary as a victim of a Russian plot on Trump's behalf than as a criminally negligent keeper of secrets.

There was much, however, CrowdStrike did not even pretend to know, including "how the hackers got in." This is where we circle back to Seth Rich. According to an unnamed confidante, the June 14 *Post* article disturbed him. "Oh, my God," Rich reportedly said. "We have a foreign entity trying to get involved in our elections??" As a DNC programmer, Rich had to be aware that CrowdStrike had started its audit two months before the article was published. That he was noisily lamenting the supposed Russian breach may have been a way of distancing himself from the hack.

Twelve days after Rich's death, WikiLeaks began releasing emails pilfered from the DNC. Although the firemen did their brutal best to kill the speculation that Rich had something to do with those emails, WikiLeaks maestro Assange made that task much more difficult. Interviewed on Dutch TV four weeks after the shooting, Assange said, unprompted, "Whistleblowers go to significant efforts to get us material and often very significant risks. There's a twenty-seven-year-old, works for the DNC, was shot in the back, murdered just a few weeks ago for unknown reasons as he was walking down the street in Washington."

The show host, a fireman of international stripe, tried to head off Assange's line of thought. He said, "That was just a robbery, I believe. Wasn't it?" Assange would not be reined in. Said he, accurately, "No. There's no finding." After the increasingly restive host intervened again, Assange asserted, "I'm suggesting that our sources take risks." Although Assange evaded the question of whether Rich was a source, his offer of a $20,000 reward to find Rich's killer raised the possibility that Rich was one.[13]

Among those who took the Assange interview seriously was Donna Brazile. She knew from experience how Assange could shape history, starting with her own employment history. On July 22, WikiLeaks began releasing the purloined DNC emails. These showed how the DNC stacked the Democratic primaries in Clinton's favor. The revelation embarrassed then DNC chair Debbie Wasserman Schultz into resigning, and Brazile got the job. Assange's leak of the John Podesta emails in October showed Brazile feeding CNN debate questions to Hillary Clinton and cost Brazile her job with CNN.

In her 2017 book *Hacks*, Brazile talks at some length about Assange's interview. She notes how he "dropped his smirk" when talking about the risks his sources took.[14] His body language causes Brazile to at least consider his insinuation that Rich was a source. For certain, Rich's murder obsesses Brazile. "All I could think about was Seth Rich," she acknowledges.[15] Although she repeats occasionally the ritualistic cant about hurtful conspiracy theories, she deliberately feeds those same theories. Brazile muses at one point whether Rich had been killed by "someone who had it out for Democrats" and at another whether the Russians had "played some part in his unsolved murder."[16] A third explanation Brazile suggests is that Rich "was murdered for being white on the wrong side of town."[17] She refers to Rich on a dozen different occasions and dedicates the book to him, despite barely knowing the young programmer.

I cite the Rich case to show just how thoroughly invested journalists had become in the care and nurturing of Obama's presidency. The major media steadfastly refused to investigate a case that worried DNC insiders and that, on its face, could have provided *House of Cards* with a season's worth of episodes. They refused to investigate because no likely outcome had useful political value, including Brazile's "being white" theory.

Although Brazile had reason to be concerned, her theories had little grounding. Rich was not on the wrong side of town when killed. He was in the District's Bloomingdale neighborhood where the median home price is north of a million. If he were feeding Assange, the Russians had no reason to kill him, as they were allegedly doing the same thing. If someone "had it out for Democrats," there were much fatter targets than Rich in a District that gave Trump only 4 percent of its vote.

Rich was one unlucky fellow. In the three months between June 1 and September 1, 2016, he was the only person murdered within five hundred yards of his home.[18] That he was murdered "about 300 steps from his front door" suggests someone was waiting for him. That possibility could not be entertained at the *Washington Post*. "What seems painfully obvious to his family is that Seth Rich was, instead, the victim of a botched holdup," the *Post*'s Manuel Roig-Franzia reported in a lengthy January 2017 article.[19] The fact remained, however, that the would-be robbers took nothing: not his wallet, not his phone, not his watch, not an expensive pendant that he wore. Six months after the shooting, the Metropolitan Police were refusing to answer questions on the case, to show a grainy video of his two assailants, to share Rich's comments in the hour or so he lived after the shooting, or to explain why it took nearly three hours for him to walk the thirty or so minutes from a local bar to his home.

The police attributed their silence to fear of compromising "an ongoing investigation." *Post* editors had no more excuse for failing to probe what Roig-Franzia called the "curiosities" of this case than they did the "curiosity" of Obama's Connecticut Social Security number. After eight years of accommodating the White House, they preferred to warn about "dark theories" in an "era of reckless information" than to assign reporters to seek the truth.

In time, the June 14 article that triggered Rich would seem like a curious artifact of a distant past. The *Post*'s Ellen Nakashima pictured Trump not as a participant in the plot, but as a target. The headline boldly stated the thesis: "Russian government hackers penetrated DNC, stole opposition research on Trump." According to Nakashima, the hackers also accessed Trump's political network, as well as that of several Republican PACs.

Rich was murdered four weeks after the *Post* article was published. In those intervening weeks, the narrative started to shift from Trump as possible victim of the hack to Trump as probable villain. The plot was in gear. On June 20, Steele introduced the first of the memos that would comprise the Steele dossier. In late June, a British counterpart allegedly tipped off CIA chief John Brennan that something was rotten at Trump Tower. On July 5, the FBI met secretly with Steele in London. On that very same day, Comey cleared Hillary Clinton of criminal charges.

The task had fallen to the now notorious Peter Strzok, the FBI's lead investigator on the Clinton email case—code name "Midyear Exam"—to align the FBI's messaging with that of the White House. It was he who changed the language in an earlier draft by Comey from "gross negligence"—the exact words in the Espionage Act—to "extremely careless," the words Obama introduced and Comey eventually used. In her testimony before the HPSCI, Strzok's FBI lover, Lisa Page, acknowledged that the directive had come from Obama's DOJ not to charge Hillary with a crime.[20] With Clinton now the certain nominee, the pressure increased to protect her candidacy and Obama's legacy.

Five days after Comey cleared Hillary, Rich was murdered. If he were supplying WikiLeaks with data as Assange suggested, or even if he knew who did, Rich had the potential to subvert the increasingly important Russian collusion theory. The *Times* later implied as much, describing Assange's implication of Rich as "an alternative narrative to the cascade of damaging revelations about the Trump administration's ties to Russian officials who meddled in the presidential election." Michael Grynbaum and Daniel Victor wrote the above in May 2017 when false collusion reports were cascading from newsrooms like water over Niagara.

Nearly a year after the murder, the *Times* reporters were content to write, "The Washington Metropolitan Police Department is still investigating the death of Mr. Rich." So locked into their own conspiracy theory were the major media that they demonized any investigator who dared propose "an alternative narrative." A "botched robbery" was all the explanation journalists needed or wanted.[21]

As the summer of 2016 progressed, Steele shared his research about Donald Trump memo by memo not just with the FBI, but with the DOJ, the State Department, and select media. The cumulative tale the Steele memos told was that Donald Trump had been compromised by the Russian government and was colluding with it to steal the upcoming election. The CIA's John Brennan got the word. According to a March

2018 HPSCI report, Brennan had become aware of "specific Russian efforts to influence the election" by that summer. It was he who "pulled together experts" from the CIA, NSA, and FBI "to focus on the issue."[22]

Strzok would head up the FBI surveillance of the Trump campaign—code name, "Crossfire Hurricane." He was excited. On July 31, the day the counterintelligence operation was formally launched, he texted Page, "Damn this feels momentous. Because this matters. The other one did, too, but that was to ensure that we didn't F something up. This matters because this MATTERS."[23] The "other one" was the investigation into Hillary's emails. For the previous few months, he and Page had been sharing their affection for each other and their loathing of Trump. Now, they could do something about it. "You're meant to protect the country from that menace," Page texted on August 5, the "menace" being Trump. "I'll try to approach it that way," the heroic Strzok responded. "I can protect our country at many levels."[24]

In June 2017, the *Washington Post* published a lengthy, breathless article detailing an early August 2016 meeting in the White House. It should be noted that the article was written to provide cover for the Obama administration's seemingly lackadaisical response to what the media imagined as the greatest provocation from Moscow since the Cuban missile crisis. According to the *Post*, the CIA's Brennan had sent an "intelligence bombshell" directly to Obama, an "eyes only" report with sourcing deep inside the Kremlin.

This report had to be some subset of Steele's memos. It allegedly detailed "Russian President Vladimir Putin's direct involvement in a cyber campaign to disrupt and discredit the U.S. presidential race." Reportedly, Putin was not just meddling in the campaign but was actively trying to defeat Hillary and elect Trump. "It took time," said the *Post*, "for other parts of the intelligence community to endorse the CIA's view."

The IG Report lacked the clarity of the *Post* article, in part because Comey and McCabe, when questioned, were both evasive about this meeting. Comey told the Office of the Inspector General (OIG) he thought it important that "the President know the nature of the FBI's efforts," but insisted he did not provide "any specifics." Well, hardly any specifics: Comey did implicate four individuals with, in his own words, "some association or connection to the Trump campaign." Comey also acknowledged that Brennan, Director of National Intelligence James Clapper, and National Security Advisor Susan Rice were in attendance as well as Obama.[25] In short, Obama knew by early August 2016 that the FBI was investigating the Trump campaign's likely involvement in the collusion plot.

In June 2017, when the *Post* article was published, its editors were still confident that "Russia's interference was the crime of the century." It was no such thing, but in documenting the White House's multilevel response to the alleged threat, the *Post* sheds unwitting light on what was the crime of the century, the White House's framing of Donald Trump for collusion with Russia.[26]

Although Strzok told the OIG "he never attended any White House briefings about Crossfire Hurricane,"[27] he certainly gave Page the impression he attended that August 2016 meeting in the White House. Later in the day on August 5, texting with Page, he quoted an unnamed bigwig, likely Brennan, as saying, "The White House is running this."[28] Curiously, the IG Report does not mention this text.

Strzok claimed to have pushed back not because of any perceived impropriety but because the White House was intruding on FBI turf. On August 15, Strzok memorably signaled the shared motive of all the conspirators. "There's no way [Trump] gets elected—but I'm afraid we can't take that risk," he texted Page. "It's like an insurance policy in the unlikely event you die before you're 40."[29]

It seems highly unlikely that Ben Rhodes designed the Russian collusion campaign or that President Barack Obama orchestrated it. Obama orchestrated almost nothing during his eight years in the White House. He fronted for stuff. That was his MO. His near immunity from criticism encouraged the conspirators to think they could take out the Republican nominee, if need be even the newly elected president of the United States, and get away with it.

Yet, there remain those damnable texts between Page and Strzok. "POTUS wants to know everything we're doing," texted Page on September 2. She was preparing talking points for then FBI Director James Comey because Obama apparently wanted to be kept abreast of the investigation.[30] When questioned by the OIG, however, Strzok insisted Obama wanted to "know everything" only about Russian interference in the campaign, not about Crossfire Hurricane.[31] Just a month earlier, as noted, Comey told Obama the FBI was investigating four individuals associated with Trump. Obama surely wanted to know "everything." Strzok here cannot be taken at his word. He was covering for Obama.

From the beginning of 2016, the conspirators had been feeding the media inside dope, some of it fictional, some of it classified. In February of that year, for instance, Mark Hosenball and Steve Holland launched the disinformation campaign against Lt. Gen. Michael Flynn in a Reuters article teasingly titled, "Trump being advised by ex-U.S. Lieutenant General who favors closer Russia ties."[32]

In September 2016, Michael Isikoff wrote a lengthy breakout article for Yahoo News based on a briefing by "multiple sources," the most notable of whom, unnamed in the article, was Steele. As Isikoff reported, intelligence officials were investigating Trump adviser Carter Page's "private communications with senior Russian officials." He reported too that Senate majority leader Harry Reid had briefed the FBI director James Comey on the "significant and disturbing ties" between the Trump campaign and the Kremlin, information Reid could only have gotten from the dossier. The word was spreading.[33]

A few weeks after its publication, the DOJ and the FBI packaged the Isikoff article in their application to the Foreign Intelligence Surveillance Court (FISC), specifically to monitor Carter Page. As the IG Report made painfully clear, despite years of denial by various parties, the FBI relied heavily upon the Steele dossier to get FISA authorization on Page. The FBI then submitted the Isikoff article as independent evidence full well knowing it was simply reheated Steele material. Upon learning how he was used, Isikoff admitted finding it "a little odd" that his article would be included in the FISA application given that Steele shared that same information with the Bureau before he shared it with Isikoff.[34]

I cite Isikoff and Hosenball for a reason. They had been carrying water for the intelligence community (IC) for at least twenty years. In 2003, I met the pair at the *Newsweek* offices where they both then worked. At the time, I was promoting *First Strike*, a book I co-authored on TWA Flight

800, the 747 that exploded off the coast of Long Island on July 17, 1996. In that pivotal election year, surely with a nod from the Clinton White House, the CIA quietly masterminded the disinformation campaign that followed TWA 800's destruction. As would happen again in 2016, the FBI publicly fronted for it. With a Democrat in the White House who needed re-electing, the media played along.

As I wrote in my 2016 book, *TWA 800: The Crash, The Cover-Up, The Conspiracy,* "Had Hosenball been on the CIA payroll he could not have done more to legitimize the agency's crude rewrite of history." When I met with the pair in 2003, Hosenball blew me off, and Isikoff asked which three pages of the book he should read. "Given that this is the great untold story of our time," I answered, "how about a chapter?" Isikoff repeated coldly, "Which three pages?"[35]

In 1996, the conspirators had to woo an unreliable media, but by 2016, after eight or so years of swooning over Obama, no courtship was necessary. "The Russiagate era has so degraded journalism," writes Taibbi in his book *Hate Inc.*, "that even once 'reputable' outlets are now only about as right as politicians, which is to say barely ever, and then only by accident."[36]

No mainstream journalist, no matter how august, seemed immune to the conspiratorial web being spun out of the White House. On August 3, 2016, *New Yorker* editor David Remnick weighed in with a catty piece in his own publication titled, "Trump and Putin: A Love Story." The same writer who could not find an unkind word to say about Stalinist pornographer Frank Marshall Davis spoke of Vladimir Putin and Donald Trump as the fraternal spawn of Satan. The same writer who consigned me to the "web's farthest lunatic orbit" for daring to suggest Bill Ayers and Barack Obama were literary collaborators, grasped at just about every conspiratorial chimera in his orbit to imagine Trump and Putin as soul mates.

"Trump sees strength and cynicism in Putin and hopes to emulate him. Putin sees in Trump a grand opportunity. He sees in Trump weakness and ignorance, a confused mind. He has every hope of exploiting him."[37] Curiously, Remnick, an Obama biographer, makes no comment at all about the relationship between Obama and Putin. This was a necessary omission. For the Trump-Russia campaign to succeed, the conspirators needed editors of Remnick's stature to erase the memory of the previous eight years. There was much to erase, starting with the fact that the Obama White House began sucking up to Russia immediately after the January 2009 inauguration.

Speaking at a February 2009 security conference in Munich, Vice President Joe Biden signaled Obama's eagerness to undo President Bush's hard line on missile defense and other issues. He told the audience, "It is time to press the reset button and to revisit the many areas where we can and should be working together with Russia."[38] A month later, Secretary of State Hillary Clinton met with the Russian foreign minister in Geneva and presented him with a red plastic "reset" button. Unfortunately, whoever was responsible for finding the Russian word for "reset" used the Russian word for "overcharged" instead. Much awkwardness ensued, but the meeting otherwise went swimmingly.[39]

Two years after proposing the reset button, Biden made an extraordinary speech at Moscow State University. There he listed the many new areas of cooperation between Russia and the United States and cited with pride the fruits of that relationship. Just two years prior, only 17 percent of Russians held a positive view of the United States, said Biden. By the time of his speech in March 2011, that figure had increased to 60 percent.[40] Russians had good cause to favor team Obama. As Andy McCarthy observes in his 2019 book, *Ball of Collusion*, Obama and company had spent the previous two years "improving our declining but dangerous rival's military and cyber capabilities and fortifying its capacity to extort the European nations and former Soviet republics that rely on Russia for their power needs."[41]

During his 2011 speech, Biden boasted of visiting a high-tech hub on the outskirts of Moscow called "Skolkovo." Biden thought Skolkovo held the potential to become Russia's Silicon Valley. With a proven talent for taking care of those close to him, a talent he would hone in the Ukraine, Biden encouraged American venture capitalists to invest there. Among the Russian investors who got involved in Skolkovo was oligarch Viktor Vekselberg, a donor to the Clinton Foundation. Several American donors to the foundation invested as well. Hillary's State Department greased the skids.

Even apolitical observers were troubled by an exchange of capital and information that recalled the woolly pay-for-play days of the Clinton presidency. EUCOM, the American military's leading intelligence think tank in Europe, called American involvement in Skolkovo "an overt alternative to clandestine industrial espionage—with the additional distinction that it can achieve such a transfer on a much larger scale and more efficiently."[42]

Always on the prowl for a quick buck, Bill Clinton secured State's permission to meet with Skolkovo honcho Vekselberg. Clinton happened to be in Russia at the time to give his infamous $500,000 speech, paid for by a Russian investment bank with ties to the Kremlin. On that same trip, Clinton met with senior Rosatom official Arkady Dvorkovich. The media scarcely noticed.

Rosatom was the entity that controlled all things nuclear in Russia, including the arsenal. Rosatom also built the controversial Bushehr reactor in Iran and supplied it with uranium. The unfussy Rosatom executives also counted among their clients North Korea, Venezuela, and Myanmar. At the time, Rosatom was seeking the State Department's permission to buy Uranium One, a Canadian company with vast U.S. uranium reserves.

This deal raised eyebrows even at the *New York Times*. As Jo Becker and Mike McIntire reported in April 2015, too late to make a difference, the Russians took control of Uranium One in three discrete transactions from 2009 to 2013, during which time "a flow of cash made its way to the Clinton Foundation." The Chairman of Uranium One alone donated $2.35 million. For Russian President Vladimir Putin, securing Uranium One was like finding a pony under his tree on Christmas morning. As Rosatom CEO Sergei Kiriyenko told Putin in a staged interview, "Few could have imagined in the past that we would own 20 percent of U.S. reserves."[43]

In an unusual grace note, the *Times* reporters credited Peter Schweizer, a star of the samizdat, with providing the research material on which they built their story; this despite Schweizer's association with the "right-leaning Hoover Institution." In his books, *Clinton Cash*, *Secret Empires*, and *Profiles in Corruption*, Schweizer does a heroic job documenting the labyrinthine transactions facilitated by Obama's State Department. If Becker and McIntire, like most mainstream reporters, more or less absolved Obama of Hillary Clinton's failings as secretary of state, Schweizer does not. As he observes, the Clinton camp signed a memorandum of understanding with the White House imposing certain restrictions on foreign donations to the foundation and speaking fees to the former president, but no one paid it much mind. Writes Schweizer, "The claimed commitment to transparency was fleeting."[44] At an opportune moment in the not too distant past, the reader may recall, Obama even claimed ownership of Hillary's credits and debts. "She works for me," he proudly said of Hillary during the 2012 Town Hall debate with Romney. "I'm the president, and I'm always responsible."

Obama was just as careless about potential corrupt dealings with Ukraine as he was about those with Russia. Although not overtly involved in Trump's botched impeachment, Obama's indifference to the scheming of Biden father and son in Ukrainian intrigue set in motion all that followed. "We do know that questions were raised about the Ukraine deal with Burisma almost immediately," said Schweizer after Hunter Biden's wildly overpaid gig with the Ukrainian gas company became a political issue. "But apparently, he was allowed to continue to do it." Schweizer believes that Obama and other relevant parties were well aware of the undisguised exploitation of Biden's office. What he does not understand is why someone did not tell the Bidens just how bad it looked.[45]

If Ukraine was still on the back burners in 2012, Russia was front and center. During the campaign Obama put his own stamp of approval on the felicitous state of U.S.-Russia affairs. In March 2012, Obama met with outgoing Russian President Dmitry Medvedev in Seoul, South Korea. A live microphone picked up a conversation between the two men that was supposed to be private. "On all these issues, but particularly missile defense, this can be solved, but it's important for him to give me space," said Obama, the "him" being incoming president Putin. Obama continued, "This is my last election. After my election I have more flexibility." Replied Medvedev, "I understand. I will transmit this information to Vladimir."[46]

Obama did his Russia-friendly flexing center stage during his final debate with Mitt Romney in 2012. Earlier in that year, Romney had called out Obama for his overture to Putin. "This is without question our No. 1 geopolitical foe," said Romney. "They fight for every cause for the world's worst actors. The idea that he has more flexibility in mind for Russia is very, very troubling indeed."

During the debate, Obama countered with a scripted zinger: "The 1980s are now calling to ask for their foreign policy back because the Cold War's been over for twenty years." He then added, "When it comes to our foreign policy, you seem to want to import the foreign policies of the 1980s, just like the social policies of the 1950s, and the economic policies of the 1920s." As *Washington Post* fact checker Glenn Kessler noted, the jab "spawned approving headlines."[47] The media laughed off the Russian threat along with Obama. Unremarked by Kessler was Obama's sly coupling of Romney's Russia anxiety with his fondness for the presumably racist "social policies of the 1950s." This is the way Obama and his people rolled.

Vladimir Putin served as prime minister during Obama's first term and was elected president eight months before Obama humbled Romney on national TV. Obama had a productive relationship with Russia during those first four years and expected more of the same, especially with his newfound flexibility. As should have been expected, the newly re-elected Putin read Obama's flexibility for the weakness it was. Russia annexed the Crimea, refused to accept international inspection of its nuclear sites, and gave rogue NSA contractor Edward Snowden safe harbor. Putin even showed up forty-five minutes late for his first meeting with Obama post-reelection, an offense memorialized by a huffy Ben Rhodes in his book, *The World As It Is*.[48] That said, as late as March 2014, Obama was dismissing Russia as a "regional power" and no real threat to world order.[49]

In July 2015, whatever tensions existed between the White House and the Kremlin eased considerably when Obama called Putin thanking him for his help securing the Iran nuclear pact. Obama had reason to be grateful. No foreign leader had more influence over the mullahs than Putin. As Obama told Tom Friedman of the *New York Times*, "We would have not achieved this agreement had it not been for Russia's willingness to stick with us and the other P5-Plus members in insisting on a strong deal."[50]

In July 2015, it was still respectable for an American president to collaborate with Putin. Putin's darker deeds seemed largely behind him. These included not only his annexation of Crimea but also a string of suspected political assassinations. Among the more prominent victims was whistleblower lawyer Sergei Magnitsky. Magnitsky died in police custody in November 2009, the same year as the "reset." In his honor, Congress passed a human rights law in 2012 just weeks after Obama ridiculed Romney's concern about Russia.

Also murdered was dissident Boris Nemtsov. In echoes of the Seth Rich case, an unknown assailant shot Nemtsov in the back in *his* nation's capital. The shooting took place in February 2015, just months before Putin helped Obama seal the Iran deal. With the deal pending, Obama made sure not to mention Putin in his official communiqué on the Nemtsov assassination. Rather, he called upon "the Russian government to conduct a prompt, impartial, and transparent investigation," an inquiry that was denied Seth Rich.[51] In Moscow, unlike in Washington, the media felt free to probe the rationale for the shooting. The speculation did not include as possible motive "botched robbery."[52]

In 2015, no one would have predicted that within a year Russia would emerge as a monstrously subversive country hell-bent on throwing the 2016 election to Donald Trump. No one would have predicted this scenario because it defied common sense. "Putin's Russia got what it paid for," observed author Diana West, "from those infamous U.S. uranium stocks, to Obama's 'flexibility,' to hypersonic missile engine technology to WTO membership and more."[53] Russia had a proven pawn in Obama and a friend in Hillary. It did not need an unpredictable Donald Trump. "Putin has eaten Obama's lunch, therefore our lunch, for a long period of time," said Trump in 2014 while slamming Obama's failure to stand up to Putin in Crimea.[54] Russia was never a real concern of Obama's, but to frame Trump, the White House had to frame Russia too.

In his memoir, Obama adviser Ben Rhodes attempts to explain the apparent chill between Putin and Obama, but Rhodes was writing after the Russian collusion narrative had become set, if not in stone, at least in type, thousands of times over. Rhodes had a hand in creating that narrative and shows it in the book when, remarkably, he fails to give Putin any credit for his essential role in Obama's signature foreign policy achievement, the Iran deal. His account of the Obama-Putin relationship strikes the reader as still more messaging for the "know nothing" crowd, this time after the fact.

"In Obama's view," writes Rhodes, "Putin was a white man standing up for a politics rooted in patriarchy, tribe, and religion, the antiglobalist."[55] For all of Putin's nationalist posturing, to cast the drama as racial is as perverse as it is predictable. No, what seems clear in retrospect is that Obama and his allies projected Trump's personality onto Putin and pushed the "Putin as evil conspirator" message as shamelessly as they pushed "if you like your health care plan," "the video caused Benghazi," and "we waited until Iran elected moderates."

Until they could attach Trump's name to tales of Russian espionage, the media largely ignored Russian intrigue. Reportedly, there had been an ongoing FBI investigation into Russia's cyber-espionage dating back to 2014, but no one much cared.[56] As the HPSCI reported, "Russia's interference in the 2016 election was nothing novel for the Kremlin."[57] Russia had been messing with American politics since its manipulation of the Sacco-Vanzetti case in the 1920s.

Historically, however, the Kremlin intervened to bolster progressive causes and/or cause chaos. From Stalin on, Russian leaders had no illusions about being able to elect American lawmakers, let alone the president. America, they knew, was no Estonia. As McCarthy writes of Putin, "His realistic hope for us is destabilization: raising hot-button issues, exploiting racial divisions and economic anxieties, inciting tensions between rivals but not necessarily picking one over the other."[58]

If inciting tension was part of Putin's game plan, he was about to see his hopes realized. On November 8, 2016, the Lilliputians of the samizdat and a few loyal allies in the larger conservative media shocked the world. They showed that when the moment was right, they had as much power to effect outcomes as did the political, media, tech, and academic elites combined.

If Hillary won the election, as expected, peace would have returned to the land, maybe not to the hinterland, but certainly to the places where it mattered—Washington, New York, Hollywood, Silicon Valley. But Trump won. Post-election, the Trump-Russia business would no longer be background noise. Shocked and understandably frightened by their loss of the White House, the conspirators turned up the volume. For the next three years, even Putin's laughter would scarcely be heard above the din. For the conspirators, it was time to cash in on that "insurance policy."

In his 2018 memoir, Rhodes offered a sneak preview of President Obama's final messaging campaign. Rhodes, it should be noted, was no Page or Papadopoulos. According to the two dozen insiders David Samuels spoke to for his controversial piece in the *New York Times*, Rhodes was the "single most influential voice shaping American foreign policy aside from Potus himself." Rhodes borrowed the Star Trek phrase "mind meld" to describe how closely he and Obama were aligned on foreign policy issues, none more important down the home stretch than Russia's meddling in the American election.[59] Writing of a time a week or two before Election Day 2016, Rhodes makes a claim so deep in exculpatory BS it needs to be read in full:

> Of course, we had no idea—Obama had no idea—at the time that there was an FBI investigation into the Trump campaign's contacts with Russia; that information was walled off from the White House, and I wouldn't even learn about it until long after I left government, in the press.[60]

This was an extraordinary claim, one that Andy McCarthy, among others, has proved to be hogwash. "The Obama White House had been involved in the Trump-Russia investigation from the first," writes McCarthy. "That is not a dig. That is the way it is supposed to be.

Trump-Russia was a counterintelligence investigation, and such investigations are done for the president."[61]

Obama found just the right people to move the investigation forward. From the beginning, as we've seen, Obama affiliated with communists and fellow travelers: his Hawaiian mentor Frank Marshall Davis, his Marxist pals at Occidental, the small "c" communist Bill Ayers, the openly socialist New Party and ACORN. In 1983, he wrote his first published essay. It just happened to be in support of the KGB-initiated anti-nuke movement sweeping the western world, Christopher Steele's Cambridge included.

Once elected president, Obama surrounded himself with kindred spirits. In nominating John Brennan first as deputy national security advisor and later as director of the CIA, Obama picked the rare American intel chief openly fond of Marxism. From the beginning, Brennan served as Obama's fixer. He came to the job well prepared, having written in his graduate thesis, "The democratic process may involve, at some point, the violation of personal liberties and procedural justice."[62] Only mainstream journalists could believe Brennan had nothing to do with his employee's breach of Obama's passport files in 2008. As Sharyl Attkisson has documented, his fingerprints were all over Fast and Furious and possibly her own harassment as well.

Brennan met at least one potential fellow traveler in Obama's inner intelligence circle. In 2013, the same year Brennan was named director of the CIA, Obama chose the seemingly apolitical James Comey to head the FBI. Like Brennan, however, Comey had a past. In 2003, he acknowledged his leftist roots in a *New York* magazine interview, telling reporter Chris Smith, "I'd moved from Communist to whatever I am now." Despite an impending appointment by George W. Bush to serve as deputy attorney general, Comey used the Smith interview to signal his independence: "I'm not even sure how to characterize myself politically. Maybe at some point, I'll have to figure it out."[63] As with Brennan, much would depend on the situation. In his graduate thesis, Comey wrote, "The Christian in politics must be willing to transgress any purely Christian ethic. He must be willing to sin in the name of justice."[64]

Contemporaries remember "Chris" Steele as an "avowedly Left-wing student with CND credentials."[65] CND is shorthand for "Campaign for Nuclear Disarmament," a British organization that was particularly active when Steele arrived at Cambridge in the early 1980s. Obama, meanwhile, was applauding the same KGB agitprop at Columbia. "Millions of people were infected by this madness," writes Vladimir Bukovsky. "They will hardly wish to dig out the archives that contain the indisputable proof of their folly."[66]

MI5 monitored CND for its reported communist ties, but not closely enough. In the unfortunate Cambridge tradition—Kim Philby, Guy Burgess, John Cairncross, and the like—Steele joined MI6 upon graduation. He spent at least three years in Russia and worked the Russian desk in London for three more years. History will remember Steele for attaching his name to a massive disinformation campaign that sowed disorder in the western world. One has to wonder in whose interest he was really working.

One other conspirator with a strong Russian background deserves attention. At the time the dossier was being compiled, Nellie Ohr worked as Russian expert for Fusion GPS. Married to a high-ranking DOJ official and associated with the CIA, Nellie was as wired into the nation's intelligence networks as anyone in Washington. Meanwhile, her husband, Bruce Ohr, served as unofficial DOJ contact with Steele. In fact, Ohr introduced Steele to the FBI in 2010 and "provided the FBI with all of his wife's opposition research."[67] It doesn't get much cozier than that. Even after the FBI severed its relationship with Steele in late 2016, Bruce Ohr met with Steele an additional thirteen times.[68]

Before she got into the conspiracy business, Nellie Ohr was a scholar with a specialty in Russian history and literature. In 1990, Ohr completed her PhD dissertation at Stanford, titled, "Collective farms and Russian peasant society, 1933-1937: The stabilization of the kolkhoz order."[69] In her dissertation, Ohr tried to find the silver lining in a terror-famine that left as many as six million dead. Like many "revisionist" historians, she had an ill-concealed soft spot for Josef Stalin.

In her provocative book, *The Red Thread*, Diana West makes a lively case that the coming together of such unrepentant fans and friends of the

Soviet Union was more than mere coincidence. Like Van Jones or Bill Ayers, these were Obama's kind of people. Given the company he kept, it made sense that a progressive president would support a Russian regime that refused to apologize for its Soviet past and was manned by many of the same Soviet apparatchiks. "From earliest days," writes West, "the 'new' Russian government served to protect the 'old' Soviet government. Which suggests there is more than a thread of continuity between the two."[70] As Putin is fond of saying, "There is no such thing as a former K.G.B. man."[71] As Obama might say if he were more honest, "There is no such thing as a former Marxist." As history reminds us, Marxists have always depended on the KGB or something like it to enforce their will.

A globalist and a cradle progressive, National Security Advisor Susan Rice shared with Brennan and Comey a penchant for situational ethics. At an interagency teleconference in April 1994, Rice, then a "rising star" on President Clinton's National Security Council, offered her own take on the proper response to the ongoing genocide in Rwanda. "If we use the word 'genocide' and are seen as doing nothing," she asked rhetorically, "what will be the effect on the November [congressional] election?" She stunned those who heard her, not by thinking what she said, but by saying it out loud. Rice would later claim she did not recall the incident.[72]

Like her boss, Susan Rice also had a gift for being surprised by information she already knew. In the waning days of the Obama administration, Rice "unmasked" the identities of several incoming Trump officials. She would not have done something this provocative without Obama's approval. When the controversy first surfaced in April 2017, Rice played dumb. PBS's Judy Woodruff asked Rice whether it was true that President Trump and the people around him "may have been caught up in surveillance of foreign individuals in that their identities may have been disclosed." Said Rice, "I know nothing about this. I was surprised to see reports from Chairman [Devin] Nunes on that count today."[73] It was not until her September 2017 appearance before a House subcommittee that Rice admitted that, yes, she had unmasked those individuals.

On the unmasking front, Rice was a piker compared to Obama's Ambassador to the United Nations, Samantha Power. In September 2017, Fox News reported that in the final months of Obama's tenure, the London-born Power unmasked individuals, many of them affiliated with Trump, at the rate of several a day. During a House Oversight Committee hearing, Power tried the Anthony Weiner gambit. Yes, she admitted, there was exposure going on, but someone else was doing it under her name.[74] Speaking of unmasking, it was Power who, as a young reporter for the *Atlantic*, busted Rice for her cold-blooded quote on the Rwanda dead and dying. Small world.

Thanks to another Rice misjudgment, we know about an unusual meeting that took place in the White House on January 5, 2017. In conference with Obama was his national security team including all the usual suspects: Comey, Brennan, Biden, Rice, James Clapper, and acting attorney general Sally Yates. Following the meeting, Obama asked Yates and Comey to stick around along with Rice, his trusted scribe and factotum. Obama had a reason for singling out Comey and Yates. Unlike the others, they were staying on in their jobs. On the very day at the very moment Trump was being inaugurated, Rice sent to "self" a peculiar email. It read:

> President Obama began the conversation by stressing his continued commitment to ensuring that every aspect of this issue is handled by the Intelligence and law enforcement communities "by the book." The President stressed that he is not asking about, initiating or instructing anything from a law enforcement perspective. He reiterated that our law enforcement team needs to proceed as it normally would by the book.

In September 2012, Rice marked herself as a paid shill with her quintuple "the video caused it" deceptions on the Sunday shows following the Benghazi fiasco. What credibility she had to spare she squandered with this comically disingenuous email. Like Rhodes, Rice was trying to absolve Obama of signing off on the coup. Unfortunately for Obama, she proved to be just as clumsy and obvious as on the fateful Sunday shows. Senators Charles Grassley and Lindsey Graham saw right through the smokescreen. "Despite your claim that President Obama repeatedly told Mr. Comey to proceed 'by the book,'" the good senators responded to Rice upon discovering the email, "substantial questions have arisen about whether officials at the FBI, as well as at the Justice Department and the State Department, actually did proceed 'by the book.'"[75]

There is no "book" that justifies what Comey and pals did in the weeks immediately following this meeting while Obama was still president. The next day, January 6, 2017, the conspirators released the declassified version of the Intelligence Community Assessment (ICA). Commissioned a month earlier by Obama, the ICA was John Brennan's way of welcoming the president-elect to Washington. Titled "Assessing Russian Activities and Intentions in Recent US Elections," the report concluded that Putin "ordered" an influence campaign, the goal of which was "to undermine public faith in the US democratic process, denigrate Secretary Clinton, and harm her electability and potential presidency." The corollary of this, of course, was that "Putin and the Russian Government developed a clear preference for President-elect Trump." Interestingly, although the FBI and CIA had "high confidence" in this judgment, the National Security Agency (NSA), headed by Adm. Mike Rogers, had only "moderate confidence," a demurral that passed without explanation.[76]

The "Obama dossier," as Nunes called the ICA, reads like one of my college term papers, filled with sundry bits of information gathered from here and there just hours before the due date. Although Comey lobbied to have the Steele dossier included in the body of the text, wiser heads prevailed, and it was relegated to the appendices.[77]

Among the ICA's more obvious shortcomings is its failure to provide a credible rationale for Putin to disfavor Hillary Clinton so vehemently. According to the ICA, Putin "publicly blamed her since 2011 for inciting mass protests against his regime" and "holds a grudge for comments he almost certainly saw as disparaging him." The ICA does not mention Hillary's more than compensatory assets, an oversight that is at the heart of the larger disinformation campaign.

Many of the report's assertions were made with evidence no more convincing than that which tied Putin to Trump, including some in bold face such as "Putin Ordered Campaign To Influence US Election" or the

"Influence Effort Was Boldest Yet in the US." Lacking human intelligence in the Kremlin, the report writers had no idea what Putin did or did not order. They conceded that, beginning in June 2016, Putin ceased "directly praising President-elect Trump" for the probable reason that "any praise from Putin personally would backfire in the United States." Unaddressed is why Putin showed such discretion in this regard and yet authorized a "multi-faceted" campaign so maladroit that it damaged Trump's campaign and almost destroyed his presidency.

As the report writers admitted, Russian influence campaigns were "designed to be deniable" and "false-flag operations" were a staple in their bag of tricks. Given this history, author Diana West has asked the logical question, namely whether "the Putin-wants-Trump line" might have been "a classic Moscow influence operation, another iteration of 'fake newski' to manipulate the ignorant West."[78]

Much of the ICA bordered on irrelevance. If Russia's primary television network, RT, favored Trump, it surely had less influence than the BBC or the scores of other networks, foreign and domestic, that favored Hillary. The various trolls and bots on social media, if actually Russian in origin, had even less influence. These desultory strands of information mostly just took up space in the assessment, much more space than the one "facet" of Putin's influence campaign that actually merited the interest of the intelligence community, the cyber operations.

"In July 2015," reported the ICA, "Russian intelligence gained access to Democratic National Committee (DNC) networks and maintained that access until at least June 2016." The report writers claimed that the GRU, the intelligence arm of the Russian military, hacked data "from the DNC and senior Democratic officials" and relayed it to WikiLeaks for publication. Despite the protestations of various Democrats to the contrary—sorry, Ms. Brazile—the WikiLeaks dumps did not contain "any evident forgeries."

The evidence for the hacking claim was much sketchier than the public has been led to believe. One reason the report spent so much pointless time on RT's programming and Julian Assange's past was to compensate for the absence of real proof. "An assessment of attribution usually is not a simple statement of who conducted an operation," the

ICA insisted, "but rather a series of judgments that describe whether it was an isolated incident, who was the likely perpetrator, that perpetrator's possible motivations, and whether a foreign government had a role in ordering or leading the operation." This was a long-winded way of saying there was no DNA, and the cyber fingerprints left behind could just as easily have been false-flagged. It raises the question, too, of who was making the "judgments." John Brennan? Peter Strzok? James Comey? Mueller would indict a dozen Russians for interference only because he knew they would never show up in court. The evidence was not there to convict them. He declined, however, to indict Assange. Assange would have shown up.

Undermining the whole study was one extraordinary failure by the FBI: the Bureau did not examine the servers the Russians allegedly hacked. The ICA concealed this fact, but the truth came to light in a public feud between the DNC and the FBI. "*The FBI never requested access to the DNC's computer servers*," Eric Walker, the DNC's deputy communications director, emphatically told *BuzzFeed* in an email two days before the ICA was released.[79] The FBI insisted otherwise. A day later, a senior FBI official fired back, "The FBI repeatedly stressed to DNC officials the necessity of obtaining direct access to servers and data, only to be rebuffed until well after the initial compromise had been mitigated."[80] If DNC staffers repeatedly "rebuffed" the FBI, they may well have had something to hide, starting with the opposition research done on Donald Trump. This was a dispute that needed airing, but the drive-by media just drove by. They had a conspiracy to peddle.

Having rejected the FBI's offer to examine its servers, the DNC contracted, as mentioned earlier, with the private cybersecurity firm CrowdStrike. "CrowdStrike is pretty good. There's no reason to believe that anything that they have concluded is not accurate," an intelligence official told *BuzzFeed*.[81] On an investigation of this magnitude, "pretty good" does not inspire confidence. Nor does "pretty good" have anything to do with "non-partisan," something CrowdStrike certainly was not.

"CrowdStrike is a deeply Democratic firm," observes McCarthy.[82] The same law firm that served as a cutout on the Steele dossier, Perkins Coie, recommended CrowdStrike to the DNC. In April 2016, just before CrowdStrike started its research, Obama appointed the company's legal counsel, Steven Chabinsky, to a White House commission on cyber security. One of its two co-founders, the Russian-born Dmitri Alperovitch, is a senior fellow at the globalist Atlantic Council, many of whose members served in the Obama administration. More worrisome still, the firm's primary investor, Eric Schmidt of Google fame, showed up in one of Podesta's hacked emails. "I met with Eric Schmidt tonight," wrote Podesta in 2014 to Robby Mook, the man who would manage Hillary's 2016 campaign. "He's ready to fund, advise, recruit talent, etc... Clearly wants to be head outside advisor."[83]

Scandalous in its own right was the willingness of the Obama DOJ to allow the DNC to sidestep the FBI and hire this firm on a matter of the highest national security. It's as if Nixon's DOJ allowed the RNC to hire Republican-friendly Pinkertons to investigate the Watergate break-in. To the IT-savvy, Russian-American journalist Yasha Levine, this whole affair read "like a plotline from a vintage James Bond film." Truth, Levine learned through experience, is the first casualty even in a cyber war. "Far from establishing an airtight case for Russian espionage," Levine concluded, "CrowdStrike made a point of telling its DNC clients what it already knew they wanted to hear: after a cursory probe, it pronounced the Russians the culprits."[84]

On the CrowdStrike blog, Alperovitch proudly described how quickly his tech crew identified the hackers, the *soi-disant* "Cozy Bear" and "Fancy Bear." Wrote Alperovitch, "We've had lots of experience with both of these actors attempting to target our customers in the past and know them well."[85] If KGB-veteran Putin "ordered" this intervention on *Trump's* behalf, one has to wonder why he would use hackers who could be easily busted and tracked back to the GRU. If Russia did intervene, which is altogether possible, sowing chaos would seem to have been the most likely motive. If so, Putin succeeded beyond his most feverish dream.

On the same day the ICA was released, January 6, Comey, Clapper, Brennan, and Mike Rogers briefed the incoming president at Trump Tower, sort of. "[W]e were not investigating him and the stuff [in the dossier] might be totally made up but it was being said out of Russia and our job was to protect the president from efforts to coerce him," Comey wrote in *his* notes to self following the meeting.[86] At least three of the four men were investigating Trump, and it was not the Russians who were doing the coercing.

Only Comey stayed behind to brief Trump about the Steele dossier. It had not yet been published. CNN had the story, Comey knew. He also knew that by telling the president about the dossier, he would give CNN the necessary news hook to report the dossier's allegations, at least the more plausible ones. One of the conspirators promptly leaked the news of the more intimate briefing to CNN. On January 8, deputy FBI director Andrew McCabe emailed his senior FBI colleagues. "CNN is close to going forward with the *sensitive* story," wrote McCabe, emphasis his. "The trigger for [CNN] is they know the material was discussed in the brief and presented in an attachment." McCabe sent this email under the heading, "The flood is coming."[87]

On January 10, 2017—for Lee Smith, the day the media "imploded"—a heavy-hitting quartet of CNN reporters including Watergate vet Carl Bernstein broke the story of the Steele dossier. In the first paragraph, readers learned that "Russian operatives claim to have compromising personal and financial information about Mr. Trump." In the second, they learned that "the allegations came, in part, from memos compiled by a former British intelligence operative, whose past work US intelligence officials consider credible."[88] This was the closest Bernstein had come to matching his past glory in more than forty years, but as some Roman once shrewdly said, *sic transit gloria mundi*, "So passes the glory of the world."

Unfortunately for Bernstein and crew, hours later on that same January day, *BuzzFeed* served up the ultimate buzz kill. It went ahead and ran the complete dossier under the headline, "These Reports Allege Trump Has Deep Ties To Russia." Edited by fireman extraordinaire Ben Smith, *BuzzFeed* claimed to publish the dossier "so that Americans can make up their own minds about allegations about the president-elect that have circulated at the highest levels of the US government."[89] Given Smith's history, he had to have chuckled his way through that explanation.

The CNN crew was outraged. "Collegiality wise," wrote Jake Tapper to Smith, "it was you stepping on my dick."[90] CNN had an exclusive. Steele himself had briefed its reporters. They could have milked the story for weeks. *BuzzFeed* blew their cover. Even at a glance, the casual reader could see what a pile of rubbish the whole thing was.

As spelled out in its subhead, the dossier purports to detail "Republican candidate Donald Trump's activities in Russia and compromising relationship with the Kremlin." This subhead hints at a pattern obvious throughout the document, namely that it appears to be written by a non-native English speaker. The phrase should read, "Republican candidate Donald Trump's activities in Russia and *his* compromising relationship with the Kremlin." Several sentences, in fact, are missing pronouns or articles. For instance, the phrase "to encourage splits and divisions in western alliance" is missing a "the" before "western alliance." The phrase "anchored upon countries' interest" should read, in context, "anchored upon *the country's* interest." The author omits an article and misuses the possessive.

More problematic is that the dossier introduced the narrative that would bolster the FISA applications and shape media coverage for the next three years: "Russian regime has been cultivating, supporting and assisting TRUMP for at least 5 years." Only a complicit media could have taken seriously a claim this extravagant or the claim that Putin was "motivated by fear and hatred of Hillary CLINTON." Hatred maybe; Hillary can be difficult. But fear? Fear of what?

The complicit media included *Times* top gun Tom Friedman.

A day after the dossier was published, in an op-ed with the creepy title "Online and Scared," Friedman repeated his overripe observation that the internet was "an open sewer of untreated, unfiltered information." Incredibly, he managed to say this without identifying the dossier as the textbook case of untreated and unfiltered sewage. Indeed, Friedman proved no more equipped to "bring skepticism and critical thinking" to what he read than did the imaginary school children he presumed to lecture. For him and his colleagues, the fact that Russia "intervene[d] on Trump's behalf with hacks of Democratic operatives' computers" was already gospel.[91] They would spend the next two years preaching it.

A year after the dossier was published, independent filmmaker Joel Gilbert and I wrote an article in *American Thinker* highlighting its rampant errors in content and style.[92] To that point, no one in major media had challenged, as we did, Steele's authorship. "Chris Steele," his byline at the Cambridge University student publication, knew the language too well to have written this dossier unless he wrote the dossier to mimic the way a native-Russian speaker might have written it. This is possible.

When Christopher Steele started trotting his seamy material around Washington in July 2016, its provenance was still unknown. Incredibly, not until October 2017 did America learn who paid for the dossier. This they learned only through the relentless probing of Devin Nunes and the HPSCI team of investigators. Knowing Nunes had uncovered the funding source, the conspirators fed the story to the *Washington Post*. Its editors would know how to massage the revelation. Had the editors found the source on their own a year earlier as they should have, they could have spared the president and the nation a world of trouble.

During the 2016 campaign, inconvenient facts such as the funding of the dossier or its authorship had to drop-kick MSM journalists in the teeth before they noticed, let alone investigated. By contrast, writes Taibbi, the media "swallowed whole a massive disinformation campaign."[93] Even after journalists could see what a mess the dossier was, even after they learned it was simply bad opposition research, they continued to talk about its allegations as if they meant something.

The telling of this story showed contemporary journalism at its most partisan and most predictable. The major media did as they had been doing for the previous eight years. They followed leads that supported their narrative and largely ignored those that did not. "For years," observes Taibbi, "every hint the dossier might be true became a banner headline, while every time doubt was cast on Steele's revelations, the press was quiet."[94] Stories generated outside their newsrooms bored them. The serious reporting done by people like *National Review*'s Andy McCarthy, Gregg Jarrett and Sara Carter of Fox News, John Solomon of *The Hill*, Mollie Hemingway and Margot Cleveland of the *Federalist*, Kimberley Strassel of the *Wall Street Journal*, Lee Smith of the Hudson Institute, Diana West, and Peter Schweizer, among others, went largely unread.

The third major phase of the Democratic messaging campaign was submitted to Attorney General William Barr in March 2019. Three years of steady disinformation had disarmed the true believers. They were as shocked to learn that Mueller cleared Trump of collusion as they were to learn in 2016 that Trump beat Hillary. As to Page and Papadopoulos, both got their "Get Out of Jail Free" cards. Mueller and his people found "no documentary evidence" that Papadopoulos had shared news of the Russian dirt on Hillary with anyone in the Trump campaign. They also found no evidence that "Page coordinated with the Russian government in its efforts to interfere with the 2016 presidential election."[95]

After months of very expensive legal harassment, Jerry Corsi also escaped the guillotine. The report even quoted Corsi to the effect that he was "not going to sign a lie" to accept a favorable plea deal. As for Christopher Steele, the report mentioned the dossier on several occasions but never critically. There was no apparent inquiry into its origins or its funding, no mention of Glenn Simpson or Fusion GPS. These mysteries were apparently beyond Mueller's famed "purview."

Unlike the media, Mueller thought Seth Rich worth discussing. The report focused on Assange and quoted him at length about his insinuation that Rich had been a source. "According to media reports," Mueller notes, "Assange told a U.S. congressman that the DNC hack was an 'inside job,' and purported to have 'physical proof' that Russians did not give materials to Assange."[96] Given his centrality to the whole investigation, Assange should have been the first person Mueller's crew interviewed. He wasn't interviewed at all. Mueller was content to link him to Russia through the enigmatic Guccifer 2.0 and dismiss his inferences about Rich as false.

Mueller's people did not even attempt to discover who did kill the unfortunate DNC analyst. Their failure to interview Ellen Ratner was indicative. On the day after the 2016 election Ratner, a veteran news analyst, participated in a recorded symposium at Embry-Riddle Aeronautical University. "I spent three hours with Julian Assange on Saturday at the Ecuadorian Embassy in London," said Ratner more than an hour into the conversation. "One thing he did say was the leaks were not from, they were not from the Russians. They were an internal source from the

Hillary Campaign."[97] An admitted Hillary Clinton supporter, Ratner had no reason to make this up. She had access to Assange through her brother Michael Ratner, a left-wing civil rights attorney who defended WikiLeaks before his death in May 2016. Her fellow panelists, one a former Republican congressman, let Ratner's blockbuster remark pass without comment. The media missed the revelation altogether.

According to Ed Butowsky, a high-profile author and financial adviser, Ratner knew more than she shared at the symposium. "Seth Rich and his brother, Aaron, were responsible for releasing the DNC emails to Wikileaks,"[98] Assange allegedly told Ratner, and she in turn told Butowsky. Butowsky made this claim in a complex, multi-party defamation lawsuit filed in July 2019.

When Ratner failed to go public with what she knew, Butowsky texted her on December 16, 2016. He asked, in hasty text English, "Why don't you speaking up about email hack?" Ratner texted back, "I have." As related in the suit, Ratner subsequently told Butowsky that she had spoken with two people at Fox News about her meeting with Assange, co-president Bill Shine and producer Malia Zimmerman.

On December 17, at Ratner's request, Butowsky informed Rich's parents of Assange's comments. He later referred the Rich family to a Fox News contributor and former DC homicide detective named Rod Wheeler. The well-intentioned Butowsky had no idea how ferocious was the Hydra-headed monster he had just prodded. For the next three years and counting he was slandered, defamed, physically threatened, had his property vandalized, and was dragged into court for his indirect involvement with the Seth Rich saga.

The major media were relentless in their assault on Butowsky. The headline of an August 2017 NPR piece perfectly captured the firehouse dynamics of Obama-era news: "The Man Behind The Scenes In Fox News' Discredited Seth Rich Story."[99] Below the headline on the NPR website was a large photo of Butowsky captioned, "A lawsuit accuses Ed Butowsky, a Fox News reporter and the network of concocting a story about Seth Rich's death in an effort to help President Trump." In fact, Butowsky was not a reporter but an occasional Fox News contributor on economic issues. He was not "concocting a story about Seth Rich's death" but attempting to solve a genuine mystery. He had information that the major media did not, including Ratner's testimony and unfiltered conversations with Rich's parents.

NPR reporter David Folkenflik had less interest in solving Rich's murder than he did in slandering Butowsky. He dug into the educational background of this amateur investigator more aggressively than NPR had ever dug into Barack Obama's. Other samizdat journalists, most notably the irrepressible Matt Couch, faced similar legal and media harassment. Eventually, Fox News was sued into silence. This widespread suppression would have had some justification if major media journalists knew *anything* about Rich's murder, but they did not. In 2017, they were not even aware of Ratner's role. Butowsky had protected her identity. If anyone knew about Assange's source, it was Assange, and the media did their shameful best to ignore him or shut him up.

The Mueller report failed to vindicate those who investigated the Rich murder and vindicated Trump only left-handedly. The document was littered with generous droppings of gossip, innuendo, and unfiltered sewage from the Steele dossier. Indeed, Mueller left enough detritus in his wake to give Democrats hope that they could massage it into something impeachment worthy. Nunes labeled this report the "Mueller dossier," the third "dossier" in a series of smears. In the samizdat, the name caught on.

One person the Mueller report spared was President Obama. The name "Barack Obama" appears only twice in the report and both times inconsequentially. There were other references to the "Obama administration" and "President Obama," but sufficiently few that Obama did not seem like a major player in the drama that unfolded on his watch. The IG Report likewise reports the mischief of Obama's subordinates without any negative insinuations about the president himself.

There was a pattern here. Throughout his presidency, Obama insisted he learned about various scandals—from Fast and Furious to IRS abuse of the Tea Party—only through the media. No serious person, however, could believe for a moment Rhodes's claim that as late as October 2016 Obama "had no idea" the FBI was investigating the Trump campaign's contacts with Russia. It needs to be repeated that Comey told the OIG about his August briefing of Obama regarding four targeted individuals associated with the Trump campaign.

Obama's grounding in Marxist theory is well enough known, as is his weakness for redistributionist policies. Overlooked, however, even by his critics, was the relentless invasiveness and quiet brutality of his regime. Like England's Henry II, who reportedly said of Thomas Becket, "Will no one rid me of this turbulent priest," Obama seems to have led by way of suggestion. His henchmen and women did the dirty work. They sent Nakoula Basseley Nakoula to prison for making a video. They watched in silence as Lt. Col. Terry Lakin was dispatched in shackles to Leavenworth. They had James O'Keefe and David Daleiden arrested for undercover reporting. They cyber harassed reporter Sharyl Attkisson. They used search warrants on reporter James Rosen and several Associated Press reporters. They punished whistleblowers. They helped frame George Zimmerman and Officer Darren Wilson. They used the IRS to crush the Tea Party. They turned a blind eye to the New Black Panther goons. They conspired to clear Hillary Clinton of criminal charges. They discouraged all serious investigation into the death of Seth Rich. And even before the election, they breached Obama's passport file and probably doctored it.

Deceit came easily to Obama and his people as well. There were his speechwriters, Jon Favreau and Jon Lovett, joking with Charlie Rose on national TV about who came up with the punch line, "If you like your health care plan, you can keep your health care plan." There was Jonathan Gruber insisting that "lack of transparency [was] a huge political advantage" in selling Obamacare to voters, whose "stupidity" made them easy marks. There was Ben Rhodes saying of the very reporters who did his bidding, "They literally know nothing." There was the State Department's Jen Psaki who sold her "useful lie" about Iran, saying, "There are times when diplomacy needs privacy in order to progress." There was Susan Rice telling the same Benghazi lie on five different shows one Sunday morning. There were Brennan, Clapper, and Comey, whose multiple deceits could fill a book. And then there is Obama who built his political career on a series of fables, most fundamentally that his parents shared an "improbable love" and "an abiding faith in the possibilities of this nation."

"He weaponized information and showed a willingness to lie, using traditional media like television, and new media platforms like Twitter, Facebook, and YouTube, to spread disinformation into open, Western societies like a virus," writes Rhodes. He is writing here about Putin, but he might just as easily have been writing about his boss.[100]

Epilogue

The late *Washington Post* president and publisher Philip L. Graham is credited with the observation that "journalism is the first rough draft of history." If so, future histories of the Obama years will likely be as fawning and superficial as were the news reports. A November 2018 *Vanity Fair* article by presidential historian Jon Meacham suggests what we can expect.

"It seems safe to say," Meacham wrote, "that his background—as a child raised in Hawaii, the son of a white mother and a Kenyan father, together with the hyper-vigilant care with which he approached the task of living a life balancing disparate traditions, influences, and world-views—was critical to his rise to the pinnacle of American power."

After eight years of the Obama presidency, Meacham remained as star struck as he was at the 2004 Democratic National Convention. "Obama's personal answer to our current plight?" Meacham wrote. "Tell a better story. Insist on a more appealing counter-narrative."[1] In his upcoming memoir, Obama will surely put a good deal more meat on this counter-narrative. The problem for Meacham is one that historians of earlier presidencies never had to face, namely the samizdat. Scores of serious people, many of them not formally "journalists," have been un-telling the Obama story for the last fifteen years. Thanks to the internet, they have as much access to information as Meacham does, and they are not constrained by the polite mendacity of the liberal establishment.

Aided by the responsible right, the samizdat had considerable success in checking the progressive advance. The proof is in the numbers. In January 2009, the Democratic Party controlled both chambers of twenty-seven state legislatures. Eight years later, Democrats controlled both chambers in only thirteen states. It gets worse. On Obama's watch, his party lost a net total of thirteen governorships and 816 state legislative seats.[2] Although historians talk of the "Age of Jackson" and the "Reagan Era," when all is said and done, Barack Obama will deserve little more than an unpleasant moment.

The fault was not entirely his. Obama was tasked with selling a center-right population on policies that were widely perceived to be unworkable, unnecessary, and, in some cases, unnatural. He got away with some of it, and had it not been for the samizdat, he might have gotten away with all of it. The Lilliputians held the line.

Acknowledgments

Dedicated to the unsung warriors of the samizdat, among them: MVP Andrew Breitbart, J. Christian Adams, Sharyl Attkisson, Matthew Boyle, Ed Butowsky, Michael Cannon, Sara Carter, Vince Cefalu, Margot Cleveland, Angelo Codevilla, Jerry Corsi, David Codrea, Matt Couch, Susan Daniels, David Daleiden, James Delingpole, Jay Dobyns, Catherine Engelbrecht, Colin Flaherty, Ryan Geiser, Joel Gilbert, Hannah Giles, Shawn Glasco, Doug Hagmann, Mollie Hemingway, Greg Jarrett, KC Johnson, Paul Kengor, Phil Kerpen, Cliff Kincaid, Les Kinsolving, Stanley Kurtz, Terry Lakin, Michael Patrick Leahy, Laura Loomer, Trevor Loudon, Heather Mac Donald, Andy McCarthy, Sandra Merritt, Frank Miele, Steve Milloy, Marc Morano, Melissa Ohden, James O'Keefe, Camille Paglia, Katie Pavlich, Jesse Lee Peterson, Joel Pollak, Lila Rose, James Sanders, Paul Schiffer, Peter Schweizer, Lee Smith, John Solomon, Christina Hoff Sommers, Kimberly Strassel, Sundance and his fellow Treepers, Stuart Taylor, Ken Timmerman, Mike Vanderboegh, Rich Weinstein, Diana West, and the folks at Legal Insurrection, the American Center for Law and Justice, and Judicial Watch as well as scores more still unsung.

Endnotes

Prologue: Michael Cohen Calling

[1] Dennis Wagner, "ATF gun probe: Behind the fall of Operation Fast and Furious," *Arizona Republic*, November 27, 2011, http://www. bikernews.org/wtn/news.php?extend.13833.

[2] Vladimir Bukovsky, *Judgment in Moscow* (New York: Ninth of November Press, 2019), 170, Nook edition.

[3] Ray Bradbury, *Fahrenheit 451* (New York: Simon & Schuster, Inc., 1951), 6.

[4] Sharyl Attkisson, *Stonewalled: My Fight for Truth Against the Forces of Obstruction, Intimidation, and Harassment in Obama's Washington* (New York: HarperCollins, 2014), 258, Kindle edition.

[5] Michael Calderone, "JournoList: Inside the echo chamber," *Politico*, March 17, 2009, https://www.politico.com/story/2009/03/journolist-inside-the-echo-chamber-020086.

[6] Alvin Felzenberg, *A Man and His Presidents: The Political Odyssey of William F. Buckley Jr*, (New Haven: Yale University Press, 2017), 140.

[7] Rich Lowry, "A Personal Retrospective," *National Review*, November 17, 2005, https://www.nationalreview.com/2005/11/personal-retrospective-rich-lowry-2/.

[8] Christopher Andersen, *Barack and Michelle: Portrait of an American Marriage* (New York: HarperCollins, 2009), location 2622-2693, Kindle edition.

[9] Mark Summer, "Donald Trump's astounding racist projections," *Daily Kos*, September 19, 2016, https://www.dailykos.com/stories/2016/9/19/1571956/-Donald-Trump-s-astounding-racist-projections.

10 Transcript, Chris Matthews, *Hardball,* MSNBC, September 22, 2009, http://www.nbcnews.com/id/32984839/ns/msnbc-hardball_with_chris_matthews/t/hardball-chris-matthews-tuesday-september/#.XK9emYRTVIY.

11 Original article is no longer available. Quote can be found in Ta-Nehisi Coates, "Epic Fail—Ayers ghost-wrote Obama's memoir," the *Atlantic,* October 12, 2008, https://www.theatlantic.com/entertainment/archive/2008/10/epic-fail-ayers-ghost-wrote-obama-apos-s-memoir/6026/.

12 Ta-Nehisi Coates, "Epic Fail—Ayers ghost-wrote Obama's memoir," the *Atlantic,* October 12, 2008, https://www.theatlantic.com/entertainment/archive/2008/10/epic-fail-ayers-ghost-wrote-obama-apos-s-memoir/6026/.

13 Ibid.

14 David Remnick, *The Bridge: The Life and Rise of Barack Obama* (New York: Random House, 2010), pp. 253-254.

15 Ronald Radosh, "Remnick Takes Up Obama's Critics," Hudson Institute, April 12, 2010, https://www.hudson.org/research/6917-remnick-takes-up-obama-s-critics.

16 Ibid., p. 253.

17 Ibid., p. 254.

The Front Man

1   John Kerry, *Every Day Is Extra* (New York: Simon & Schuster, 2018), 62, Kindle edition.

2   Angelo Codevilla, "The Rise of Political Correctness," Independent Institute, November 28, 2016.

3   Ibid.

Scandal Free

1   Lisa Hagen, "Obama: Proud administration was 'without significant scandal,'" *The Hill,* November 14, 2016, https://thehill.com/blogs/blog-briefing-room/305955-obama-proud-administration-was-without-significant-scandal.

2   Nicole Goodkind, "Barack Obama Takes Jab at Donald Trump: 'I Did Not Have Scandals As President,'" *Newsweek*, May 24, 2018, https://www.newsweek.com/barack-obama-donald-trump-scandal-white-house-943806.

3   Jonathan Alter, "The Obama Miracle, a White House Free of Scandal," Bloomberg, October 27, 2011, https://www.bloomberg.com/opinion/articles/2011-10-27/obama-miracle-is-white-house-free-of-scandal-commentary-by-jonathan-alter.

4   Paul Bremmer, On PBS, David Remnick Praises Obama Administration As Scandal-Free, Pro-Science, *Newsbusters*, January 21, 2014, https://www.newsbusters.org/blogs/nb/paul-bremmer/2014/01/21/pbs-david-remnick-praises-obama-administration-scandal-free-pro.

5   David Brooks, "I Miss Barack Obama," *New York Times*, February 9, 2016, https://www.nytimes.com/2016/02/09/opinion/i-miss-barack-obama.html.

6   Douglas Brinkley, CNN, January 19, 2017, https://www.newsbusters.org/blogs/nb/brad-wilmouth/2017/01/20/cnns-brinkley-gushes-unimpeachable-obama-eisenhower-highest-ethics.

7   "Obama's Speech on Health Care Reform," *New York Times*, June 15, 2009, https://www.nytimes.com/2009/06/15/health/policy/15obama.text.html?pagewanted=3&_r=0.

8   Kevin Wacasey blog, Healthcareonomics, #49, May 13, 2019, https://www.youtube.com/watch?v=ZZYMB2qrn7M.

9   Michael Cannon, "ObamaCare Architect Jonathan Gruber: 'If You're A State And You Don't Set Up An Exchange, That Means Your Citizens Don't Get Their Tax Credits,'" *Forbes*, July 25, 2014, https://forbes.com/sites/michaelcannon/2014/07/25/obamacare-architect-jonathan-gruber-if-youre-a-state-and-you-dont-set-up-an-exchange-that-means-your-citizens-dont-get-their-tax-credits/#211f06f15438.

10 Patrick Howley, "Obamacare Architect: Lack of Transparency Was Key Because 'Stupidity Of The American Voter' Would Have Killed Obamacare," *Daily Caller*, November 9, 2014, https://dailycaller.com/2014/11/09/obamacare-architect-lack-of-transparency-was-

key-because-stupidity-of-the-american-voter-would-have-killed-obamacare/.

[11] Becket Adams, "New York Times ignored Jonathan Gruber bombshell," *Washington Examiner,* May 28, 2015, https://www.washingtonexaminer.com/new-york-times-ignored-jonathan-gruber-bombshell.

[12] Karen Tumulty, "What exactly was Gruber's role in the creation of the health law?" *Washington Post,* November 16, 2004, https://www.washingtonpost.com/news/post-politics/wp/2014/11/16/what-exactly-was-grubers-role-in-the-creation-of-the-health-law/.

[13] Neil Irwin, "The Jonathan Gruber Controversy and Washington's Dirty Little Secret," *New York Times,* November 12, 2014, https://www.nytimes.com/2014/11/13/upshot/the-jonathan-gruber-controversy-and-washingtons-dirty-little-secret.html?abt=0002&abg=0.

[14] Zachary Pleat, "The Fraudulent Media Campaign To Scandalize Obamacare's Passage," Media Matters for America, November 13, 2014, https://www.mediamatters.org/bill-oreilly/fraudulent-media-campaign-scandalize-obamacares-passage?redirect_source=/research/2014/11/13/the-fraudulent-media-campaign-to-scandalize-oba/201549.

[15] "Charlie Rose and Obama Speechwriters Laugh At Those Who Lost Health Insurance," *CNS News,* May 10, 2016, https://www.cnsnews.com/video/charlie-rose-and-obama-speechwriters-laugh-those-who-lost-health-insurance.

[16] David French, "A Broad-Based IRS Assault on the Tea Party?" *National Review,* March 2, 2012, https://www.nationalreview.com/corner/broad-based-irs-assault-tea-party-david-french/.

[17] Abraham Miller, "The VanderSlooting of America," *American Spectator,* May 28, 2013, https://spectator.org/55516_vanderslooting-america/.

[18] Treasury Inspector General for Tax Administration, May 14, 2013, p. 31, https://www.treasury.gov/tigta/auditreports/2013reports/201310053fr.html.

19 Jillian Kay Melchior, "True Scandal," *National Review*, May 20, 2013, https://www.nationalreview.com/2013/05/true-scandal-jillian-kay-melchior/.

20 Charlie Savage, "Holder Signals Tough Review of New State Laws on Voting," *New York Times*, December 13, 2011, https://www.nytimes.com/2011/12/14/us/politics/in-speech-holder-to-critique-new-voting-laws.html.

21 Catherine Engelbrecht IRS Targeting Speech, C-SPAN, February 8, 2014, https://www.c-span.org/video/?c4483865/user-clip-catherine-engelbrecht-irs-targeting-speech.

22 Stephanie Saul, "Looking, Very Closely, for Voter Fraud," *New York Times*, September 16, 2012, https://www.nytimes.com/2012/09/17/us/politics/groups-like-true-the-vote-are-looking-very-closely-for-voter-fraud.html.

23 William Mullen and George Bliss, "Poll Judge Violations Condoned in Election Office," *Chicago Tribune*, September 12, 1972, http://archives.chicagotribune.com/1972/09/12/page/2/article/poll-judge-violations-condoned-in-election-office.

24 Melchior, May 20, 2013.

25 Virginia Allen, "This Conservative Group Fought IRS for Years. Now a Court's Given It a Victory," *Daily Signal*, June 12, 2019, https://www.dailysignal.com/2019/07/12/this-conservative-group-fought-irs-for-years-now-a-courts-given-them-a-victory/.

26 Ian Haney López, *Dog Whistle Politics: How Coded Racial Appeals Have Reinvented Racism and Wrecked the Middle Class* (New York: Oxford University Press, 2013), 159.

27 Eric Felten, "The Kadzik Affair: Clintonesque Corruption," *Washington Examiner*, June 22, 2018, https://www.washington examiner.com/weekly-standard/the-kadzik-affair-clintonesque-corruption.

28 Jonathan Weisman, "I.R.S. Apologizes to Tea Party Groups Over Audits of Applications for Tax Exemption," *New York Times*, May 10, 2013, https://www.nytimes.com/2013/05/11/us/politics/irs-apologizes-to-conservative-groups-over-application-audits.html?_r=0.

29 Pete Sepp, "Learning the Cost of Lois Lerner's Pension," National Taxpayers Union, September 30, 2013, https://www.ntu.org/publications/detail/learning-the-cost-of-lois-lerners-pension.

30 Interview, Susan Daniels, April 8, 2019.

31 "Gibbs sidesteps Obama's Social Security Number," *WND,* June 10, 2010, https://www.wnd.com/2010/06/165225/.

32 David Mikkelson, "Did Barack Obama Steal His Social Security Number?" *Snopes.com,* June 13, 2011, https://www.snopes.com/fact-check/false-obama-stole-his-social-security-number-from-paul-ludwig/.

33 "Social Security Number Randomization," https://www.ssa.gov/employer/randomization.html.

34 "Social Security Claim Vanishes From O'Reilly Podcast," *WND,* April 16, 2011.

35 "Birthers' new fixation: Obama's Social Security number?" *The Week,* May 14, 2010, https://theweek.com/articles/494358/birthers-new-fixation-obamas-social-security-number.

36 Jonathan Strong, *Daily Caller,* March 20, 2010.

The Home Front

1 "Barack Obama's Remarks to the Democratic National Convention," *New York Times,* July 27, 2004, https://www.nytimes.com/2004/07/27/politics/campaign/barack-obamas-remarks-to-the-democratic-national.html.

2 Remnick, 360.

3 John Kerry's speech to the Democratic National Convention, *Guardian,* July 29, 2004, https://www.theguardian.com/world/2004/jul/30/uselections2004.usa5.

4 Ralph Blumenthal and Robert Worth, "For Kerry's Chief Accuser, a Flashback to a Political Battle From 1971," *New York Times,* August 28, 2004.

5 Wikipedia, https://en.wikipedia.org/wiki/Swiftboating. In the author's opinion, Wikipedia provides an excellent service except on political topics. These are almost inevitably hijacked by volunteer editors with a leftist agenda.

6   Martha Gessen, "The Hustlers and Swindlers of the Mueller Report," *New Yorker*, April 18, 2019, https://www.newyorker.com/news/our-columnists/the-hustlers-and-swindlers-of-the-mueller-report.

7   Cyber Alert, Morning Edition, September 3, 2004, https://www.mrc.org/profiles-bias/media-vs-swift-boat-veterans-truth?gclid=EAIaIQobChMIlaDotq_X4QIVUZ7ACh0vrwKdEAAYASAAEgKLYvD_BwE.

8   Rebecca Leung, "New Questions on Bush Guard Duty," *60 Minutes*, CBSnews.com, September 8, 2004, https://www.cbsnews.com/news/new-questions-on-bush-guard-duty-08-09-2004/.

9   Scott Johnson, "The Sixty-First Minute," *Power Line*, September 9, 2004, https://www.powerlineblog.com/archives/2004/09/007699.php.

10 Maureen Balleza and Kate Zernike, "Memos on Bush Are Fake But Accurate, Typist Says," *New York Times*, September 15, 2004, https://www.nytimes.com/2004/09/15/us/the-2004-campaign-national-guard-memos-on-bush-are-fake-but-accurate.html.

11 "For the Record: Bush Documents," CBS News, https://www.cbsnews.com/news/for-the-record-bush-documents-15-09-2004/.

12 "Special Report With Brit Hume," Fox News, Sept. 14, 2004, https://www.foxnews.com/story/how-the-blogosphere-took-on-cbs-docs.

13 "Obama's Speech," *Atlantic*, August 28, 2008, https://www.theatlantic.com/daily-dish/archive/2008/08/obamas-speech/212373/.

14 Michael Patrick Leahy, *What Does Barack Obama Believe?* (Nashville: Harpeth River Press, 2008). I relied on an extract of the book, no page number available, https://archive.org/details/TheMythOfBarackObamasEarlyLife.

15 David Mendell, *Obama: From Promise to Power* (New York: Arsenal, 2007) 28, Kindle edition.

16 Excerpted from *What Does Barack Obama Believe?*

17 Ibid.

18 Phone interview, Michael Patrick Leahy, May 15, 2019.

19 David Maraniss, "Though Obama Had to Leave to Find Himself, It Is Hawaii That Made His Rise Possible," *Washington Post*, August

22, 2008, http://www.washingtonpost.com/wp-dyn/content/article/
2008/08/22/AR2008082201679.html.

[20] "When and where Obama lived on this Capitol Hill," *Capitol Hill Seattle Blog*, January 7, 2009, http://www.capitolhillseattle.com/2009/01/when-and-where-obama-lived-on-this-capitol-hill/.

[21] Ibid.

[22] David Remnick, *The Bridge: The Life and Rise of Barack Obama* (New York, Knopf Doubleday Publishing Group, 2010) Kindle edition, 56.

[23] Ibid., 57.

[24] Ibid., 56.

[25] David Mendell, *Obama: From Promise to Power* (New York: Arsenal, 2007) 28, Kindle edition.

[26] Janny Scott, *A Singular Woman: The Untold Story of Barack Obama's Mother* (New York: Riverhead Books, 2011), 46.

[27] Sally Jacobs, *The Other Barack: The Bold and Reckless Life of President Obama's Father* (New York: Public Affairs, 2011) 125.

[28] Ibid.

[29] David Maraniss, *Barack Obama: The Story* (New York: Simon & Schuster, 2012) Kindle edition, 177-179.

[30] David Garrow, *Rising Star, The Making of Barack Obama* (New York: William Morrow, 2017), Kindle edition, location 1153.

[31] Ibid., 1222.

The Red Front

[1] Paul Kengor, *The Communist—Frank Marshall Davis: The Untold Story of Barack Obama's Mentor* (New York: Threshold Editions, 2012), Kindle edition, 4.

[2] Ibid., 242.

[3] Yvonne Shinhoster Lamb, "Vernon Jarrett, 84; Journalist, Crusader," *Washington Post*, May 25, 2004, http://www.washingtonpost.com/wp-dyn/articles/A53239-2004May24.html.

[4] Kengor, 111.

5 Jodi Kantor, "Valerie Jarrett," *The New York Times*, November 5, 2008, https://www.nytimes.com/2008/11/06/us/politics/06jarrett. html?searchResultPosition=1.

6 Cliff Kincaid, "Obama's Red Mentor Was a Pervert," *Accuracy in Media*, September 1, 2008, http://www.conservativetruth.org/article. php?id=661.

7 Maraniss, *Barack Obama: The Story*, 382, Kindle edition.

8 Jack Cashill, "What the Media Won't Say about Frank Marshall Davis," *American Thinker*, July 24, 2012, https://www. americanthinker.com/articles/2012/07/what_the_media_wont_ say_about_frank_marshall_davis.html.

9 David Maraniss, "The Red Scare targeted my family. America hasn't shaken its demons yet," *Washington Post*, May 13, 2019, https://www.washingtonpost.com/outlook/the-red-scare-targeted-my-family-america-hasnt-shaken-its-demons-yet/2019/05/10/ 1c941e68-7077-11e9-9eb4-0828f5389013_story.html?utm_term= .9551810c59a6.

10 Maraniss, *Barack Obama: The Story*, 270, Kindle edition.

11 Paul Kengor, "The Washington Post Sugarcoats Obama's Communist Mentor," *American Thinker*, March 26, 2015, http:// www.americanthinker.com/articles/2015/03/the_washington_ empostem_sugarcoats_obamas_communist_mentor.html#ixzz3 VanoJC9E.

12 Gerald Horne, "Rethinking the History and Future of the Communist Party," *People's World*, April 6, 2007, https://www. peoplesworld.org/article/rethinking-the-history-and-future-of-the-communist-party/.

13 "An Interview with Trevor Loudon," Capital Research Center, February 24, 2017, https://capitalresearch.org/article/an-interview-with-trevor-loudon/.

14 Trevor Loudon, "Barack Obama's Marxist Mentor," March 28, 2007, *New Zeal*, https://www.trevorloudon.com/2007/03/barack-obamas-marxist-mentor/.

15 Cliff Kincaid, "Obama's Communist Mentor," *Accuracy in Media*, February 18, 2008, https://www.aim.org/aim-column/ obamas-communist-mentor/.

16 Frank Marshall Davis to Margaret Burroughs, November 1, 1968, Margaret Burroughs Papers, the DuSable Museum of African American History.

17 Sudhin Thanawala, "Writer offered a young Barack Obama advice on his life," Associated Press, August 2, 2008, https://www.foxnews.com/printer_friendly_wires/2008Aug02/0,4675,ObamaMentor,00.html.

18 Kengor, 156, Kindle edition.

19 Jon Meacham, "What Barack Obama Learned From His Father," *Newsweek,* August 22, 2008, https://www.newsweek.com/what-barack-obama-learned-his-father-88011.

20 Kengor, 277, Kindle edition.

21 Ibid., 278.

22 Remnick, 97, Kindle edition.

23 Ibid., 254.

24 Ibid., 106.

25 Garrow, location 2936, Kindle edition.

26 Ibid., location 27412.

27 Rudolph Giuliani, "Fox News interview with Megyn Kelly," Fox News, Feb. 20, 2015, https://www.foxnews.com/transcript/2015/02/20/giuliani-doubles-down-on-obama-criticism-on-kelly-file/.

28 Cliff Kincaid, "Frank Marshall Davis: Obama's 'Communist mentor'?" *Accuracy in Media*, March 23, 2019.

29 Michelle Ye Hee Lee, "Frank Marshall Davis: Obama's 'Communist mentor'?" *WashingtonPost,*March23,2015,https://www.washingtonpost.com/news/fact-checker/wp/2015/03/23/frank-marshall-davis-obamas-communist-mentor/?utm_term=.d2b89f792815.

30 Cliff Kincaid, *Accuracy in Media*, March 23, 2019.

31 Stanley Kurtz. *Radical-in-Chief: Barack Obama and the Untold Story of American Socialism* (New York: Pocket Books, 2010), p. 6. Kindle Edition.

32 "Obama's 1983 College Magazine Article," *New York Times,* https://www.nytimes.com/interactive/projects/documents/obama-s-1983-college-magazine-article.

33 Janny Scott, "Obama's Account of New York Years Often Differs From What Others Say," *New York Times,* October 30, 2007, https://www.nytimes.com/2007/10/30/us/politics/30obama.html.

34 Barack Obama, *Dreams from My Father* (New York: Crown Publishers, 1995), 69.

35 Kurtz, 7, Kindle edition.

36 Ibid., 5.

37 Bill Ayers, *Fugitive Days: Memoirs of an Antiwar Activist* (Boston: Beacon Press, 2001), 286.

38 Garrow, location 11190.

39 "Professor Bernardine Dohrn remarks on her Manson Family remarks," C-SPAN, June 7, 2009, https://www.c-span.org/video/?c4460430/professor-bernardine-dohrn-remarks-manson-family-remarks.

40 Ibid., location 12472.

41 Ibid., location 18317.

42 Peter Hitchens, "The Black Kennedy: But does anyone know the real Barack Obama?" *Daily Mail,* February 2, 2008, https://www.dailymail.co.uk/debate/article-511901/The-Black-Kennedy-But-does-know-real-Barack-Obama.html.

43 Michael Dobbs, "Obama's 'Weatherman' Connection," *Washington Post,* February 19, 2008, http://voices.washingtonpost.com/fact-checker/2008/02/obamas_weatherman_connection.html.

44 Larry C. Johnson, "No, He Can't Because Yes, They Will," *Huffington Post,* February 16, 2008, https://www.huffpost.com/entry/no-he-cant-because-yes-th_b_87036.

45 Robert Bidinotto, "Getting away with murder," *Reader's Digest,* July 1988.

46 Eugene Scott, "How the Willie Horton ad factors into George H.W. Bush's legacy," *Washington Post,* December 3, 2018, https://en.wikipedia.org/wiki/George_H._W._Bush.

47 Pennsylvania Democratic Presidential Candidates Debate, C-SPAN, April 16, 2008, https://www.c-span.org/video/transcript/?id=691.

48   "George Stephanopoulos Taking Notes From Sean Hannity for Tomorrow Night's Debates," *Democratic Underground*, April 15, 2008, https://www.democraticunderground.com/discuss/duboard. php?az=view_all&address=132x5518957.

49   Jonathan Strong, "Documents show media plotting to kill stories about Rev. Jeremiah Wright," *Daily Caller*, July 20, 2010, https://dailycaller.com/2010/07/20/documents-show-media-plotting-to-kill-stories-about-rev-jeremiah-wright/print/.

50   Faiz Shakir, "AUDIO: Hannity Feeds Stephanopoulos Debate Question On Weather Underground," *ThinkProgress*, April 17, 2008, https://thinkprogress.org/audio-hannity-feeds-stephanopoulos-debate-question-on-weather-underground-62d87b4d3e9d/.

51   Jason Linkins, "Hannity Spoonfed Left-Field Debate Question To Stephanopoulos," *Huffington Post*, April 24, 2008, https://www. huffpost.com/entry/stephanopoulos-left-field_n_97136.

52   Robin Abcarian, "Stephanopoulos defends his questions to Obama," *Los Angeles Times*, April 17, 2008, https://latimesblogs.latimes.com/ showtracker/2008/04/stephanopoulos.html.

53   Tom Shales, "In Pa. Debate, The Clear Loser Is ABC," *Washington Post*, April 17, 2008, http://www.washingtonpost.com/wp-dyn/ content/article/2008/04/17/AR2008041700013.html.

54   Email exchange, September 18, 2019.

55   Larry Rohter, "Real Deal on 'Joe the Plumber' Reveals New Slant," *New York Times*, October 16, 2008, https://www.nytimes. com/2008/10/17/us/politics/17joe.html.

56   James Kloppenberg, *Reading Obama: Dreams, Hope, and the American Political Tradition* (Princeton: Princeton University Press, 2011), 270, Kindle Edition.

57   Ibid., 248.

58   Ibid., 153.

59   Ibid., 69.

60   Jack Cashill, "Who Wrote 'Audacity of Hope'?" *American Thinker*, July 12, 2009, http://www.cashill.com/intellect_fraud/who_wrote_ audacity.htm.

61 Michiko Kakutani, "Obama's Foursquare Politics, With a Dab of Dijon," *New York Times,* October 17, 2006, https://www.google.com/?client=safari.

62 Remnick, 444.

63 Ibid., 7.

64 "Terrorist Ayers Confesses Sharing Obama's 'Dreams,'" *Investor's Business Daily,* November 26, 2013, https://www.investors.com/politics/policy-analysis/bill-ayers-claims-authorship-of-obama-dreams-memoir/.

65 "We are five days away from fundamentally transforming the United States of America," YouTube, October 31, 2008, https://www.youtube.com/watch?v=PI8P4-pgkYw.

66 Krissah Thompson, "Cornel West's criticism of Obama sparks debate among African Americans," *Washington Post,* May 18, 2011, https://www.washingtonpost.com/politics/cornel-wests-criticism-of-obama-sparks-debate-among-african-americans/2011/05/18/AFlGTf6G_story.html?utm_term=.efbabfc84246.

67 Alter, 271, Kindle edition.

The Black Front

1 Jack Cashill, "How a Missouri Rodeo Became A Phony Scandal," *American Thinker,* August 19, 2013, http://www.cashill.com/intellect_fraud/how_a_missouri.htm.

2 The View, March 25, 2011, https://ricorant.blogspot.com/2011/03/oh-what-can-we-dig-up-on-him.html.

3 Jacobs, p. IX.

4 Michael Dobbs, "Citizen McCain," *Washington Post,* May 2, 2008, http://voices.washingtonpost.com/fact-checker/2008/05/citizen_mccain.html.

5 Joel Pollak, "The Vetting—Exclusive—Obama's Literary Agent in 1991 Booklet: 'Born in Kenya and raised in Indonesia and Hawaii,'" *Breitbart,* May 17, 2012, https://www.breitbart.com/politics/2012/05/17/The-Vetting-Barack-Obama-Literary-Agent-1991-Born-in-Kenya-Raised-Indonesia-Hawaii/.

6   Karen Tumulty, "The birthers are back! The birthers are back!" *Washington Post*, May 19, 2012, https://www.washingtonpost.com/blogs/she-the-people/post/the-birthers-are-back-the-birthers-are-back/2012/05/19/gIQAw8nObU_blog.html?utm_term=.ea8ab0ab10bb.

7   Obama, *Dreams from My Father*, 72.

8   David Burgess, *A Tale of Two Brothers: The Keith Kakugawa Story*, (Self-published 2009-2012), 18. The book is written in the first person from Kakugawa's perspective.

9   John Carucci, "Bernie Sanders calls Trump a racist before Apollo event," Associated Press, April 5, 2019, https://www.telegram.com/ZZ/news/20190405/bernie-sanders-calls-trump-racist-before-apollo-event.

10   Ron Kampeas, "Bernie Sanders calls Trump a racist in MLK Day speech," *Times of Israel*, January 22, 2019, https://www.timesofisrael.com/bernie-sanders-calls-trump-a-racist-in-mlk-day-speech/.

11   Maraniss, "The Red Scare targeted my family."

12   Gregory Krieg, "14 of Trump's most outrageous 'birther' claims—half from after 2011," *CNN Politics*, September 16, 2016, https://www.cnn.com/2016/09/09/politics/donald-trump-birther/index.html.

13   Ryan Struyk, "67 Times Donald Trump Tweeted About the 'Birther' Movement," ABC News, September 16, 2016, https://abcnews.go.com/Politics/67-times-donald-trump-tweeted-birther-movement/story?id=42145590.

14   Maureen Dowd, "Usurper in Chief?" *New York Times*, December 14, 2010, https://www.nytimes.com/2010/12/15/opinion/15dowd.html.

15   Interview with Terry Lakin, Pueblo, Colorado, May 3, 2019.

16   Jon Greenberg, *PolitiFact*, September 23, 2015, https://www.politifact.com/truth-o-meter/statements/2015/sep/23/donald-trump/hillary-clinton-obama-birther-fact-check/.

17 Gabriella Schwartz, "Trump again questions Obama's birthplace," *CNN Politics*, March 23, 2011, http://politicalticker.blogs.cnn. com/2011/03/23/trump-again-questions-obamas-birthplace/.

18 "Jeff Daniels: It's The End of Democracy If We Lose 2020," MSNBC, May 20, 2019, https://www.youtube.com/watch?v=tubBx 97lwHM.

19 "Obama, Clinton Speeches in Selma, Alabama," CNN.com, March 4, 2007, http://www.cnn.com/TRANSCRIPTS/0703/04/le.02.html.

20 Patrick Healy and Jeff Zeleny, "Clinton and Obama Unite in Pleas to Blacks," *New York Times*, March 5, 2007, https://www.nytimes. com/2007/03/05/us/politics/05selma.html.

21 Richard Cohen, "From Obama, a Map for a New March," *Washington Post*, March 6, 2007, http://www.washingtonpost.com/wp-dyn/ content/article/2007/03/05/AR2007030501188.html.

22 Ibid., 13.

23 Jodi Kantor, "A Candidate, His Minister and the Search for Faith," *New York Times*, April 30, 2007, https://www.nytimes. com/2007/04/30/us/politics/30obama.html?scp=1&sq=a+ candidate%2C+his+minister&st=nyt.

24 Neela Banerjee, "Obama walks a difficult path as he courts Jewish voters," *New York Times*, February 29, 2008, https://www.nytimes. com/2008/03/01/world/americas/01iht-01obama.10602004. html?searchResultPosition=1.

25 Chris Suellentrop, "A Sermon's Echoes Threaten Obama," *New York Times*, March 13, 2008, https://opinionator.blogs. nytimes.com/2008/03/13/a-sermon-echoing-around-obama/? searchResultPosition=9.

26 Jodi Kantor, "The Wright Controversy," *New York Times*, March 13, 2008, https://thecaucus.blogs.nytimes.com/2008/03/13/the- wright-controversy/?searchResultPosition=10.

27 Katharine Seelye and Julie Bosman, "Ferraro's Obama Remarks Become Talk of Campaign," *New York Times*, March 12, 2008, https://www.nytimes.com/2008/03/12/us/politics/12campaign. html.

28 "Sen. Barack Obama Addresses Race at the Constitution Center in Philadelphia," *Washington Post*, March 18, 2008, http://www.washingtonpost.com/wp-dyn/content/article/2008/03/18/AR2008031801081.html?sid=ST2008031801183.

29 Obama, *Dreams*, 67.

30 Barack Obama interview, 610 WIP morning show, WIP Radio, March 24, 2008, http://www.redlasso.com/ClipPlayer.aspx?id=8a521134-e10b-4bfb-8aec-690d61794d50.

31 "Sen. Obama's Speech on Race," *Philadelphia Inquirer*, March 19, 2008, https://www.inquirer.com/philly/opinion/inquirer/20080319_Editorial__Sen__Obamas_Speech_on_Race.html.

32 Janny Scott, "Obama Chooses Reconciliation Over Rancor," *New York Times*, March 19, 2008, https://www.nytimes.com/2008/03/19/us/politics/19assess.html.

33 Roy Peter Clark, "Why it worked: A rhetorical analysis of Obama's speech on race," *Poynter*, October 20, 2017, https://www.poynter.org/reporting-editing/2017/why-it-worked-a-rhetorical-analysis-of-obamas-speech-on-race-2/.

34 "Mr. Obama and Rev. Wright," *New York Times*, April 30, 2008, https://www.nytimes.com/2008/04/30/opinion/30wed1.html.

35 Jonathan Strong, *Daily Caller*, July 20, 2010.

36 David Squires, "Rev. Jeremiah Wright says 'Jews' are keeping him from President Obama," *Daily Press,* June 10, 2009, https://www.dailypress.com/news/dp-local_wright_0610jun10-story.html.

37 "Obama's Father's Day Remarks," *New York Times*, June 15, 2008, https://www.nytimes.com/2008/06/15/us/politics/15text-obama.html.

38 Jeff Zeleny, "Jesse Jackson Apologizes for Remarks on Obama," *New York Times*, July 10, 2008, https://www.nytimes.com/2008/07/10/us/politics/10jackson.html.

39 Jonathan Martin, "Jackson used racial epithet," *Politico*, July 16, 2008, https://www.politico.com/blogs/jonathanmartin/0708/Jackson_used_racial_epithet_.html#site-content.

40 Jonathan Weisman, "It's Jackson vs. Jackson on 'Ugly' and 'Demeaning' Obama Remarks," *Washington Post*, July 9, 2008,

http://voices.washingtonpost.com/44/2008/07/09/rep_jackson_blasts_his_father.html.

[41] Suzanne Goldenberg, "'I want to cut his nuts out'—Jackson gaffe turns focus on Obama's move to the right," *Guardian*, July 10, 2008, https://www.theguardian.com/world/2008/jul/11/barackobama.uselections2008.

[42] "Megyn Kelly Interviews Renowned Civil Rights Attorney Bartle Bull," Fox News, July 2, 2010, https://www.youtube.com/watch?v=Vn6h-xeXwcM.

[43] J. Christian Adams, "Inside the Black Panther case," *Washington Times*, June 25, 2010, https://www.washingtontimes.com/news/2010/jun/25/inside-the-black-panther-case-anger-ignorance-and-/.

[44] Megyn Kelly Interview.

[45] Adam Serwer, *American Prospect*, December 23, 2009, https://prospect.org/article/about-black-panther-case.

[46] Andrew Cohen, "On Voting Rights, Discouraging Signs From the Hill," *Atlantic*, July 18, 2013, https://www.theatlantic.com/national/archive/2013/07/on-voting-rights-discouraging-signs-from-the-hill/277894/.

[47] "J. Christian Adams," Media Matters for America, undated profile.

[48] Matthew Boyle, "Emails reveal Justice Dept. regularly enlists Media Matters to spin press," *Daily Caller*, September 18, 2012, https://dailycaller.com/2012/09/18/emails-reveal-justice-dept-regularly-enlists-media-matters-to-spin-press/.

[49] Krissah Thompson, "2008 voter-intimidation case against New Black Panthers riles the right," *Washington Post*, July 15, 2010, http://www.washingtonpost.com/wp-dyn/content/article/2010/07/14/AR2010071405880.html.

[50] Andrew Alexander, "Why the silence from The Post on Black Panther Party story?" *Washington Post*, July 18, 2010, http://www.washingtonpost.com/wp-dyn/content/article/2010/07/16/AR2010071604081.html.

[51] Becket Adams, "Joe Biden parrots laughable falsehood that the Obama administration was scandal-free," *Washington Examiner*, April 26, 2019, https://www.washingtonexaminer.com/opinion/joe-

biden-parrots-laughable-falsehood-that-the-obama-administration-was-scandal-free.

52 Jonathan Alter, *The Center Holds: Obama and His Enemies* (New York: Simon & Schuster, 2013), 75, Kindle edition.

53 Robin Mordfin, "From the Green Lounge to the White House," The University of Chicago Law School, August 20, 2009, https://www.law.uchicago.edu/news/green-lounge-white-house.

54 John Fund, *How the Obama Administration Threatens to Undermine Our Elections* (New York: Encounter Books, 2009), 1.

55 Seth Stern, "Obama-Schumer Bill Proposal Would Criminalize Voter Intimidation," *New York Times*, January 31, 2007, https://archive.nytimes.com/www.nytimes.com/cq/2007/01/31/cq_2213.html.

56 Josh Gerstein, "Eric Holder: Black Panther case focus demeans 'my people,'" *Politico*, March 1, 2011, https://www.politico.com/blogs/under-the-radar/2011/03/eric-holder-black-panther-case-focus-demeans-my-people-033839.

57 Jack Cashill, "Wally and the Beav Join the Thought Police," *WND*, May 5, 2011, http://www.cashill.com/intellect_fraud/wally_and_beaver.htm.

58 Stanley Kurtz, "Inside Obama's ACORN, *National Review*, May 29, 2008, https://www.nationalreview.com/2008/05/inside-obamas-acorn-stanley-kurtz/.

59 Stanley Kurtz, *Radical-in-Chief: Barack Obama and the Untold Story of American Socialism* (New York: Pocket Books, 2010), 210, Kindle edition.

60 "It's War Between 'The Factor' and The New York Times," Fox News, May 19, 2009, https://www.foxnews.com/transcript/its-war-between-the-factor-and-the-new-york-times.

61 Matthew Vadum, "New York Times Finally Admits It Spiked Obama/ACORN Corruption Story," *American Spectator*, May 18, 2009, https://spectator.org/18757_new-york-times-finally-admits-it-spiked-obamaacorn-corruption-story/.

62 James O'Keefe, *Breakthrough: Our Guerilla War to Expose Fraud and Save Democracy* (New York: Simon & Schuster, 2013), 38.

63 Ibid., 40.

64 Ibid., 58.

65 Ibid., 47.

66 "Official Statement from ACORN Housing President Alton Bennett, Executive Director Mike Shea," *Breitbart,* September 11, 2009, https://www.breitbart.com/politics/2009/09/11/official-statement-from-acorn-housing-president-alton-bennett-executive-director-mike-shea/.

67 Transcripts, CNN.com, September 10, 2009, www.cnn.com › TRANSCRIPTS › ldt.01.html.

68 goodidealist, "The Acorn Pimp: The bully behind the costume. (I found his blog)," *Daily Kos,* September 15, 2009, https://www.dailykos.com/stories/2009/9/14/782156/-.

69 Darryl Fears, "ACORN to review actions," *Washington Post,* September 17, 2009, https://www.spokesman.com/stories/2009/sep/17/acorn-to-review-actions/.

70 Darryl Fears and Carol Leonnig, "Duo in Sting Video Say Their Effort Was Independent," *Washington Post,* September 18, 2009, https://www.pressreader.com/usa/the-washington-post/20090918/textview.

71 Scott Whitlock, "Former Dem Aide Stephanopoulos Lectures James O'Keefe: 'You're More of a Political Activist Than a Journalist,'" *Media Research Center,* June 1, 2010, https://archive2.mrc.org/bias-alerts/former-dem-aide-stephanopoulos-lectures-james-okeefe-youre-more-political-activist-journ.

72 James O'Keefe, "James O'Keefe Interviews Jack Cashill Part I: Journalism Ethics," projectveritas.com, August 10, 2016, https://www.projectveritas.com/2016/08/10/james-okeefe-interviews-jack-cashill-part-i-journalism-ethics/.

73 Kerry Picket, "AUDIO: Origin of Rep. Carson's racism accusation toward health care protesters," *Washington Times,* April 6, 2010, https://www.washingtontimes.com/blog/watercooler/2010/apr/6/audio-rep-carson-first-peddles-out-racism-story-re/.

74 "Video Proof: The NAACP Rewards Racism," *Breitbart,* July 19, 2010, https://www.breitbart.com/politics/2010/07/19/video-proof-the-naacp-awards-racism-2010/.

75 Ibid.

76 Krissah Thompson, "Shirley Sherrod reflects on her link to Andrew Breitbart," *Washington Post,* March 1, 2012, https://www.washingtonpost.com/blogs/she-the-people/post/shirley-sherrod-reflects-on-her-link-to-andrew-breitbart/2012/03/01/gIQAgP8ykR_blog.html?utm_term=.0066ce0cb05b.

77 Caroline May, "Will Pigford Vindicate Andrew Breitbart," *Daily Caller,* December 9, 2010, https://dailycaller.com/2010/12/09/will-pigford-vindicate-andrew-breitbart/.

78 "Transcript of Obama's Press Conference," *Real Clear Politics,* September 10, 2010, https://www.realclearpolitics.com/articles/2010/09/10/transcript_of_obama_press_conference_107112.html.

79 Sharon LaFraniere, "U.S. Opens Spigot After Farmers Claim Discrimination," *New York Times,* April 26, 2013, https://www.nytimes.com/2013/04/26/us/farm-loan-bias-claims-often-unsupported-cost-us-millions.html.

80 Conor Friedersdorf, "Andrew Breitbart and James O'Keefe Ruined Him, and Now He Gets $100,000," *Atlantic,* March 8, 2013, https://www.theatlantic.com/politics/archive/2013/03/andrew-breitbart-and-james-okeefe-ruined-him-and-now-he-gets-100-000/273841/.

81 James O'Keefe, Twitter, January 17, 2020, https://twitter.com/JamesOKeefeIII/status/1218359754747269120.

82 Glenn Kessler, "Has the Obama White House been 'historically free of scandal'?" *Washington Post,* January 19, 2017, https://www.washingtonpost.com/news/fact-checker/wp/2017/01/19/has-the-obama-white-house-been-historically-free-of-scandal/?utm_term=.cf678a44af85.

83 Attkisson, *Stonewalled,* 278, Kindle edition.

84 Incident Report 9005127, Cambridge Police Department, July 16, 2009, http://www.samefacts.com/archives/Police%20report%20on%20Gates%20arrest.PDF.

85 Abby Goodnough, "Harvard Professor Jailed; Officer Is Accused of Bias," *New York Times,* July 20, 2009, https://www.nytimes.com/2009/07/21/us/21gates.html.

86 Helene Cooper, "Obama Criticizes Arrest of Harvard Professor," *New York Times,* July 22, 2009, https://www.nytimes.com/2009/07/23/us/politics/23gates.html?auth=login-email.

87 Andrew Breitbart, "On Race, 'No, He Can't'," *Real Clear Politics,* August 3, 2009, https://www.realclearpolitics.com/articles/2009/08/03/on_race_no_he_cant_97747.html.

88 Jack Cashill, *If I Had a Son: Race, Guns, and the Railroading of George Zimmerman* (Nashville: WND Books, 2013), 6-20.

89 "Trayvon 'hunted down like rabid dog,'" *IOL,* March 28, 2012, https://www.iol.co.za/news/world/trayvon-hunted-down-like-rabid-dog-1265264.

90 *Good Morning America,* ABC, March 10, 2012.

91 "Trayvon Martin shooting: Black leaders press White House," *Politico,* March 23, 2012, https://www.politico.com/news/stories/0312/74385_Page2.html.

92 President Obama statement on Trayvon Martin case, *The 1600 Report,* March 23, 2012, http://whitehouse.blogs.cnn.com/2012/03/23/president-obama-statement-on-trayvon-martin-case/.

93 Sundance, "Look, I'm as concerned at Trayvon Martin's shooting as anyone," *Conservative Treehouse,* March 23, 2012, https://theconservativetreehouse.com/2012/03/23/look-im-as-concerned-at-trayvon-martins-shooting-as-anyone-but-a-million-hoodie-march-really-cmon/.

94 Sundance, "Trayvon Martin was apparently a 17 year old undisciplined punk thug, drug dealing, thief and wanna be gangsta," *Conservative Treehouse,* March 31, 2012, https://theconservativetreehouse.com/2012/03/27/trayvon-martin-was-apparently-a-17-year-old-undisciplined-punk-thug-drug-dealing-thief-and-wannabe-gangsta/.

95 Elspeth Reeve, "Profiles in October Surprise: Obama's 'Real' Dad," *Atlantic,* October 15, 2012, https://www.theatlantic.com/

politics/archive/2012/10/profiles-october-surprise-obamas-real-dad/322541/.

[96] Miami Herald Editorial Board, "He killed Trayvon Martin, now George Zimmerman is suing — everyone. Why?" Miami Herald, December 4, 2019, https://www.miamiherald.com/opinion/editorials/article238044044.html.

[97] Lisa Bloom, *Suspicion Nation: The Inside Story of the Trayvon Martin Injustice and Why We Continue to Repeat It* (Berkeley: Counterpoint, 2015), 155.

[98] Victor Li, "Judge throws out George Zimmerman's libel lawsuit against NBC," *ABA Journal*, June 30, 2014, http://www.abajournal.com/news/article/judge_throws_out_george_zimmermans_libel_lawsuit_against_nbc.

[99] Miami Herald Editorial Board, "He killed Trayvon Martin, now George Zimmerman is suing — everyone. Why?" *Miami Herald*, December 4, 2019, https://www.miamiherald.com/opinion/editorials/article238044044.html.

[100] Ta-Nehisi Coates, "Did George Zimmerman Use A Racial Slur?" *Atlantic*, March 22, 2012, https://www.theatlantic.com/national/archive/2012/03/did-george-zimmerman-use-a-racial-slur/254925/.

[101] "Our Mission: America's Peacemaker," Department of Justice, https://www.justice.gov/crs/about.

[102] "Documents Obtained by Judicial Watch Detail Role of Justice Department in Organizing Trayvon Martin Protests," *Judicial Watch*, July 10 2013, https://www.judicialwatch.org/press-releases/documents-obtained-by-judicial-watch-detail-role-of-justice-department-in-organizing-trayvon-martin-protests/.

[103] David Maraniss, "The first black president has rarely put the focus on his race. But on Friday, he spoke first as a black American," *Washington Post*, July 21, 2013, https://www.pressreader.com.

[104] Neil King and Rebecca Ballhaus, "Views on Race Relations Sour, Especially Among Blacks," *Wall Street Journal*, July 24, 2013, https://www.wsj.com/articles/SB10001424127887324144304578624183517587130.

[105] Wesley Lowery and Todd Frankel, "Mike Brown notched a hard-fought victory just days before he was shot: A diploma," *Washington Post*, August 12, 2014, https://www.washingtonpost.com/politics/mike-brown-notched-a-hard-fought-victory-just-days-before-he-was-shot-a-diploma/2014/08/12/574d65e6-2257-11e4-8593-da634b334390_story.html?utm_term=.7a65eef9e3ce.

[106] Sundance, "The Instigator," *Conservative Treehouse*, August 29, 2014, https://theconservativetreehouse.com/2014/08/29/the-instigator-how-one-saint-louis-man-originated-the-hands-up-dont-shoot-mike-brown-controversy-and-created-the-eye-witness-testimonials/.

[107] Manny Fernandez and Campbell Robertson, "At Ferguson March, Call to Halt Traffic in Labor Day Highway Protest," *New York Times*, August 30, 2014, https://www.nytimes.com/2014/08/31/us/at-ferguson-march-call-for-labor-day-highway-protest.html.

[108] "Shooting Death of Michael Brown—Ferguson, MO," The United States Department of Justice, 2014, https://www.justice.gov/crs/timeline-event/shooting-death-michael-brown-ferguson-mo.

[109] Jonathan Capehart, "UP w/Steve Kornacki," MSNBC, August 10, 2014, http://www.msnbc.com/up-w-steve-kornacki/watch/police-shooting-of-teenager-sparks-protest-316983363930.

[110] Jonathan Capehart, "'Hands up, don't shoot' was built on a lie," *Washington Post*, March 16, 2015, https://www.washingtonpost.com/blogs/post-partisan/wp/2015/03/16/lesson-learned-from-the-shooting-of-michael-brown/?utm_term=.f29d4656f9e7.

[111] Jonathan Capehart, "Darren Wilson and guilt by association," *Washington Post*, December 1, 2014, https://www.washingtonpost.com/blogs/post-partisan/wp/2014/12/01/darren-wilson-and-guilt-by-association/?utm_term=.f9ad5428cc66.

[112] "Transcript: Obama's remarks on unrest in Ferguson, Mo., and Iraq," *Washington Post*, August 14, 2014, https://www.washingtonpost.com/politics/transcript-president-obamas-remarks-on-unrest-in-ferguson-mo-and-iraq/2014/08/14/c8ce971e-23c7-11e4-958c-268a320a60ce_story.html?utm_term=.70bfa9dfe772.

[113] David Remnick, *The Bridge*, 238.

[114] Maraniss, *Barack Obama: The Story*, 305.

115 Sam Levine, "Obama discusses Ferguson protests in personal terms," *HuffPost,* December 8, 2014, https://www.huffpost.com/entry/obama-ferguson-protests_n_6291608.

116 Ibid.

117 "Video Shows NYC Protesters Chanting for 'Dead Cops,'" News 4 New York, December 15, 2014, http://www.nbcnewyork.com/news/local/Eric-Garner-Manhattan-Dead-Cops-Video-Millions-March-Protest-285805731.html.

118 Ralph Ellis, Brian Todd, Faith Karimi, "Citing security concerns, Darren Wilson resigns from Ferguson police force," CNN, November 30, 2014, https://www.cnn.com/2014/11/29/us/ferguson-protests/index.html.

119 Heather Mac Donald, "The Ferguson Effect," *Washington Post,* July 20, 2016, https://www.washingtonpost.com/news/volokh-conspiracy/wp/2016/07/20/the-ferguson-effect/?utm_term=.fa65ecff89d2.

120 Ibid.

121 FBI Unified Crime Reports, Death Penalty Information Center, https://deathpenaltyinfo.org/facts-and-research/murder-rates.

122 Timothy Burke, "Colin Kaepernick Refuses to Stand for Anthem: 'There Are Bodies in the Street,'" *DeadSpin,* August 27, 2016, https://deadspin.com/colin-kapernick-refuses-to-stand-for-anthem-there-are-1785838030.

The Rainbow Front

1 Katharine Seelye and John Broder, "The Obama-McCain Faith Forum," August 16, 2008, https://thecaucus.blogs.nytimes.com/2008/08/16/tonights-obama-mccain-faith-forum/.

2 Ibid.

3 David Axelrod, *Believer: My Forty Years in Politics* (New York: Penguin Books, 2015), 446.

4 Email from David Garrow, January 17, 2020.

5 Garrow, *Rising Star,* (paperback edition, 2019), 113.

6 Barack Obama. "Pop," Feast, Spring 1981, Occidental College Special Collections and College Archives.

7   Neo-Neocon, "'POP' — Obama's disturbing poem on man-boy relationship." This article can now be found at https://outline.com/d7s9WR.

8   Larry Sinclair Press Conference Exposing Barack Obama, YouTube, May 17, 2012, https://www.youtube.com/watch?v=3QK0eGp3N6A.

9   Ben Smith, "Ax on Ayers," *Politico*, February 26, 2008, https://www.politico.com/blogs/ben-smith/2008/02/ax-on-ayers-006517.

10 Sarah Lai Stirland, "Bloggers Get Obama Accuser Hauled Off in Handcuffs," *Wired*, June 19, 2008, https://www.google.com/?client=safari.

11 Matthew Weaver, "Gay rage at Proposition 8," *Guardian*, November 6, 2008, https://www.theguardian.com/world/deadlineusa/2008/nov/06/usa-gayrights.

12 Jacqueline L. Salmon, Debbi Wilgoren and Peter Slevin, "Obama Defends Invocation by Conservative Pastor," *Washington Post*, December 18, 2008, http://voices.washingtonpost.com/44/2008/12/choice-of-warren-to-give-invoc.html.

13 Carrie Prejean, *Still Standing: The Untold Story of My Fight Against Gossip, Hate, and Political Attacks* (Washington: Regnery, 2009), 4.

14 Prejean, 280-282.

15 Alexander Burns, "Trump on Prejean: Same as Obama," *Politico*, May 12, 2009, https://www.politico.com/story/2009/05/trump-on-prejean-same-as-obama-022413.

16 Katharine Seelye, "Trump Rules: Miss California Is Not Fired," *New York Times*, May 12, 2009, https://thelede.blogs.nytimes.com/2009/05/12/the-donald-carrie-prejean-and-the-tiara/.

17 Joe Becker, "How the President Got to 'I Do' on Same-Sex Marriage," *New York Times*, April 16, 2014, https://www.nytimes.com/2014/04/20/magazine/how-the-president-got-to-i-do-on-same-sex-marriage.html.

18 Mark 10:7, *King James Bible*, Bible Hub, https://biblehub.com/mark/10-7.htm.

[19] Associated Press, "Black Ministers Protest Gay Marriage," *New York Times*, March 23, 2004, https://www.nytimes.com/2004/03/23/us/black-ministers-protest-gay-marriage.html.

[20] Out.com editors, "Power 50," *Out*, April 3, 2007, https://www.out.com/out-exclusives/power-50/2007/04/03/power-50.

[21] Charlie Savage and Sheryl Gay Stolberg, "In Shift, U.S. Says Marriage Act Blocks Gay Rights," *New York Times*, February 23, 2011, https://archive.nytimes.com/www.nytimes.com/2011/02/24/us/24marriage.html.

[22] Matt Apuzzo, "Holder Sees Way to Curb Bans on Gay Marriage," *New York Times*, February 24, 2014, https://www.nytimes.com/2014/02/25/us/holder-says-state-attorneys-general-dont-have-to-defend-gay-marriage-bans.html.

[23] Axelrod, 452.

[24] Valerie Jarrett, *Finding My Voice: My Journey to the West Wing and the Path Forward* (New York: Penguin Publishing Group, 2019), 277, Kindle edition.

[25] Jim Downs, "We're looking at the Masterpiece Cakeshop case all wrong. And so did the Supreme Court," *Washington Post*, June 6, 2018, https://www.washingtonpost.com/news/made-by-history/wp/2018/06/06/were-looking-at-the-masterpiece-cakeshop-case-all-wrong-and-so-did-the-supreme-court/.

The Brown Front

[1] Brian Lonergan, "Barbara Jordan's wisdom is needed in today's immigration debate," *The Hill*, January 17, 2018, https://thehill.com/opinion/immigration/369153-barbara-jordans-wisdom-is-needed-in-todays-immigration-debate.

[2] Bill Clinton, State of the Union Address, C-SPAN, January 24, 1995, https://www.google.com/?client=safari.

[3] Steven Greenhouse, "Riding Across America for Immigrant Workers," *New York Times*, September 17, 2003, https://www.nytimes.com/2003/09/17/us/riding-across-america-for-immigrant-workers.html.

4   John Wagner, "Trump touted Obama's 2005 remarks on immigration. Here's what Obama actually said," *Washington Post,* October 24, 2018, https://beta.washingtonpost.com/politics/trump-touted-obamas-2005-remarks-on-immigration-heres-what-obama-actually-said/2018/10/24/1ed845c0-d782-11e8-aeb7-ddcad4a0a54e_story, html?noredirect=on.

5   Ashley Southall, "Obama Vows to Push Immigration Changes," *New York Times,* October 25, 2010, https://thecaucus.blogs.nytimes.com/2010/10/25/in-appeal-to-hispanics-obama-promises-to-push-immigration-reform/.

6   Ibid.

7   Allahpundit, "Obama's Turnout Pitch To Latinos: Get Out There And Punish Your 'Enemies,'" *Hot Air,* October 25, 2010, https://hotair.com/archives/allahpundit/2010/10/25/obamas-turnout-pitch-to-latinos-get-out-there-and-punish-your-enemies/.

8   Stanley Renshon, "Shades of Richard Nixon: Obama to Latinos—'Punish Our Enemies,'" Center for Immigration Studies, October 27, 2010, https://cis.org/Renshon/Shades-Richard-Nixon-Obama-Latinos-Punish-Our-Enemies.

9   "Text: Obama and Calderon in Mexico City," April 17, 2009, CBS News, https://www.cbsnews.com/news/text-obama-and-calderon-in-mexico-city/.

10 J.J. Hensley, "Feds link Arizona buyers to drug cartels' guns," *Arizona Republic,* September 18, 2010.

11 Sari Horwitz, "Agent who started 'Fast and Furious' defends gun-tracking operation," *Washington Post,* June 27, 2012, https://www.washingtonpost.com/world/national-security/agent-who-started-fast-and-furious-defends-gunrunning-operation/2012/06/27/gJQAQviT7V_story.html.

12 John Hayward, "Fast and Furious: 'The Perfect Storm of Idiocy'?" *Human Events,* July 26, 2011, https://www.independentsentinel.com/fast-furious-perfect-storm-of-idiocy/.

13 Dennis Wagner, "ATF gun probe: Behind the fall of Operation Fast and Furious," *Arizona Republic,* November 27, 2011, http://www.bikernews.org/wtn/news.php?extend.13833.

14 Mike Vanderboegh, "The blame shifting & leaping to illogical exculpatory conclusions begins, but Obama's Gunwalker was a deliberate conspiracy vs. the 2nd Amendment," *Sipsey Street Irregulars*, March 8, 2011, https://sipseystreetirregulars.blogspot.com/2011/03/blame-shifting-leaping-to-illogical.html.

15 Michael Horowitz, "Report by the Office of the Inspector General on the Review of ATF's Operation Fast and Furious and Related Matters," September 20, 2012, https://oig.justice.gov/testimony/t1220.pdf.

16 Attkisson, p. 96.

17 Katie Pavlich, *Fast and Furious: Barack Obama's Bloodiest Scandal and the Shameless Cover-Up* (Washington: Regnery, 2012), 192.

18 Matt Gertz, "Fast And Spurious: Katie Pavlich's ATF Conspiracy," Media Matters, April 23, 2012, https://www.mediamatters.org/national-rifle-association/fast-and-spurious-katie-pavlichs-atf-conspiracy.

19 Matt Gertz, "Fox Hides Extremism Of Terror-Inspiring Source Of Holder Attack," Media Matters, July 12, 2012, https://www.mediamatters.org/fox-news/fox-hides-extremism-terror-inspiring-source-holder-attack?redirect_source=/blog/2012/07/12/fox-hides-extremism-of-terror-inspiring-source/187091.

20 "Obama on 'gunwalking'—'Serious mistakes' may have been made," CBS News, March 23, 2011, https://www.youtube.com/watch?v=Lh37v_NkmM4.

21 Richard Serrano, "Emails to White House didn't mention gun sting," *Los Angeles Times,* July 28, 2011, https://www.latimes.com/world/la-xpm-2011-jul-28-la-na-fast-furious-emails-20110729-story.html.

22 "AP sources: Bush-era probe involved guns 'walking,'" NBC News, updated October 5, 2011, http://www.nbcnews.com/id/44788900/ns/politics-more_politics/t/ap-sources-bush-era-probe-involved-guns-walking/.

23 Pavlich, 73.

24 Ibid., 132.

25 Horowitz, 256.

26 The Colbert Report, "Unraveling the Fast and Furious Scandal," Comedy Central, June 20, 2012, http://www.cc.com/video-playlists/kw3fj0/the-opposition-with-jordan-klepper-welcome-to-the-opposition-w–jordan-klepper/95tn0n.

27 Attkisson, 128.

28 Ibid., 298.

29 "Transcript And Audio: Second Presidential Debate," NPR, October 16, 2012, https://www.npr.org/2012/10/16/163050988/transcript-obama-romney-2nd-presidential-debate.

30 Remarks by the President on immigration, Obama White House Archives, June 15, 2012, https://obamawhitehouse.archives.gov/the-press-office/2012/06/15/remarks-president-immigration.

31 "Remarks by the President at Univision Town Hall," Obama White House Archives, March 28, 2011, https://obamawhite house.archives.gov/the-press-office/2011/03/28/remarks-president-univision-town-hall.

32 Penny Starr, "Obama Campaign Sends 'Dreamers' Fundraising Email Hours after Amnesty Announcement," *CNS News*, June 18, 2012, https://www.cnsnews.com/news/article/obama-campaign-sends-dreamers-fundraising-email-hours-after-amnesty-announcement.

33 State of the Union with Candy Crowley, CNN, June 17, 2012, http://transcripts.cnn.com/TRANSCRIPTS/1206/17/sotu.01.html.

The Green Front

1 Michael Crichton, "Remarks to the Commonwealth Club," September 15, 2003, https://www.cs.cmu.edu/~kw/crichton.html.

2 "Steven Milloy," Wikipedia, https://en.wikipedia.org/wiki/Steven_Milloy.

3 David Paul Kuhn and Ben Smith, "Messianic rhetoric infuses Obama rallies," *Politico,* December 9, 2007, https://www.poli tico.com/story/2007/12/messianic-rhetoric-infuses-obama-rallies-007281.

4   "Barack Obama's Remarks in St. Paul," *New York Times*, June 3, 2008, https://www.nytimes.com/2008/06/03/us/politics/03text-obama.html.

5   Angelo Codevilla, "The Rise of Political Correctness," https://claremontreviewofbooks.com/the-rise-of-political-correctness/.

6   Attkisson, *Stonewalled*, 153.

7   Ellen Goodman, "Can we please stop arguing and do something about the climate?" *Pittsburgh Gazette*, February 8, 2007, https://www.post-gazette.com/opinion/Op-Ed/2007/02/09/Ellen-Goodman-Global-warning/stories/200702090178.

8   Jack Cashill, "The Democratic War on Science," February 7, 2008, *American Thinker*, http://www.cashill.com/natl_general/demo_war_on%20_science.htm.

9   "A sensitive matter," *The Economist*, March 30, 2013, https://www.economist.com/science-and-technology/2013/03/30/a-sensitive-matter.

10   Barack Obama, *The Audacity of Hope* (New York: Crown Publishers, 2006), 101.

11   2009 H1N1 Pandemic, Center for Disease Control and Prevention, https://www.cdc.gov/flu/pandemic-resources/2009-h1n1-pandemic.html.

12   Jesse Lee, "Van Jones to CEQ," the White House blog, https://obamawhitehouse.archives.gov/blog/2009/03/10/van-jones-ceq.

13   Max Schulz, "Green Hustler," *City Journal*, March 16, 2009, https://www.city-journal.org/html/green-hustler-10552.html.

14   Eliza Strickland, "The New Face of Environmentalism," *East Bay Express,* November 2, 2005, https://www.eastbayexpress.com/gyrobase/the-new-face-of-environmentalism/Content?oid=1079539&showFullText=true.

15   "22 to Know," *In These Times*, September 26, 2008, http://inthesetimes.com/article/3933/twenty_two_to_know/.

16   Mark Rudd, "Let's Get Smart About Obama," November 2008, MarkRudd.com, https://www.markrudd.com/indexa2a8.html?organizing-and-activism-now/lets-get-smart-about-obama-nov-2008.html.

17 Cliff Kincaid, "The Blogger Who Nailed Van Jones," *Accuracy in Media*, September 7, 2009, https://www.aim.org/aim-column/the-blogger-who-nailed-van-jones/.

18 Grandia, September 9, 2009.

19 Jack Cashill, phone interview with Trevor Loudon, July 2, 2019.

20 Kevin Grandia, "The Right Wing Attack Machine Behind the Van Jones Affair," *Desmog*, September 9, 2009, https://www.desmogblog.com/right-wing-attack-machine-behind-van-jones-affair.

21 Johanna Neuman, "White House aide's 9/11 conspiracy theories cloud his future. It's not easy being green," *Los Angeles Times*, September 4, 2009, https://latimesblogs.latimes.com/washington/2009/09/white-house-aides-911-conspiracy-theories-cloud-his-future-its-not-easy-being-green.html.

22 John Broder, "White House Official Resigns After G.O.P. Criticism," *New York Times*, September 6, 2009, https://www.nytimes.com/2009/09/07/us/politics/07vanjones.html.

23 "Obama did not order Van Jones' resignation, adviser says," CNN, September 6, 2009, http://www.cnn.com/2009/POLITICS/09/06/obama.adviser.resigns/index.html.

24 Jack Kelly, "How Could Obama Have Hired Van Jones?" *Real Clear Politics*, September 13, 2009, https://www.realclearpolitics.com/articles/2009/09/13/how_could_obama_have_hired_van_jones_98293.html.

25 John Broder, "Energy Department Issues First Renewable-Energy Loan Guarantee," *New York Times*, March 20, 2009, https://green.blogs.nytimes.com/2009/03/20/energy-department-issues-first-renewable-energy-loan-guarantee/.

26 Tim Dickinson, "The Climate Killers," *Rolling Stone*, January 6, 2010, https://web.archive.org/web/20100111035001/http://www.rollingstone.com/politics/story/31633524/the_climate_killers/print.

27 Submitted Written Testimony of Marc Morano, Publisher of CFACT's Climate Depot, House Natural Resources Committee, May 22, 2019, https://naturalresources.house.gov/imo/media/doc/

Morano%20Testimony%20WOW%20Ov%20Hrg%2005.22.19.
pdf.

28 John Richardson, "This Man Wants to Convince You Global
Warming Is a Hoax," *Esquire*, March 30, 2010, http://joannenova.
com.au/2010/03/esquire-mag-does-the-full-marc-morano-
climategate-story/.

29 Phone interview, Marc Morano, June 26, 2019.

30 Andrew Revkin and John Broder, "In Face of Skeptics, Experts
Affirm Climate Peril," *New York Times*, December 6, 2009, https://
www.nytimes.com/2009/12/07/science/earth/07climate.html.

31 Naomi Klein, "Copenhagen's failure belongs to Obama,"
Guardian, Decmeber 21, 2009, https://www.theguardian.com/
commentisfree/cif-green/2009/dec/21/copenhagen-failure-obama-
climate-change.

32 Jackie Calmes, "Invoking the Oil Crisis, Obama Lauds Clean
Energy," *New York Times,* May 26, 2010, https://green.blogs.
nytimes.com/2010/05/26/invoking-the-oil-crisis-obama-
lauds-clean-energy/?searchResultPosition=26.

33 Matthew Wald, "Solar Firm Aided by Federal Loans Shuts
Doors," *New York Times*, August 31, 2011, https://www.nytimes.
com/2011/09/01/business/energy-environment/solyndra-solar-
firm-aided-by-federal-loans-shuts-doors.html.

34 Matthew Wald and Michael Kanellos, "F.B.I. Raids Solar Firm That
Got U.S. Loans," *New York Times,* September 8, 2011, https://www.
nytimes.com/2011/09/09/business/solar-company-is-searched-by-
fbi.html?searchResultPosition=37.

35 Marc Morano, Neil Cavuto Show, Fox News, September 24, 2011,
http://coyoteblog.com/coyote_blog/2011/09/more-on-solyndra.
html.

36 Joe Nocera, "The Phony Solyndra Scandal," *New York Times,*
September 23, 2011, https://www.nytimes.com/2011/09/24/opinion/
the-phony-solyndra-scandal.html.

The Pink Front

1   Anemona Hartocollis and Yamiche Alcindor, "Women's March Highlights as Huge Crowds Protest Trump: 'We're Not Going Away,'" *New York Times*, January 21, 2017, https://www.nytimes.com/2017/01/21/us/womens-march.html.

2   Women's March Global, https://womensmarchglobal.org/about/.

3   "Remarks by the President at United States of Women Summit," June 14, 2016, https://obamawhitehouse.archives.gov/the-press-office/2016/06/14/remarks-president-united-states-women-summit.

4   Melanie Garunay, "Taking Action to Advance Equal Pay," White House blog, January 29, 206, https://obamawhitehouse.archives.gov/blog/2016/01/29/taking-action-advance-equal-pay.

5   David Nakamura, "Obama to propose new rule to examine gender pay inequity," *Washington Post*, January 29, 2016, https://www.washingtonpost.com/news/post-politics/wp/2016/01/29/obama-to-propose-new-rule-to-examine-gender-pay-inequity/?utm_term=.3fc5b03928a4.

6   Julie Hirschfeld Davis, "Obama Moves to Expand Rules Aimed at Closing Gender Pay Gap," *New York Times*, January 29, 2016, https://www.nytimes.com/2016/01/29/us/politics/obama-moves-to-expand-rules-aimed-at-closing-gender-pay-gap.html.

7   State of the Union 2014 Address: President Obama's FULL SOTU Speech, *The New York Times*, January 28, 2014, https://www.youtube.com/watch?v=hed1nP9X7pI.

8   Glenn Kessler, Fact Checking the 2014 State of the Union address, *Washington Post*, January 28, 2014, https://www.washingtonpost.com/news/fact-checker/wp/2014/01/28/fact-checking-the-2014-state-of-the-union-address/?utm_term=.749cd0f4b6e1.

9   Glenn Kessler, "The White House's use of data on the gender wage gap," *Washington Post*, June 5, 2012, https://www.washingtonpost.com/blogs/fact-checker/post/the-white-houses-use-of-data-on-the-gender-wage-gap/2012/06/04/gJQAYH6nEV_blog.html?utm_term=.665d34215ccb.

10 Christina Hoff Sommers, "No, Women Don't Make Less Money Than Men," *Daily Beast*, February 1, 2014, https://

www.thedailybeast.com/no-women-dont-make-less-money-than-men?ref=scroll.

11 Dear Colleague Letter, Office of the Assistant Secretary, US Department of Education, April 4, 2011, https://www2.ed.gov/about/offices/list/ocr/letters/colleague-201104_pg19.html.

12 Camille Paglia, "The Modern Campus Cannot Comprehend Evil," *Time*, September 29, 2014, https://time.com/3444749/camille-paglia-the-modern-campus-cannot-comprehend-evil/.

13 Sam Dillon, "Biden to Discuss New Guidelines About Campus Sex Crimes," *New York Times*, April 4, 2011, https://www.nytimes.com/2011/04/04/education/04violence.html.

14 Staff, "The feds' mad assault on campus sex," *New York Post*, July 20, 2011, https://nypost.com/2011/07/20/the-feds-mad-assault-on-campus-sex/.

15 Christina Hoff Sommers, "In Making Campuses Safe for Women, a Travesty of Justice for Men," *Chronicle of Higher Education*, June 5, 2011, https://www.chronicle.com/article/In-Making-Campuses-Safe-for/127766/.

16 "Alcohol and Other Drug Use at UMass Amherst: Results from 2012 Campus-wide Student Survey," https://www.umass.edu/ccc/sites/default/files/Campus%20wide%20Survey%202012%20%20final%20report%204-23.pdf.

17 Paglia, September 29, 2014.

18 Emma Paul, "Students Protest Sommers' Lecture," *Oberlin Review*, April 24, 2015, https://oberlinreview.org/8088/news/students-protest-sommers-lecture/.

19 Mairead McArdle, "Law-School Students Shout Down 'Known Fascist' Christina Hoff Sommers," *National Review*, March 6, 2018, https://www.nationalreview.com/2018/03/christina-hoff-sommers-lewis-clark-law-students-shout-down/.

20 Anna Orso, "UArts students protest professor Camille Paglia for comments on transgender people, sexual assault survivors," Philadelphia Inquirer, April 15, 2019, https://www.inquirer.com/news/camille-paglia-u-arts-professor-philadelphia-protest-petition-transgender-survivors-sexual-assault-david-yager-20190415.html.

21 Laura Kipnis, *Unwanted Advances: Sexual Paranoia Comes to Campus* (New York; Harper Collins, 2017), 1.

22 "Rolling Stone and UVA: The Columbia University Graduate School of Journalism Report," *Rolling Stone*, April 5, 2015, https://www. rollingstone.com/culture/culture-news/rolling-stone-and-uva-the-columbia-university-graduate-school-of-journalism-report-44930/.

23 Bret Stephens, "Betsy DeVos Ends a Campus Witch Hunt," *New York Times*, September 8, 2017, https://www.nytimes.com/2017/09/08/opinion/betsy-devos-title-iv.html.

24 Nancy Flanders, "Dave Chappelle calls out Planned Parenthood 'spin' in new comedy special," Live Action, March 25, 2017, https:// www.liveaction.org/news/dave-chappelle-calls-planned-parenthood-spin-new-comedy-special/.

25 "Full Transcript: Saddleback Presidential Forum, Sen. Barack Obama, John McCain; Moderated by Rick Warren," Vote Smart, August 17, 2008, https://votesmart.org/public-statement/658545/full-transcript-saddleback-presidential-forum-sen-barack-obama-john-mccain-moderated-by-rick-warren/?search=saddleback#.XSMqdi2ZPcg.

26 Jeffrey Ressner and Ben Smith, "Exclusive: Obama's lost law review article," *Politico*, August 22, 2008, https://www.politico.com/story/2008/08/exclusive-obamas-lost-law-review-article-012705.

27 Ibid.

28 Josh Hicks, "Did Obama deny rights to infants who survive abortion?," *Washington Post*, September 10, 2012, https://www.washingtonpost.com/blogs/fact-checker/post/did-obama-vote-to-deny-rights-to-infant-abortion-survivors/2012/09/07/9852895a-f87d-11e1-8398-0327ab83ab91_blog.html?utm_term=.59e9978055e7.

29 Tabitha Hale, "Stupak: HHS Mandate Violates My Obamacare Compromise," *Breitbart*, September 4, 2012, https://www.breitbart.com/politics/2012/09/04/Stupak-President-Played-Me-with-Obamacare-Deal/.

30 O'Keefe, *Breakthrough*, 27.

31 Ibid., 28.

32 Jeremy Peters, "Republicans Alter Script on Abortion, Seeking to Shift Debate," *New York Times*, July 26, 2015, https://www.nytimes. com/2015/07/27/us/politics/republicans-alter-script-on-abortion-seeking-to-shift-debate.html.

33 "Planned Parenthood VP Says Fetuses May Come Out Intact, Agrees Payments Specific to the Specimen," Center for Medical Progress, July 30, 2015, http://www.centerformedicalprogress.org/cmp/investigative-footage/.

34 "Planned Parenthood VP Says Fetuses May Come Out Intact, Agrees Payments Specific to the Specimen," Center for Medical Progress, July 30, 2015, https://www.youtube.com/watch?v=GWQuZMvcFA8.

35 Tim Hains, "Earnest: Unsure If Obama Has Seen 'Selectively' Edited Planned Parenthood Videos From 'Extremists On The Right,'" *Real Clear Politics*, July 30, 2015, https://www.realclearpolitics.com/video/2015/07/30/earnest_unsure_if_obama_has_seen_selectively_edited_planned_parenthood_videos_from_extremists_on_the_right.html.

36 Liz Kreutz, "Hillary Clinton Calls Planned Parenthood Videos 'Disturbing,'" ABC News, July 29, 2015, https://abcnews.go.com/Politics/hillary-clinton-calls-planned-parenthood-videos-disturbing/story?id=32757475.

37 Sandhya Somashekhar, "Videos deceptively edited, Planned Parenthood tells Congress," *Washington Post*, August 27, 2015, https://www.washingtonpost.com/national/videos-deceptively-edited-planned-parenthood-tells-congress/2015/08/27/5633612c-4cdd-11e5-902f-39e9219e574b_story.html?utm_term=.84ccc271cf80.

38 Jackie Calmes, "Planned Parenthood Videos Were Altered, Analysis Finds," *New York Times*, August 27, 2015, https://www.nytimes. com/2015/08/28/us/abortion-planned-parenthood-videos.html?_r=0.

39 Kelli, "Multiple reports confirm that Planned Parenthood videos were not manipulated," Live Action, April 25, 2016, https://www. liveaction.org/news/faked-criminal-videos-planned-parenthood-lies-again-on-twitter/.

The Crescent Front

1   This Week with George Stephanopoulos, ABC News, September 7, 2008, https://archive.org/details/WJLA_20140907_140000_This_Week_With_George_Stephanopoulos.

2   Peter Wallsten, "Allies of Palestinians see a friend in Obama," *Los Angeles Times*, April 10, 2008, https://www.latimes.com/archives/la-xpm-2008-apr-10-na-obamamideast10-story.html.

3   John Stephenson, "LA Times Withholds Video of Obama Toasting Former PLO Operative at Jew Bashing Dinner," *Newsbusters*, October 25, 2010, https://www.newsbusters.org/blogs/nb/john-stephenson/2008/10/25/la-times-withholds-video-obama-toasting-former-plo-operative-jew.

4   Andy McCarthy, "The L.A. Times Suppresses Obama's Khalidi Tape," *National Review*, October 27, 2008, https://www.nationalreview.com/2008/10/la-times-suppresses-obamas-khalidi-bash-tape-andrew-c-mccarthy/.

5   Marc Santora and Elissa Gootman, "Political Storm Finds a Columbia Professor," *New York Times,* October 30, 2008, https://www.nytimes.com/2008/10/31/nyregion/31khalil.html.

6   Richard Pérez-Peña, "McCain Attacks Los Angeles Times Over Its Refusal to Release '03 Obama Video," *New York Times*, October 29, 2008, https://www.nytimes.com/2008/10/30/us/politics/30campaign.html.

7   Hazel Trice Edney, "Photo of Sen. Barack Obama with Minister Louis Farrakhan surfaces," *North Star News Today*, January 20, 2018, http://www.northstarnewstoday.com/history/10867/.

8   "Louis Farrakhan," Southern Poverty Law Center, https://www.splcenter.org/fighting-hate/extremist-files/individual/louis-farrakhan.

9   Amanda Svachula, "Netflix Won't Offer Louis Farrakhan Documentary," *New York Times,* August 1, 2018, https://www.nytimes.com/2018/08/01/arts/television/louis-farrakhan-netflix.html.

10 "Moderate Muslims Speak Out on Capitol Hill," The Investigative Project on Terrorism, October 1, 2010, https://www.facebook.com.

11 "The Accord on Racism: The Declaration; Regrets for Past Wrongs And Hopes for Peace," *New York Times*, September 9, 2001, https://www.nytimes.com/2001/09/09/world/the-accord-on-racism-the-declaration-regrets-for-past-wrongs-and-hopes-for-peace.html?searchResultPosition=4.

12 Sheryl Gay Stolberg, "Obama Strongly Backs Islam Center Near 9/11 Site," *New York Times*, August 13, 2010, https://www.nytimes.com/2010/08/14/us/politics/14obama.html.

13 Jack Cashill, "Is Khalid al-Mansour the Man Behind the Obama Myth," *WND*, August 28, 2008, https://www.wnd.com/2008/08/73649/. Video can be viewed at https://www.conservativedailynews.com/2010/08/meet-dr-khalid-abdullah-tariq-al-mansour-an-obama-backer/.

14 "Mayor spurns Saudi's $10m," *Guardian*, October 12, 2001, https://www.theguardian.com/world/2001/oct/12/israeland thepalestinians.september11.

15 Ken Timmerman, phone interview, August 1, 2019.

16 Ken Timmerman, "Who is Khalid al-Mansour?" *Newsmax*, September 4, 2008, https://www.newsmax.com/newsfront/khalid-al-mansour-obama/2008/09/04/id/325191/.

17 "Update," Smith, September 4.

18 Ben Smith, "Sutton family retracts Obama story," *Politico*, September 6, 2008, https://www.politico.com/blogs/ben-smith/2008/09/sutton-family-retracts-obama-story-011622.

19 Ken Timmerman, "Obama's Harvard Years: Questions Swirl," *Newsmax*, September 23, 2008, https://www.newsmax.com/kentimmerman/obama-harvard-/2009/12/14/id/342454/.

20 Arif Khatib, "The National and International Roundtable," Blog Talk Radio, September 19, 2012, http://www.blogtalkradio.com/afterthoughtswithdenice/2012/09/19/the-national-and-international-roundtable#.UFptoKF6-yA.blogger.

21 Vernon Jarrett, "Will Arabs Back Ties To Blacks With Cash?" *St. Petersburg Independent*, November 6, 1979, 19-a, https://

news.google.com/newspapers?nid=950&dat=19791106&id=
RcFaAAAAIBAJ&sjid=GFkDAAAAIBAJ&pg=6597,1456637&
hl=en.

22 Frank Miele, "Does 1979 Newspaper Column Shed Light On 2008
Campaign Story," *Daily Inter Lake,* September 23, 2008, https://
www.dailyinterlake.com/news/20120923/does_1979_newspaper_
column_shed_light_on_2008_campaign_story.

23 Ben Smith, "What Percy Sutton Might Have Been Talking
About," *BuzzFeed News,* September 24, 2012, https://www.buzz
feednews.com/article/bensmith/what-percy-sutton-might-have-
been-talking-about. Frank Miele, "Khalid al-Mansour and his
'Terrible, Horrible, Not Good, Very Bad' Luck with Dear Friends
and Reporters," *Daily Inter Lake,* September 29, 2012, https://www.
dailyinterlake.com/archive/article-bb250fec-09db-11e2-b508-
001a4bcf887a.html.

24 Ibid.

25 Adam Johnson, "BuzzFeed's Obama Coverage Is 99 Percent
Uncritical—and Borderline Creepy," FAIR, https://fair.org/home/
buzzfeeds-obama-coverage-is-99-percent-uncritical-and-borderline-
creepy/.

26 Remnick, 112-113.

27 "Obama passport files violated; 2 workers at State fired;
1 rebuked," *Washington Times,* March 20, 2008, https://www.
washingtontimes.com/news/2008/mar/20/obama-passport-files-
violated-2-workers-at-state-f/.

28 Helene Cooper and Michael Grynbaum, "Passport Files of 3
Candidates Were Improperly Viewed," *New York Times,* March
21,2008,https://www.nytimes.com/2008/03/21/us/politics/21cnd-
passport.html.

29 Helene Cooper, "Passport Files of 3 Candidates Were Pried
Into," *New York Times,* March 22, 2008, https://www.nytimes.
com/2008/03/22/us/politics/22passport.html.

30 Tal Kopan, "Polygraph panic: CIA director fretted his vote for
communist," CNN, September 15, 2016, https://www.cnn.

com/2016/09/15/politics/john-brennan-cia-communist-vote/index.html.

31 Ibid.

32 "Islamophobe John Guandolo Claims CIA Director John Brennan is a Secret Muslim," YouTube, https://www.youtube.com/watch?v=aieUdwZoYMg.

33 Kate Bolduan, "Chief of firm involved in breach is Obama adviser," CNN, March 22, 2008, http://edition.cnn.com/2008/POLITICS/03/22/passport.files/index.html.

34 Glenn Kessler, "Rice Apologizes For Breach of Passport Data," *Washington Post*, March 22, 2008, http://www.washingtonpost.com/wp-dyn/content/article/2008/03/21/AR2008032100377.html?sid=ST2008032101821.

35 R. Jeffrey Smith, "Obama Taps CIA Veteran As Adviser On Terror; Brennan Has Drawn Fire on Interrogations," *Washington Post*, January 9, 2009, A-1.

36 Ken Timmerman, "Obama's Intelligence Adviser Involved in Security Breach," Newsmax, January 12, 2009, https://www.newsmax.com/kentimmerman/brennan-passport-breach/2009/01/12/id/337482/.

37 Kenneth Timmerman, *Deception: The Making of the Youtube Video Hillary and Obama Blamed for Benghazi* (Nashville: Post Hill Press, 2016), 132-3. Kindle edition.

38 "Key witness in passport fraud case fatally shot," *Washington Times*, April 19, 2008, https://www.washingtontimes.com/news/2008/apr/19/key-witness-in-passport-fraud-case-fatally-shot/.

39 Timmerman, *Deception*, 132.

40 Interview with Dan Pfeiffer, Fox News Sunday, May 19, 2013, http://www77.realclearpolitics.com/video/2013/05/19/obama_aide_pfeiffer_largely_irrelevant_fact_where_obama_was_during_benghazi_attack.html.

41 Timmerman, *Deception*, 161.

42 Max Fisher, "The Movie So Offensive That Egyptians Just Stormed the U.S. Embassy Over It," *Atlantic*, September 11, 2012, https://www.theatlantic.com/international/archive/2012/09/

the-movie-so-offensive-that-egyptians-just-stormed-the-us-embassy-over-it/262225/.

43 Timmerman, *Deception,* 312.

44 Max Blumenthal, "Meet The Right-Wing Extremist Behind Anti-Muslim Film That Sparked Deadly Riots," *The Exiled,* September 12, 2012, http://exiledonline.com/max-blumenthal-meet-the-right-wing-extremist-behind-anti-muslim-film-that-sparked-deadly-riots/.

45 Timmerman, *Deception,* 340-342.

46 "Benghazi Documents Point to White House on Misleading Talking Points," Judicial Watch, April 29, 2014, https://www.judicialwatch.org/press-releases/judicial-watch-benghazi-documents-point-white-house-misleading-talking-points/.

47 "Flashback: What Susan Rice Said About Benghazi," *Wall Street Journal,* November 16, 2012, https://blogs.wsj.com/washwire/2012/11/16/flashback-what-susan-rice-said-about-benghazi/.

48 Ben Rhodes, *The World As It Is: A Memoir of the Obama White House* (New York: Random House, 2018), 244.

49 Christian Toto, "David Letterman Mocks Pope, Catholic Church," *Breitbart,* July 24, 2013, https://www.breitbart.com/entertainment/2013/07/24/letterman-mocks-pope-crowd-not-amused/.

50 Tom Bevan, "What the President Said About Benghazi," *Real Clear Politics,* November 30, 2012, https://www.realclearpolitics.com/articles/2012/11/30/what_the_president_said_about_benghazi_116299.html.

51 Madeleine Kearns, "An Interview with Douglas Murray: Gender, Race, and Identity," *National Review,* October 1, 2019, https://www.nationalreview.com/2019/10/douglas-murray-book-the-madness-of-crowds-gender-race-and-identity/.

52 Serge Kovaleski and Adam Nagourney, "Man of Many Names Is Tied to a Video," *New York Times,* September 13, 2012, https://www.nytimes.com/2012/09/14/us/origins-of-provocative-video-are-shrouded.html.

53 Ibid.

54 Timmerman, *Deception*, 96.

55 Phone interview with Nakoula Basseley Nakoula, November 28, 2013.

56 Ian Lovett, "Man Linked to Film in Protests Is Questioned," *New York Times*, September 15, 2012, https://www.nytimes.com/2012/09/16/world/middleeast/man-linked-to-film-in-protests-is-questioned.html.

57 "Full 2012 town hall Presidential Debate," YouTube, October 16, 2012, https://www.youtube.com/watch?v=Mc0P5sZzlo0.

58 "President Obama Speaks on the Attack on Benghazi," YouTube, September 12, 2012, https://www.youtube.com/watch?v=rDAN caPx1xg.

59 Attkisson, *Stonewalled*, 5.

60 Attkisson, 298.

61 Debra Heine, "New Lawsuit Claims Rod Rosenstein Led Task Force that Spied on Sharyl Attkisson's Computers," *American Greatness*, January 9, 2020, https://amgreatness.com/2020/01/09/new-lawsuit-claims-rod-rosenstein-led-task-force-that-spied-on-sharyl-attkissons-computers/.

62 Erik Wemple, "Sharyl Attkisson's computer intrusions: 'Worse than anything Nixon ever did,'" *Washington Post*, October 27, 2014, https://www.washingtonpost.com/blogs/erik-wemple/wp/2014/10/27/sharyl-attkissons-computer-intrusions-worse-than-anything-nixon-ever-did/?utm_term=.cd5032979936.

63 Ann Marimow, "A rare peek into a Justice Department leak probe," *Washington Post*, May 19, 2013, https://www.washingtonpost.com/local/a-rare-peek-into-a-justice-department-leak-probe/2013/05/19/0bc473de-be5e-11e2-97d4-a479289a31f9_story.html?utm_term=.fa0a9059b918.

64 Josh Gerstein, "Fox reporter confronts State Department on Iran denial," *Politico*, December 2, 2013, https://www.politico.com/blogs/under-the-radar/2013/12/fox-reporter-confronts-state-department-on-iran-denial-178651.

65 Major Garrett, "The Allure of the Useful Lie," *National Journal*, December 3, 2013, https://www.nationaljournal.com/s/65243.

66 Major Garrett, "The Obama administration's useful lie about Iran Talks," CBS News, December 4, 2013, https://www.cbsnews.com/news/the-obama-administrations-useful-lie-about-iran-talks/.

67 David Simpson and Josh Levs, "Israeli PM Netanyahu: Iran nuclear deal 'historic mistake,'" CNN, November 25, 2013, https://www.cnn.com/2013/11/24/world/meast/iran-israel/index.html.

68 James Hannaham, "David Samuels' Doubleheader," *Village Voice*, April 15, 2008, https://www.villagevoice.com/2008/04/15/david-samuels-doubleheader/.

69 David Samuels, "The Aspiring Novelist Who Became Obama's Foreign-Policy Guru," *New York Times Magazine*, May 5, 2016, https://www.nytimes.com/2016/05/08/magazine/the-aspiring-novelist-who-became-obamas-foreign-policy-guru.html?_r=1.

70 Eric Levitz, "10 Problems With That *New York Times Magazine* Profile of White House Aide Ben Rhodes," *New York Magazine*, May 10, 2016, http://nymag.com/intelligencer/2016/05/10-problems-with-nyt-mags-ben-rhodes-profile.html.

71 David Samuels, "Through the Looking Glass With Ben Rhodes," *New York Times Magazine*, May 13, 2016, https://www.nytimes.com/2016/05/12/magazine/through-the-looking-glass-with-ben-rhodes.html.

The Eastern Front

1 Maggie Haberman, "Jerome Corsi, Conspiracy Theorist, Is Subpoenaed in Mueller Investigation," *New York Times,* September 5, 2018, https://www.nytimes.com/2018/09/05/us/politics/jerome-corsi-subpoena-mueller-investigation.html.

2 Office of the Inspector General US Department of Justice, Office of the Inspector General US Department of Justice, Review of Four FISA Applications and Other Aspects of the FBI's Crossfire Hurricane Investigation, (IG Report), 312, https://oig.justice.gov/reports/2019/o20012.pdf.

3   Lee Smith, *The Plot Against the President: The True Story of How Devin Nunes Uncovered the Biggest political Scandal in U.S. History* (New York: Hachette Book Group, 2019), 134, Kindle edition.

4   Pat Collins and Andrea Swalec, "27-Year-Old DNC Staffer Seth Rich Shot, Killed in Northwest DC," NBC Washington, July 11, 2016, https://www.nbcwashington.com/news/local/Man-Shot-Killed-in-Northwest-DC-386316391.html.

5   Marlow Stern, "Bill Maher and Michael Moore Turn on Julian Assange: 'I Feel Like He's Drifted,'" *Daily Beast,* October 29, 2016, https://www.thedailybeast.com/bill-maher-and-michael-moore-turn-on-julian-assange-i-feel-like-hes-drifted.

6   Matt Taibbi, *Hate Inc.: Why Today's Media Makes Us Despise One Another* (New York: OR Books, 2019), 262, Nook edition.

7   Lee Smith, 44.

8   Ibid., 277-78.

9   David Cloud, "Obama says Hillary Clinton was careless with emails but didn't jeopardize national security," *Los Angeles Times,* April 10, 2016, https://www.latimes.com/politics/la-na-obama-clinton-20160410-story.html.

10 Ibid., 47.

11 Ibid., 45.

12 Mark Tran, "WikiLeaks to publish more Hillary Clinton emails—Julian Assange," *The Guardian,* June 12, 2016, https://www.theguardian.com/media/2016/jun/12/wikileaks-to-publish-more-hillary-clinton-emails-julian-assange.

13 "Julian Assange on Seth Rich," YouTube, https://video.search.yahoo.com/yhs/search?fr=yhs-pty-pty_news&hsimp=yhs-pty_news&hspart=pty&p=%22seth+rich%22+%22julian+assange%22+Dutch+TV#id=51&vid=1652f94fbbb5a7e840eedd1a8d587bf1&action=click.

14 Donna Brazile, *Hacks, The Inside Story of the Break-ins and Breakdowns That Put Donald Trump in the White House* (New York: Hachette Books, 2017), 141, Nook edition.

15 Ibid.,168.

16 Ibid., 83.

[17]   Ibid., 83.

[18]   Metropolitan Police Department, Crime Map, http://crimemap. dc.gov/Report.aspx.

[19]   Manuel Roig-Franzia, "Seth Rich wasn't just another D.C. murder victim. He was a meme in the weirdest presidential election of our times," *Washington Post,* January 18, 2017, https://www. washingtonpost.com/lifestyle/style/seth-rich-wasnt-just-another-dc-murder-victim-he-was-a-meme-in-the-weirdest-presidential-election-of-our-times/2017/01/18/ee8e27f8-dcc0-11e6-918c-99ede3c8cafa_story.html.

[20]   Greg Jarrett, 28-31.

[21]   Michael Grynbaum and Daniel Victor, "Fox News Retracts Seth Rich Story That Stirred Controversy," *New York Times,* May 23, 2017, https://www.nytimes.com/2017/05/23/business/media/fox-news-seth-rich.html.

[22]   House Permanent Select Committee on Intelligence, "Report on Russian Active Measures"—Majority and Minority Reports, March 22, 2018, https://archive.org/stream/Russian-Active-Measures-House-Intel-2018/HRPT-115-1_djvu.txt.

[23]   Greg Jarrett, 5.

[24]   "Explosive Texts Point To FBI, Not Russian, Meddling In 2016 Election," *Investor's Business Daily,* December 13, 2017, https://www.investors.com/politics/editorials/fbi-text-message-russia-clinton-email-investigations/.

[25]   IG Report, 77.

[26]   Greg Miller, Ellen Nakashima, Adam Entous, "Obama's secret struggle to punish Russia for Putin's election assault," *Washington Post,* June 23, 2017, https://www.washingtonpost.com/graphics/2017/world/national-security/obama-putin-election-hacking/?utm_term=.fe600dca2ee1.

[27]   IG Report, 77.

[28]   McCarthy, 4.

[29]   Greg Jarrett, 38.

[30]   Adam Edelman and Mike Memoli, "FBI texts: Obama 'wants to know everything we're doing,'" NBC News, February 7,

2018, https://www.nbcnews.com/politics/politics-news/fbi-texts-obama-wants-know-everything-we-re-doing-n845531.

[31] IG Report, 76.

[32] Mark Hosenball, Steve Holland, "Trump being advised by ex-U.S. Lieutenant General who favors closer Russia ties," Reuters, February 26, 2016, https://www.reuters.com/article/us-usa-election-trump-advisor/trump-being-advised-by-ex-u-s-lieutenant-general-who-favors-closer-russia-ties-idUSMTZSAPEC2Q6G3JRH.

[33] Michael Isikoff, "U.S. intel officials probe ties between Trump adviser and Kremlin," *Yahoo! News*, September 23, 2016, https://news.yahoo.com/u-s-intel-officials-probe-ties-between-trump-adviser-and-kremlin-175046002.html.

[34] Chuck Ross, "Isikoff Stunned That His Carter Page Article Was Used To Justify Spy Warrant," *Daily Caller*, February 2, 2018, https://dailycaller.com/2018/02/02/isikoff-stunned-carter-page/.

[35] Jack Cashill, *TWA 800: The Crash, the Cover-Up, the Conspiracy* (Washington: Regnery, 2016), 149-150.

[36] Taibbi, 255.

[37] David Remnick, "Trump and Putin: A Love Story," *New Yorker*, August 3, 2016, https://www.newyorker.com/news/news-desk/trump-and-putin-a-love-story.

[38] Helene Cooper and Nicholas Kulish, "Biden Signals U.S. Is Open to Russia Missile Deal," *New York Times*, February 7, 2009, https://www.nytimes.com/2009/02/08/washington/08biden.html.

[39] Mark Landler, "Lost in Translation: A U.S. Gift to Russia," *New York Times*, March 6, 2009, https://www.nytimes.com/2009/03/07/world/europe/07diplo.html.

[40] "Vice President Biden's Remarks at Moscow State University," Obama White House Archives, March 10, 2011, https://obamawhitehouse.archives.gov/the-press-office/2011/03/10/vice-president-bidens-remarks-moscow-state-university.

[41] Andy McCarthy, *Ball of Collusion: The Plot to Rig an Election and Destroy a Presidency*, (New York: Encounter Books, 2007), 7, Kindle edition.

[42] John Solomon, "The case for Russia collusion … against the Democrats," *The Hill*, February 19, 2019, https://thehill.com/opinion/white-house/429292-the-case-for-russia-collusion-against-the-democrats.

[43] Jo Becker and Mike McIntire, "Cash Flowed to Clinton Foundation Amid Russian Uranium Deal," *New York Times*, April 23, 2015, https://www.nytimes.com/2015/04/24/us/cash-flowed-to-clinton-foundation-as-russians-pressed-for-control-of-uranium-company.html?_r=1.

[44] Peter Schweizer, *Clinton Cash: The Untold Story of How and Why Foreign Governments and Businesses Helped Make Bill and Hillary Rich* (New York: HarperCollins, 2015), 19, Nook edition.

[45] Tim Hains, Schweizer: "Obama Administration Was 'Certainly Aware' Of Biden's Son's Business In Ukraine," *Real Clear Politics*, October 4, 2019, https://www.realclearpolitics.com/video/2019/10/04/schweizer_obama_administration_was_certainly_aware_of_bidens_sons_business_in_ukraine.html#!.

[46] David Goodman, "Microphone Catches a Candid Obama," *New York Times*, March 26, 2012, https://www.nytimes.com/2012/03/27/us/politics/obama-caught-on-microphone-telling-medvedev-of-flexibility.html.

[47] Glenn Kessler, "Flashback: Obama's debate zinger on Romney's '1980s' foreign policy," *Washington Post*, March 20, 2014, https://www.washingtonpost.com/news/fact-checker/wp/2014/03/20/flashback-obamas-debate-zinger-on-romneys-1980s-foreign-policy/.

[48] Rhodes, 483.

[49] Julian Borger, "Barack Obama: Russia is a regional power showing weakness over Ukraine," *Guardian*, March 25, 2014, https://www.theguardian.com/world/2014/mar/25/barack-obama-russia-regional-power-ukraine-weakness.

[50] Thomas Friedman, "Obama Makes His Case on Iran Nuclear Deal," *New York Times*, July 14, 2015, https://www.nytimes.com/2015/07/15/opinion/thomas-friedman-obama-makes-his-case-on-iran-nuclear-deal.html?auth=login-email&login=email.

51 "Statement by the President on the Murder of Boris Nemtsov," The White House, February 27, 2015, https://obamawhitehouse.archives. gov/the-press-office/2015/02/27/statement-president-murder-boris-nemtsov.

52 David Filipov, "Here are 10 critics of Vladimir Putin who died violently or in suspicious ways," *Washington Post,* March 23, 2017, https://www.washingtonpost.com/news/worldviews/wp/2017/03/23/here-are-ten-critics-of-vladimir-putin-who-died-violently-or-in-suspicious-ways/.

53 Diana West, "Nellie Ohr: Woman in the Middle," *American Spectator,* February 22, 2018, https://spectator.org/nellie-ohr-woman-in-the-middle/.

54 Eun Kyung Kim, "Donald Trump: 'Putin has eaten Obama's lunch' on Ukraine," USA Today, March 13, 2014, https://www.today.com/news/donald-trump-putin-has-eaten-obamas-lunch-ukraine-2D79372098.

55 Rhodes, 272.

56 Ali Watkins, "Obama team was warned in 2014 about Russian interference," *Politico,* August 14, 2017, https://www.politico.com/story/2017/08/14/obama-russia-election-interference-241547.

57 "Report on Russian Active Measures"—Majority and Minority Reports, March 22, 2018.

58 McCarthy, 301.

59 Samuels, May 5, 2016.

60 Rhodes, 398.

61 McCarthy, 288.

62 John Brennan, "MA thesis at UT-Austin," https://www.scribd.com/document/121759580/John-Brennan-MA-thesis-at-UT-Austin.

63 Chris Smith, "Mr. Comey Goes To Washington," *New York Magazine,* October 10, 2003, https://nymag.com/nymag/features/n_9353/.

64 West, 12.

65 Hannah Dawson, "Everything we know about Christopher Steele, the Cambridge MI6 spy," *The Tab,* January 13, 2107, https://web.archive.org/web/20170113192708/http:/thetab.com/uk/

cambridge/2017/01/13/everything-know-christopher-steele-cambridge-mi6-spy-86612.

66 Bukovsky, 66.

67 "Report on Russian Active Measures"—Majority and Minority Reports, March 22, 2018.

68 IG Report, x.

69 West, 7.

70 West, 15.

71 Remnick, August 3, 2016.

72 Samantha Power, "Bystanders to Genocide," *Atlantic*, September 2001, https://www.theatlantic.com/magazine/archive/2001/09/bystanders-to-genocide/304571/.

73 David Harsanyi, "Reminder: Susan Rice Lied About Her Role In The Obama Admin Unmasking Scandal," *Federalist*, September 14, 2017, https://thefederalist.com/2017/09/14/reminder-susan-rice-lied-role-obama-admin-unmasking-scandal/.

74 Bret Baier and Catherine Herridge, "Gowdy: Former UN Ambassador Samantha Power claims others unmasked in her name," Fox News, October 18, 2017, https://www.foxnews.com/politics/gowdy-former-un-ambassador-samantha-power-claims-others-unmasked-in-her-name.

75 Chuck Grassley, "Grassley, Graham Uncover 'Unusual Email' Sent by Susan Rice to Herself on President Trump's Inauguration Day," February 12, 2018, https://www.grassley.senate.gov/news/news-releases/grassley-graham-uncover-unusual-email-sent-susan-rice-herself-president-trump-s.

76 Office of the Director of National Intelligence, "Assessing Russian Activities and Intentions in Recent US Elections," January 6, 2017, https://www.dni.gov/files/documents/ICA_2017_01.pdf.

77 IG Report, 384.

78 West, "Nellie Ohr: Woman in the Middle."

79 Ali Watkins, "The FBI Never Asked For Access To Hacked Computer Servers," *BuzzFeed News*, January 4, 2017, https://www.

buzzfeednews.com/article/alimwatkins/the-fbi-never-asked-for-access-to-hacked-computer-servers#.su1OoNAqJx.

80 Lily Hay Newman, "The FBI repeatedly stressed to DNC officials the necessity of obtaining direct access to servers and data, only to be rebuffed until well after the initial compromise had been mitigated," *Wired*, January 5, 2016, https://www.wired.com/2017/01/fbi-says-democratic-party-wouldnt-let-agents-see-hacked-email-servers/.

81 Ali Watkins, *BuzzFeed News*, January 4, 2017.

82 McCarthy, 202.

83 Tim Fernholz, "Hacked emails show Eric Schmidt played a crucial role in Team Hillary's election tech," *Quartz*, November 1, 2016, https://qz.com/823922/eric-schmidt-played-a-crucial-role-in-team-hillarys-election-tech/.

84 Yasha Levine, "From Russia, with Panic," *The Baffler*, March 2017, https://thebaffler.com/salvos/from-russia-with-panic-levine.

85 Dmitri Alperovitch, "Bears in the Midst: Intrusion into the Democratic National Committee," CrowdStrike.com, June 15, 2016, https://www.crowdstrike.com/blog/bears-midst-intrusion-democratic-national-committee/.

86 Philip Bump, "What the Comey memos say," *Washington Post*, April 19, 2018, https://www.washingtonpost.com/news/politics/wp/2018/04/19/what-the-comey-memos-say/.

87 Letter from Sen. Ron Johnson to FBI Director Christopher Wray, May 21, 2018, https://www.hsgac.senate.gov/imo/media/doc/2018%2005%2021%20RHJ%20to%20FBI%20Director%20Wray%20re%20Steele%20Dossier.pdf.

88 Evan Perez, Jim Sciutto, Jake Tapper, and Carl Bernstein, "Intel Chiefs Presented Trump with Claims of Russian Efforts to Compromise Him," CNN, updated January 12, 2017, https://www.cnn.com/2017/01/10/politics/donald-trump-intelligence-report-russia/index.html.

89 Ken Bensinger, Miriam Elder, Mark Schoofs, "These Reports Allege Trump Has Deep Ties To Russia," BuzzFeed News, January 10, 2017, https://www.buzzfeednews.com/article/kenbensinger/these-reports-allege-trump-has-deep-ties-to-russia.

[90] Lee Smith, 120.

[91] Thomas Friedman, "Online and Scared," *New York Times*, January 11, 2017, https://www.nytimes.com/2017/01/11/opinion/online-and-scared.html.

[92] Jack Cashill and Joel Gilbert, "Did Christopher Steele Write His Dossier or Did a Russian Associate?" *American Thinker*, January 19, 2018, http://www.cashill.com/natl_general/did-chris_steele_write_his-dossier.htm.

[93] Taibbi, 251.

[94] Ibid., 250.

[95] Robert Mueller, "Report On The Investigation Into Russian Interference In The 2016 Presidential Election," US Department of Justice, March 2019, 94-95, https://www.justice.gov/storage/report.pdf.

[96] Ibid., 182.

[97] Speaker Series: John LeBoutillier and Ellen Ratner, YouTube, November 9, 2016, https://www.youtube.com/watch?v=gdtkACCxdnc.

[98] Edward Butowsky v. Michael Gottlieb et al., Case 4:19-cv-00180-ALM-KPJ, July 15, 2019, http://lawflog.com/wp-content/uploads/2019/07/2019.07.15-Amended-complaint-stamped.pdf.

[99] David Folkenflik, "The Man Behind The Scenes In Fox News' Discredited Seth Rich Story," NPR, August 16, 2017, https://www.npr.org/2017/08/16/543830392/the-role-of-ed-butowsky-in-advancing-retracted-seth-rich-story.

[100] Rhodes, 383.

Epilogue

[1] Jon Meacham, "Obama Would Appreciate the Irony," *Vanity Fair*, November 2018, https://www.vanityfair.com/news/2018/10/letter-from-dc-jon-meacham-on-obamas-super-ego.

[2] "Under Obama, Democrats suffer largest loss in power since Eisenhower," *Quorum*, January 2017, https://www.quorum.us/data-driven-insights/under-obama-democrats-suffer-largest-loss-in-power-since-eisenhower/291/.